THE SOULMATE MYTH

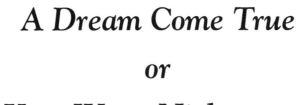

A Dream Come True

or

Your Worst Nightmare?

Judy Hall

Flying Horse Books

Published in 2010 by
Flying Horse Publications
an imprint of
The Wessex Astrologer Ltd
4A Woodside Road
Bournemouth
BH5 2AZ
England

www.wessexastrologer.com

ISBN 9781902405452

A catalogue record of this book is available at The British Library

Cover design by Dave at Creative Byte, Poole, Dorset

Original photograph © Ben Cahill
http://www.flickr.com/photos/greeng90/

Contents

List of Exercises

Acknowledgements

I would like to thank all my friends and clients who offered their case histories for this book. You know who you are so I do not need to name anyone specifically although the twinflame stories appear under people's own names and I thank them for that (most of the names in the soulmate stories have been changed to protect people's privacy and for reasons which are obvious when you read the stories). Celia Gunn and Anthony Thorley deserve a special acknowledgement and a thank you from my heart for all the learning they have offered. I would also like to acknowledge Zaidee Grofton for being such an effective catalyst. Margaret Cahill of The Wessex Astrologer, a very special soul companion, deserves eternal gratitude but, for reasons she will well understand, I offer a huge thank you instead!

For details of Judy Hall's workshops and readings please see
www.judyhall.co.uk

Introduction

You meet someone and you're sure you were lovers in a past life. After two weeks with them, you realize why you haven't kept in touch for the last two thousand years.

Al Cleathan[1]

You meet. Bells ring, the world turns rosy pink, bluebirds weave their dancing flight, and for a few weeks – or months, perhaps even years – everything is sublime, you are with 'The One'. The one person who can make you happy, complete. The person you love without question or restraint. The one you've searched for all your life, were created for. But then it begins, little niggling doubts that you push aside until the next time, or a monstrous great betrayal you cannot ignore. Is this really the one, can your other half really be the source of so much pain, so much soul scouring?

Wonderful, marvellous, the best thing that ever happened, your other half – or the biggest delusion ever? A dream come true, or your worst nightmare? This is the question that lies at the heart of the soulmate dilemma. Many people are still reeling from meeting a soulmate years after the event, others yearn for what might have been, if only...

Soulmates are both a powerful fact and one of the biggest illusions of all time. They are 'an eager wonder' that can cross time, as Tagore suggests:

> We two shall build, a bridge forever
> Between two beings, each to the other unknown,
> This eager wonder is at the heart of things.[2]

and can transform a life, but in the process they can scour us until we are raw and bleeding. When people so eagerly seek their soulmate and

---

1. Source unknown. This quotation was sent to me by a friend, any further information would be welcomed.
2. Tagore, Rabindranath *Later Poems*, trans. Aurobino Bose (Minerva Press, 1976), p.62.

yearn for their one and only love, they have no idea what they may be opening themselves up to, or the heartbreak that can follow a soulmate meeting.

These wondrous beings sweep into our life, lust and desire in their wake, they fire up our lower chakras pushing out all that is outworn and outgrown. They prod and poke, wake us up, drive us from a stultifying relationship or into living out our soul's purpose – or not as the case so often is if the initial attraction is misunderstood. Sometimes, they offer us love ever after, but equally often they flow out of our lives again when their task is done. But they inevitably leave a gift behind, if only we can identify it.

The stories in this book have been chosen because they are everyone's story. You may recognise yourself, or think you recognise another person. Who it is does not matter, it is the eternal and, sometimes it seems inevitable, soulmate story in all its glorious variety that is being told here. Some are case histories I have used before but make no apology for using them again because they are so universal and, for this book, I have endeavoured to identify the why of the experience and the gift behind it.

Soulmates are summed up in Thomas Hardy's poem, which though not explicitly about these partnerships across time highlights the questions they provoke:

Yes, I have re-entered your olden haunts at last;
(Is it really a surprise to hear me again?)
Through the years, through the dead scenes I have tracked you,
(Why should it be, when I have never forgotten you?)
What have you now found to say of our past –
(Will you not grant me one boon – to speak of that which divided us?)
Scanned across the dark space therein I have lacked you?
(For it is true – I have never recovered from the loss of you).

There are many words to describe these beings who make us feel so right, as though we have been waiting for them all our life – or lives. And, it sometimes appears that it is a question of semantics. What I now call a twinflame is someone else's soulmate or twin soul. A soul friend can be a soul companion or a soulmate. These are all terms in common use. So, what exactly is a soulmate according to popular definition?

Thomas Moore sees a soulmate as someone to whom we are 'profoundly connected', something which is brought about by 'divine grace' rather than an intentional act on our part.[3] Leslie Bach (wife of author Richard Bach) described a soulmate as someone 'who has a lock to which we have the key, and we in turn have a key to fit their lock. With this person we can be our true self. They bring out the best in us. We share with them a purpose, direction and our deepest longings'.[4] Brian Weiss said that a soulmate is someone who crosses time to be with us, someone whom we instinctively recognise from our heart, to whom we are 'bonded throughout eternity'.[5] Soulmates occur in fiction time after time:

> He's more myself than I am. Whatever our souls are made of, his and mine are the same… Nelly, I am Heathcliff. He's always, always in my mind – not as a pleasure, anymore than I am always a pleasure to myself – but as my own being.[6]

This book explains why we so desperately seek a soulmate, and why some people do not find it the blissful experience they expect. It will show why it might perhaps be better to avoid a soulmate altogether for the time being, and how to take back your heart if you have left it in the keeping of a false soulmate. It will also help you to have a realistic enough picture of what a 'soul mate' could be to attract a true companion of the heart – what I have come to call a twinflame. And, on the other hand, it will help you to understand why your soulmate may also be an invaluable tool in your karmic learning and show why there is no such thing as a wrong relationship or a mistaken connection because there is always a gift in the experience.

Your soulmate is rarely a person new to you, you have almost always met before in some other existence either in a former life on earth or another dimension – and you don't necessarily need to accept reincarnation to believe that your soul has existed in another dimension before birth onto this earth. A soulmate may well stem back to an earlier

---

3. Moore, Thomas *Soulmates*, (Shaftesbury: Element Books, 1994), p.xviii.
4. Bach, Richard *The Bridge Across Forever* (London: Pan, 1985) [hereinafter Richard Bach] p.265.
5. Weiss, Brian *Only Love is Real* (London: Piatkus, 1996) [hereinafter Brian Weiss] p.1.
6. Bronte, Emily *Wuthering Heights*.

stage of the present incarnation, someone met once in youth and never forgotten, for instance. It is often when sex enters a soulmate equation that the real problems start, and that could well be because the purpose of meeting that particular soulmate is not a sexual one in the present lifetime, as we shall see. As we will also see, we all have more than one soulmate.

My own definition of a soulmate is:

'A soul companion who helps us to grow'.

This is the person who applies a spiritual brillo pad to scour our soul to remove the encrustations of karmic and emotional patterning that have prevented us from moving into our full potential. The term spiritual brillo pad comes from author Sue Minns, who herself went through a devastating soulmate experience but one from which she emerged stronger and wiser, and wrote a book to share her insights.[7] She says that, in her view soulmates are unavoidable. 'The trick is to dance with the devil and know when to change partners/music or whatever'.

The experience of soul scouring is beautifully epitomised in this poem by Jane Lyle, which arose out of a soulmate experience that Jane saw as spun by the Fates, the three sisters who weave the threads of human destiny:

To A Soulmate
And the three sisters spun
At the edge of the World
While our love came unbidden
Our future unfurled

Time circled about us
As shadows grew deep
While the web became darker
And tangled with sleep

Then you begged for my soul
For you'd none of your own
And I gave it you gladly:
Blood, flesh and bone

---

7. Minns, Sue *Soulmates* (London: Hodder Mobius, 2004).

And the three sisters spun
In the black of the night
Whispering shadows
Cursing the light

Though I dreamed of redemption
In sunlight and rain
I had bitten your apple
And slept in my pain

At last your betrayal
Cut clean, like a knife,
Yet the husk of my spirit
Clung fiercely to life
At the edge of the World
The three sisters spin
And the price of my freedom
Is a knowledge of sin

Soul scouring

Just how soul scouring and yet soul expanding some soulmate experiences can be is seen in this story from a soul friend of mine:

Meeting my soul mate has been life changing, unexpected, empowering and very unsettling.

I was 45 when I met Charles. He telephoned me to ask about joining a networking group.

We had an instant friendly rapport. He sounded fun, interesting, light, and had a sense of humour. I imagined him to be very tall and raffish, Byronic and a bit of a flirt.

In the flesh, he was shorter, fatter, balder, very direct and very challenging almost to the point of rudeness. Mercurial, and somehow also dangerous but intriguing. I certainly wasn't attracted in any physical way.

A few weeks later he and his sister invited me and my husband for dinner. We got on better. He chatted easily with my husband and over dinner we talked about writing and various unfinished projects.

Suddenly, over a bowl of raspberries, he looked at me with such an intensity; a laser beam gaze that startled me. It wasn't a cheesey romantic moment. It was a sharp, slicing knowingness. A feeling of total exposure.

He looked right in to my soul. It felt exhilarating, but the feeling of having nowhere to hide was very disconcerting as I was always playing the role of successful woman and wonderful wife and loving mother with the seemingly perfect life

A week later, I had a very strange dream that I walked up the path to an ancient cottage in Ireland. In the dream, I knocked on the door. It was opened by an immensely loving, ebullient, warm, bosomy woman who recognised me and announced to all the people – there was a throng of them beavering in the house behind her,

"Charles's bride has arrived".

Bemused, I realised that a wedding feast was being prepared. Music was playing. Delicious food was being prepared, tables were being decorated with garlands and flowers, it was completely enchanting. But I stood in the doorway saying,

"I'm so sorry there has been a terrible mistake, you see, I'm already married".

As I said it, everything in the dream wound down, the music slurred, the woman's face turned to dismay, spoons dropped onto the floor, there was a terrible air of doom. Hopes dashed, I felt I'd let every one down.

I woke up laughing at the strangeness of it all. It was complete madness. I didn't even fancy this man let alone harbour any romantic fantasies.

But after that, it was as if I'd been kidnapped. Something wasn't quite right with me. I couldn't stop thinking about this man. The gaze, the voice, the vivid and powerful oracular dream. I felt as if a spell had been cast. I wanted to say to him, "Okay please call the fairies off. Good joke. Let me have my life back"; but how do you say that to a relative stranger. I certainly didn't feel like sharing it with him.

It was so dream-like and baffling that I wanted to get to the bottom of it. I started to visit him often. For coffee, a cup of tea. We got to know each other well. There was empathy, an easiness. We shared stories about childhood etc. I had always been a sensitive child. I had imaginary friends, I saw invisible people in our house. I knew when people were ill or dying. I saw an angel when I was six. I made medicines out of plants, I was often ill with rashes, fevers, tummy problems. To him this wasn't weird and unusual. He was not only a sympathetic and wise ear, but authoritative, all encompassing and fantastically sane. Nothing shocked him.

I had a lonely, unconventional childhood. But as I grew up, apart from becoming a healer, I didn't discuss these things much. I buried it under many layers and rarely spoke about it as I tried to live a very stable, normal and happy life.

I'd like to say things felt deeply familiar with Charles, but they weren't really. I don't think that I particularly shared past lives with him, despite the dream, But, whenever I am with him, there is a sense of deep love and a tuning into something profoundly soulful. Although very guarded and quite shy he also feels a strong connection with me.

Four months after meeting him, I became mediumistic. Spirits started to talk to me thick and fast – the main one claiming to be Charles's dead mother. Then I 'saw' and 'knew' things, became intensely psychic. Almost overnight I became clairvoyant, clairsentient and started channelling some very high level beings. I was in a very ecstatic heightened state and was in danger of having all my circuits blown. Kettles blew up, light bulbs exploded, the car broke down… everything around me was in chaos.

Fearing that my sanity was in total danger I looked around for some help and guidance as to what it all meant. Fortunately a shaman (who quite synchronistically appeared) did a 'journey' with me, and a very intense initiation, and told me that every thing that had happened was meant to be, all the psychic gifts were there to be used for the work I would now be doing and that finally, I would step into my power. He predicted that life would never be the same again, also that I would drop my well paid work to begin my real vocation in connecting people back with their ancestors on the deepest level within the community… something that I had already done over many life times. I had no real idea what this would entail. He warned that my life and practically everybody else's life around me would be turned upside down. It would be a bumpy ride – a total understatement!

Charles gave me the inner strength for all this. He guided me. He was a rock. He was not only a discerning listener but he also reinforced, confirmed, pressed all my hot spots, mirrored me, exposed my shadows, unravelled stuff I'd hidden, made me question everything I did and thought.

None of this was comfortable, it was compelling, difficult and left my nerves raw. There weren't any safe places left to rest. But I trusted him and felt complete truth in all that was happening. All the while I channelled extremely complex information to help him. At one stage

I was clearly 'told' during channelling that his contract was to help me step into my power and that in return, mine was to show him complete, total and unconditional love, and to clear a lot of unresolved past life 'overlaps' and to also hold a mirror to his own dark shadows.

Although we are very close, he says he has no strong feelings of connection with my story... and that he is a symptom of all that happened to me rather than a cause.

A year later, I visited Ireland with my husband. On a very, very remote country road miles from anywhere I found the cottage from the dream. It was exactly as I had seen it, although a heap of scrap cars were piled to one side of it. I had absolutely no doubt that it was where the wedding feast had been prepared. We stopped the car and I walked up and down the lane taking mental pictures of it. When I got home and told Charles he said that he'd stayed in that same hamlet, perhaps even in that cottage, as a child, for childhood holidays!

Three years on, as the shaman predicted, my life has certainly changed. I gave up my job and started a project partly enabled by my new understanding of the dynamics of death and what follows. I teach people how to die well and others how to become soul healers, I also teach about death and spirituality. All this is possible because of the psychic revolution that went on inside me.

Charles is still a catalyst, a profound shape shifter, prodding my psyche, an initiator, a mentor. I don't believe this was a chance meeting or happening. I know that there is a deep and profound karmic connection between us. Whether or not our links will just run their course, I'll never know. From all the learning and development I've done, I know that I have to both trust and surrender.

For all the joy, creativity, illuminating and deep love the relationship has brought me, there has been a price to pay. The ruthless learning and experiencing of deeper inner truths about aspects of me has been (usually in the middle of the night) a painful and humiliating experience and the effects upon my other close relationships has been hard. I have had a personal re-birth but it's also been a heart-breaking process at times. Meeting my soulmate triggered a re-membering of who and what I am. I just hope I've done a fraction of something in return for him.

So soulmates can be wonderful and terrible all at the same time and having your soul polished does have its positive side, as we can see from this story, as it is a profound gift to find your true self. But there are times when recognising that the contract has passed its sell-by-date allows you to move on and we will explore these relationships too.

Exercises and visualisations are included in this book that have assisted my clients to break free from the desperate need for a soulmate (see the index of exercises and visualisations at the front of the book after the Contents page) and helped them to find a true soul partner. I'd love to say that these have worked for everyone, but so far I have to be honest and say I haven't found my own true soul partner although I've had a couple of powerful soulmate experiences. Nevertheless, being a romantic Sagittarian at heart and as someone who has the planet of love, Venus, in the sign of relationships, Libra, I believe there is still time and do not doubt that there is such a thing as a twinflame – which you too can find. Having put the intention in motion, I am waiting but my life isn't on hold and I do not need a partner to make me complete. I believe there is a far greater chance of my twinflame materialising when I am not desperate for love, so I am practising the art of loving myself and entering into a full relationship with my own soul.

> If love were what the rose is,
> And I were like the leaf,
> Our lives would grow together
> In sad or singing weather,
> Blown fields or flowerful closes,
> Green pleasure or grey grief.
>
> Algernon Swinburne

My clients come from many different countries and all walks of life. You will find their stories here together with historical figures, and most probably your own story. The soulmate scenario is universal and ubiquitous. The twinflame experience, my term for what I believe people are really seeking, is rare but after enough people read this book may become more commonplace.

I am aware that I may have a somewhat warped view of soulmates, both from my own experience and that of my clients. Over sixty percent of requests for my karmic readings[8] concern soulmates and few of them have been altogether happy connections, although they may have started out that way. Hundreds of my clients have asked, "Why when

---

8. See www.judyhall.co.uk. All case histories have given consent.

I've found my soulmate have I been put through hell?" So often clients say to me, "I've found my soulmate but he, (or she – it happens to men as well as women), does not want to know me". As we shall see, a soulmate contact from one life may not necessarily be intended to carry over to the present life. It may not be on the soul's lifescript this time round. (Your lifescript is the purpose you set out for yourself before you came back into incarnation which is mapped on your birthchart: astrology being an extremely useful way of mapping both the lifescript and any soul contracts you have made with another person. Your lovescript is what you expect of love and is mapped in the same way).

As we shall also see, you may not have met your soulmate for the purpose you imagine. The answer to the soulmate enigma usually lies in another life or in how we are trying to grow this time around. A soulmate may be someone with whom we have a deep soul connection and who loves us enough to help us learn a difficult lesson. But it may also be someone to whom we are drawn inexorably because we had a previous connection and now have unfinished business – and karma.

So often the soulmate we knew in another life has changed, put on a different personality. He or she, we complain, is not the same person. Of course not. We all have to develop and grow, and change is a fundamental part of this process. This is the purpose of reincarnation. We re-incarnate to change ingrained patterns, to experience the opposite of what we have been, to make reparation for what has gone before, or to learn new ways of being, to develop another side of ourselves, to achieve forgiveness as a state of being, to evolve our soul. So, someone who was our soulmate in another life may not be appropriate any longer. They may have come back into our life now for a different purpose. If we immediately act on the 'wave of lust' that so often accompanies a soulmate recognition, we may find ourselves in bed with someone with whom we had intended to work in some other way, with whom we had a mission or spiritual purpose. Having been to bed with them may not hinder this, but on the other hand it could do – especially if either of you already has a partner. As we all belong to soul groups, we may find ourselves in a new and different relationship with a previous soulmate: they may be our child, our parent, our grandparent even. The relationship cannot then be the same as it once was although it may still feel like it.

Reframing the past

> That powerful and extraordinary phenomenon – the human imagination
> – is capable of transforming everything… We are born without wings
> and we fly faster than the eagles. We plumb the depths of the ocean
> without gills… It is the nature of human nature to change our nature.[9]

Many of the exercises in this book use visualisation – an excellent
tool for transforming ourselves and for disconnecting from the past
and learning the true nature of love and what underlies the soulmate
experience. Visualisation can be used to reframe incidents, to change a
lifescript or soul contract, to put in the provisos that will make it 'as long
as appropriate' or to take positive action, it can also draw your twinflame
to you. But, if you find visualisation difficult, don't let that put you off.
There are alternatives, as you will see.

Visualisation is a powerful means of programming our subconscious
energies. It is done in a relaxed state, which creates an 'altered mode
of consciousness'. An exercise can be memorised, taped or read aloud
by a facilitator, perhaps with appropriate background music, allowing
sufficient time for each stage. The advantage of having someone else
work with you is that they can adapt to your timing and rhythm and you
don't have to worry about forgetting a step.

Whilst some people see extremely clear pictures, others find them
hazy, and some never really see anything in a visualisation. Looking up
to the point slightly above and between your eyebrows helps images to
form – and some people find they need to create an inner screen or one
out in front of them. If you are a non-visual person, try 'acting as if'.
Let yourself feel each stage of the process. Indeed, you can act it out,
moving around a room to create the right feel and having 'props' where
appropriate. All the visualisations in the book have suggestions for 'non-
visual' working as well.

You will need a comfortable place where you will not be disturbed for
half an hour or so. You may like to sit in an armchair, or to lie on a bed
but if you lie down remember to remind yourself to start – and remain –
in a state of alert relaxation rather than drifting off to sleep. Remove any
external distractions and create a quiet, peaceful atmosphere. Flowers or

---

9. Viederman, Milton *Passionate Attachments* p.xiii. Hereinafter Viederman.

perfumed oils can help to create the right ambience and crystals can assist the images to form – Apophyllite pyramids or yellow Labradorite placed on the third eye are excellent for this. The preparation for visualisation should be completed before undertaking any of the visualisations in this book.

Preparation for visualisation

Sit in a chair with your feet on the floor and your hands resting gently on your knees. When you are comfortably settled, close your eyes. Take ten slow, deep breaths. As you breathe out, let go of any tension you may be feeling. As you breathe in, draw in a sense of peace and relaxation. Consciously let go of your everyday worries and concerns and allow yourself to be at peace.

Now breathe gently, establishing an even rhythm. Allow your eyelids to grow heavy and lie softly. Then let waves of relaxation flow through your body with each breath. Draw your attention deep inside yourself allowing the outside world to simply slip away.

Without opening your eyes, look up to the point immediately above and between your eyebrows and let your inner eye open.

Close down

Closing down after a visualisation is equally important as otherwise you leave yourself open to subtle invasion or energy leaching. So follow each visualisation with the following close down.

When you are ready to close, surround yourself with a protective bubble of light that goes all around you and under your feet. Feel yourself whole and healed within that space. Then slowly return your awareness to the room and open your eyes. Feel your feet on the floor and your connection to the earth with a grounding cord going deep into the earth holding you firmly in incarnation. Get up and do something practical or have a hot drink to ground you.

1

The Soulmate Conundrum

I know that in my lives to be
My sorry heart will ache and burn,
And worship unavailingly
The woman that I used to spurn
And shake to see another have
The love I spurned, the love she gave.

John Masefield

The whole soulmate experience is much broader than popular belief would have us think. My clients and I have explored many facets of the soulmate experience over the past thirty five years and in this book I draw on case histories that are true but in which, for the most part, names and minor details have been changed to protect the confidentiality of my clients – who all willingly gave permission and chose their aliases. These case histories have been selected because the experiences they embody have been repeated over and over again by clients in regression or in their everyday lives. In essence, these are all our stories. They are part of the journey of our soul. In the last analysis, relationships are where we meet our self in another. They are the mirror of our being. After all:

> Your encounter with partnership tells you who you are, not whom you should avoid.[1]

The soulmate experience

> Two souls with but a single thought
> Two hearts that beat as one

Friedrich Halm

Ask most people what they mean by a soulmate and they will reply "the person who makes me feel complete", or "my other half". They are

---

1. Bridges, Tom, article in *The Mountain Astrologer*, Oct. 1995, p.22.

convinced that there is only one soulmate for them, and that when that soulmate comes into their life, it will bring them everything they have ever wished for. They will live happily ever after. For those who believe in reincarnation, this soulmate will be someone with whom they have shared life after life, almost certainly as lovers. But, as we will see, this 'blissful' scenario does not always work out.

Soulmates are not an either/or situation. They can be wonderful and they can be terrible, and they may be both at one and the same time. They may also start as a blissful experience and end in trauma and pain. Occasionally, the reverse happens. Sometimes the pair come through a traumatic beginning and attain peace together. One half of a 'pair' may recognise the other first and will do all in their power to help the other come to a realisation – although this in itself can involve learning that we cannot do it for someone else. Quite often, one has to support the other through some apparently destructive experiences. We may find a spurious soulmate, or one we are attempting to extricate ourselves from. So often though, we are caught in a repeating pattern of interaction, stuck on the karmic treadmill. We go into the relationship because we have always been in the relationship, and on and on. This situation feels comfortable because it is so known and familiar despite being soul constricting. There comes a time, however, when we must change the pattern, step out of the known. At other times the roles alternate, the persecutor becomes the victim, the victim the persecutor, life after life after life. Repayment and reparation can be an endless round. Again, we must step out, break free from the cycle of the past.

There is considerable experiential evidence to show that we do not have just one soulmate, which can be confusing to say the least. We have several soulmates with whom we have been in many different relationships in the past. Regression to other lives shows that we take on many roles within loosely knit soul groups or soul families, any member of which may feel like a soulmate or our greatest enemy when we meet up again. The relationship may also change roles, or the beloved return again in some new disguise:

> Speaking through the babe now held in her embrace
> She hears again the well-known voice adored:
> 'Tis I – but do not tell!
>
> Victor Hugo

Opening Pandora's box

> If you open that Pandora's Box you never know what Trojan horses will jump out.
>
> Ernest Bevin

There is a kind of soulmate relationship that is immensely powerful, one that passes from lifetime to lifetime down through the ages, and although it is soul scouring and may appear to be far from soulmatish when viewed from outside, as this story shows, it is profoundly life changing. When I first asked her for a contribution, Jane wrote a very theoretical piece about what she'd learned about soulmates but it completely disappeared before I could type any of it up. So I asked her to tell me in her own words and typed her account straight onto the computer. Then her first account – which was in big red writing – appeared from my printer as it had somehow been scooped up with the paper on which I was printing out her story. So the experiential story had covered the underlying theoretical account, which turned out to be deeply symbolic. From what remained of the theoretical account, I gathered that in her view her soulmate was a reflection of her own soul and that what she saw she both loved and hated:

> The charm, beauty, romance and magnificence of the beast but also the rage, violence and jealousies all lying dormant under the surface waiting for my soulmate to unlock my Pandora's box. The affair – if that's what it was – continued over a 6-7 year span during which time by virtue of his comings and goings I was able to confront just about every issue and aspect of myself that I had repressed or ignored.

I'll let Jane tell the story in her own words:

> I met Jean-Marc in July of '97. I first saw him on board another boat and twenty four hours later he'd connived with a girlfriend of his to invite me out for lunch and from there it was intense; mind-blowingly intense. It was like being swept along in a hurricane that was relentless. Living on a knife edge, and yet I wasn't able to step off. It was like I just wanted to keep touching and being part of this person – and he was the same. It wasn't only in the sexual sense it was psychological as well, and we didn't have to put our hands on each other, I just had to look at him and the feeling was intense and he felt it too. I felt one of us owed

the other big time and had karmic lessons to learn. We had a language barrier and practical considerations said we couldn't stay in bed all the time. However, the relationship was literally conducted below deck on my boat, below the waterline, which turned out to be deeply symbolic. He was 16 years younger than me, which had an effect on me, but not on him, because I felt like I was with a much younger person and was his mother and his father all at once.

The relationship was very Plutonic and catalytic. It forced stuff to the surface I had never looked at. I needed to look at emotional stuff as I deceived myself about emotions, and he brought up my amniotic Moon-self and what had been dormant and hidden for aeons of lifetimes exploded.

Within the first few weeks we started talking about doing a trip to Peru in my boat. In my mind I suddenly had this picture of two small children, a little boy and girl about two and a half years old. I could see how they were dressed and, not knowing anything about past lives or anything at that time, I didn't understand the significance of this.

Probably the next significant thing in the relationship was that some people stayed on the boat and I was highly suspicious of them, had the most bizarre feelings. One guy went down in the engine room and I felt there was going to be a time in the future when I would be sailing on the boat with Jean-Marc and other people and I'd be thrown overboard because they wanted the boat off me. Two gay friends of mine seriously thought I was paranoid so I started writing everything down in minute detail with all the strong feelings of how upset and frightened I was, all that was going on in my head. I still had no understanding of why I would envisage that in my mind.

The relationship finished because it was too damaging mentally, emotionally, physically and too gut-wrenching, but the strange thing about the gut-wrenching was that it continued for the next five years, every day and all day, I just couldn't get rid of it, like heightened sensibilities because I would know when he was in the vicinity. Even years later when he'd been away sailing for a year my stomach tightened and he'd just flown back into the country from the Caribbean. The word bizarre came up constantly. I felt I needed to understand why this man had been like holding a mirror not just to my face but to my soul. There was too much similarity, too much conflict, too much love. Every thought and every feeling was intensified in this man's company. So I started asking why.

I had always been interested in astrology and had had chart readings done so I set about getting books, a computer, and a beginner's programme in astrology. I read Einstein, mythology, cosmology, Plato, Blake, Kepler and so on, and put it all into context, like putting together a huge jigsaw. I went into my own Hades, and identified with the whole. Also around that time I met a woman who was a regression-to-birth therapist and once you open a door into this other side of wanting to know, hundreds of doors open. Dream analysis and all the things that came with symbology, numerology, regression, karma, psychology and so on gave me answers to my questions and huge insights. It was like being sucked into a huge funnel, back into the past and then being shot out picking up the wisdom of all the ancients who are also a part of me.

I had by that time learned to regress myself to the point where I could remember things without going into a regressive state. What came out was where Jean-Marc fitted into all these past lives I'd had – where a lot of my feelings and fears about him – and about myself – came from. He was the catalyst and mirror image, but it was also where he fitted into the framework of who I am and what he represented. Matter, time and space all being one, he was this mirror image of a part of my own soul, a myriad of the same facets of me which I recognised in myself.

In the life in Peru, he'd been my twin and we were very close. There was a migration of this particular clan because the women were falling prey to a disease and dying at a rapid rate. The chief of the clan realised we wouldn't exist as a people any longer if we stayed where we were and we moved out of the mountainous region in a north-easterly direction to lower ground and all I remember is that somewhere along the way I lost my twin brother and was devastated.

The fear that I'd felt about Jean-Marc came back in another regression. Sometime in the 1600s on a four-masted clipper-type ship where we were becalmed at sea and a lot of crew were on deck, this young man came up trying to create a mutiny. The captain turned out to be my late husband, Ian (also a sailor in the present life), and the mutineer was Jean-Marc who whilst he was disputing with Ian told one of his motley crew to shoot the captain with an old fashioned gun. I started to remonstrate, saying "you can't just shoot the captain of the ship". I was a 15 year old cabin boy. He instructed I be thrown over the side of the ship, whereupon I promptly drowned. Hence my fear about the people on board the boat that day in Bordeaux and being 'paranoid'.

Another life came up when I introduced Jean-Marc to my two gay friends and one took exceptional dislike to him, really hated him on sight. I was in medieval England, a man of about 35, in chain mail, tall slim moustached, and a keeper of keys to the castle dungeons. I used to spend a great deal of time talking outside a door that was halfway down a staircase. I would talk to this man about what was going on within the castle and the grounds, he was a learned man who'd been manacled because of his beliefs and the writing he did wasn't in accord with the king. And whilst I was talking to him one day there was a shout from the upper staircase and a command for this man to be brought forward to be executed and the person standing at the top of the stairs was Jean-Marc and the man in the prison cell was my gay friend.

In another life that came to me rather like a daydream, I was an 18 year old native coloured girl living on an island. I was shunned because I had some very strange powers and could see things that freaked everyone out. It was an afternoon and I lived quite near the edge of the sea, all the men had gone hunting inland and this sailor turned up in a rowing boat all dishevelled, overgrown beard, filthy dirty and smelly and he kept trying to talk to the women and they wouldn't take any notice. He realised pretty quickly that there weren't any men around and raped two or three of the women. When he came out from the last place he came up to me and said "I'll be back for you". This was such a Jean-Marc characteristic in his present lifetime because he had had so many women and, in my mind, he was still going round raping and pillage and tossing aside people.

It took six years for me to understand. It was like literally having my soul destroyed and then having to put myself back together to a level where I could deal with things again – especially as he'd keep turning up out of the blue. Uncanny moments happened constantly, after a year of his absence, I'd go up on deck and he'd be there watching me from the quayside.

By going back into past lives and matching up astrologically, I was able to look in the mirror and see myself and look at other people and also see myself in everyone else and have a much clearer understanding of how we all interact with one another on subliminal levels that perhaps not everyone fully understands.

I know this is not the end of Jean-Marc and I. There are still things about myself to face through him. It may be the end of a chapter but it's not the end of the book, whether that's in this or another lifetime.

It's not finished but it sits comfortably with me now and I can deal with it. Maybe it will swing around. Because I've worked through so much now that I can virtually deal with anything that comes up without fear, apprehension, or my gut turning over, and in a more loving way. I can have more appreciation for what others go through because of what I've been through and it helps me on another level to work with people that I meet because I've adapted myself to those finite sensibilities that are able to pick up on those very deep things that people want to keep hidden. I now act as the mirror to their souls. You can't know something until you've been there, and having been there, I know. It feels like a good and comfortable place and I have no fears in that respect. My experience with Jean-Marc put me on a path of looking at my history as far back as I could go to understand why I'm here today in the way I am; a huge path of learning.

As we will see, something as simple as Jean-Marc saying, "I'll be back for you" can bring people into repeated lifetimes together. But Jane's story also illustrates how past life regression or spontaneous memories can tell our soul's story. It doesn't matter whether those lives she saw were actually, factually true, they picked up the interaction between a soul group and explained the present day antipathies and attractions. Jane finished her original written account by saying:

> In my final analysis about soulmates, I would have to say using the words of Krishnamurti that 'truth is a pathless land, that no dogma, creed or religion [takes us there]'. And that it is our true soulmates who can take us there – alone or together towards that most elusive of all elusives – LOVE – for isn't that really all we're seeing in the guise of our soulmate?

Later, when we were discussing love and relationships, Jane recalled that while she was with Jean Marc she was writing poetry at the time and that she spontaneously wrote the following words:

> Amour:
> Ca qui n'as pas de limite
> Ni de frontiers
> Mais c'est infinite dans son grace

which translates:

Love:
That which has no limits
Nor boundaries
But is infinite in its grace

The words encapsulated the state to which her soulmate experience had brought her, in which any and everything was acceptable because:

Everything that you do and aspire to be is to be in that state of grace, hence love. It is a boundless space. No matter what has gone on, it makes no difference to that which you feel, it doesn't matter what anyone else says or thinks, I am in such a comfortable space where I don't search for anything, I can accept everyone, foibles and everything. It's a difficult concept to explain unless you are there. This carried me at a very deep level through the whole experience with Jean Marc and all the way to the end – if indeed the experience of that particular soulmate journey has ended as it may continue in another life – and a state where I am today: There is nowhere else to go. It is that way. I am. It's like going through a volcanic eruption that destroys everything but opens a space for a massive evolution, and it's something I know I've worked on for many lives. I can see the beauty in everything, negativity might be there, every facet of every feeling that you go through, and can own it. The rest of my journey now is to help others to attain that same space – when I see an astrological chart it is like I get into their skin and know where they are. Which is very humbling, an experience like that cuts through everything and to the core of what everyone is going through. You can meet kings, prophets, waifs, strays and feel just as humbled by the experience of meeting them on that emotional plane as they are all trying to attain that state of grace. This sounds terribly pious but it's not, it's the only way to explain the sensibilities that I carry with me. To me a meeting of soulmates – and it doesn't have to be a physical sexual relationship – is like two souls colliding, a catalyst for the evolution of the spirit to reach that divine place.

So, why would you avoid a soulmate?

Love demands every ounce of your energy.

Edna O'Brien[2]

2. O'Brien, Edna, on *Desert Island Discs*, BBC Radio 4, 13 January 2007.

You may still be asking why would you want to avoid your soulmate? Surely this is the person who is your perfect love, your 'other half'? Someone with whom you will be eternally happy? Who will make your life complete? Is that not someone to welcome into your life? By the time you have read the rest of this book you might want to rethink that idea – you may be doing so already. As we shall see, there is someone like that, but it's not necessarily a soulmate. I prefer to use a new term, 'twinflame', as I feel there is a need to distinguish between the scourers of our soul (soulmates) and the supporters of our soul (twinflames).

Most relationships have their agenda set outside the present lifetime. They may be planned in the between-life state before incarnation, but this is not necessarily so. There may be unfinished business from the past. It is clear from regression to the between-life state that whilst some souls plan incarnations most carefully, others are drawn back into relationships by forces operating outside their control. The forces may be personal or shared by two or more people. These factors include individual expectations, ingrained personal and ancestral patterns, attraction to specific situations, mutual desires or craving, or repetition of an old interaction.

Whilst positive soulmate contacts are to be desired because of the gifts they bring, so often we meet a false soulmate who brings havoc into our lives. This may be a part of our soul's purpose, a catalyst for our growth. It may also simply be that we are caught up in a repeating pattern. Stepping out of that pattern gives us the opportunity of reassessing our part in it. Are we blindly following our past, or is this where we can move ahead and evolve?

If you easily fall instantly in lust, but believe it is true love; if you find yourself thinking, "Oh no, here we go again", or cannot understand why your soulmate wants nothing to do with you; then it may be better to learn how to avoid soulmate relationships for the time being. By stepping out of the pattern, taking a deep breath and asking "Is this really love or is it just pressing my buttons?" instead of tumbling headlong into yet another disaster, you may gain insights into why you have attracted this person. You can identify the patterns and needs behind your desperate emotional desire for your 'other half'. In time, you can find that other half inside your own self. Taking a whole person into a relationship then totally changes the outcome. Once need no longer drives the search, there is every possibility of finding true love.

Other halves

Plato's 'explanation' of soulmates, which we will examine later, is perhaps the most familiar source for the origin of the soulmate phenomena, but the idea of 'other halves' is much older than that and will be examined from both the mythic and the esoteric perspective in later chapters. However, it is Plato's view that we meet when we look at John Lennon's story. Many people have wondered what attracted, and held, John Lennon in an unconventional and symbiotic relationship with Yoko Ono. Astrologer Pauline Stone (who was married to Lennon's father) put forward the psychological view when she surmised:

> Perhaps John sensed that Yoko was the perfect embodiment of his anima, and that through her he would become complete in a way that had never been possible in his former relationships with women.[3]

John himself expressed it differently:

> Before Yoko and I met we were half a person. You know there's an old myth about a person being one half and the other half being somewhere else, in the sky or somewhere, like a mirror image. But we were two halves and now we are whole.[4]

John was here referring to Plato's explanation of the origins of soulmates, which we will be meeting further on. John believed that he and Yoko were the reincarnation of Napoleon and Josephine, and other famous lovers. He apparently purchased a mummy case, complete with occupant, from ancient Egypt in the belief that it was Yoko in a former incarnation. In his eyes they were two halves of the same soul, bonded throughout eternity. John Lennon himself was a figure who has inspired the same belief in others, as we shall see.

People often describe feeling their soulmate reach out to them across the centuries. Poets are particularly good at catching this evocation of past love:

> You have been mine before –
> How long ago I may not know,
> But just when at that swallow's soar

---

3. Stone, Pauline *Relationship, Astrology and Karma*, (London: HarperCollins 1991) [hereinafter Pauline Stone], p.189.
4. Passed to me by a personal friend of John Lennon.

Your neck turned so,
Some veil did fall – I knew it all of yore

Dante Gabriel Rossetti

Other people feel it too. In *Bridge Across Forever* author Richard Bach asked, 'Did you ever feel that you were missing someone you had never met?'[5] and went on to relate how he sought out his deeply yearned-for soulmate for many years before they met and, finally, married.

Psychiatrist and past-life therapist Dr Brian Weiss described in *Only Love is Real* how two of his patients searched the past for their soulmates only to find them in each other:

> In separate regression experiences, both were reconnecting to exactly the same lifetimes, but lived from a different perspective. Although they came from very different backgrounds, and had never met, they seemed to share a common history. Across many lifetimes, they appeared to have loved and lost each other time after time.[6]

When, finally, they passed each other in his waiting room, there was a backward glance, but that was all. No instant recognition here. On this occasion, however, destiny was at work. The two later met and fell in love on a plane high above America.

Countless people have caught a glimpse of someone and known they were fated to meet, their eyes met across a room and that was it. As Shakespeare puts it in *As You Like It*:

> Your brother and my sister no sooner met, but they looked, no sooner looked, but they loved, no sooner loved but they sighed, no sooner sighed, but they asked one another the reason, no sooner knew the reason, but they sought the remedy: and in these degrees have they made a pair of stairs to marriage, which they will climb incontinent, or else be incontinent before marriage.

Others have searched diligently for their own true love. Many have found what Brian Weiss describes as 'profound bliss and happiness, safe in the knowledge that you are together always, to the end of time'.

Whilst this scenario may well happen and you may find exactly the right person to make you feel profoundly loved and fulfilled, over thirty

---

5. Richard Bach, back cover.
6. Brian Weiss, p.48.

years of exploring karmic relationships leads me to believe it is not always this simple – and where it is the term 'twinflame' is more appropriate. Yes, I have had couples in my consulting room that, separately and together, have relived life after life where they were together. All the details clicked. The interaction was clear. But these were usually couples that had consulted me because of difficulties in their relationship. Soulmates can drift apart over the period that is eternity. Even when they meet, they may not necessarily reunite. One may recognise the other, but be spurned. Karma is a cycle of action and reaction. What goes round, comes round. Yes. But karma is also dynamic, we can set new things in motion and we may need to experience myriad facets of love.

We all have lessons that our soulmates willingly enter into with us, experiences that we share and a soulmate experience can be an enormous inspiration and life-changing event – even where the soulmate is not physically present.

Two souls colliding

The poet Dante was inspired by a soulmate. The divine Beatrice, glimpsed, adored, but never possessed. He met her when he was nine and although she didn't speak to him, he fell in love at first sight and thought her an angel. When they next glimpsed each other he was eighteen, she greeted him and he thought he was in paradise:

> This marvel appeared before me again, dressed in purest white … she turned her eyes toward me where I stood in fear and trembling, and with her ineffable courtesy, which is now rewarded in eternal life, she greeted me; and such was the virtue of her greeting that I seemed to experience the height of bliss. It was exactly the ninth hour of day when she gave me her sweet greeting… I glowed with a flame of charity which moved me to forgive all who had ever injured me; and if at that moment someone had asked me a question, about anything, my only reply would have been, "Love", with a countenance clothed with humility. When she was on the point of bestowing her greeting, a spirit of love, destroying all the other spirits of the senses, drove away the frail spirits of vision and said, "Go and pay homage to your lady"; and Love himself remained in their place. Anyone wanting to behold Love could have done so then by watching the quivering of my eyes. And when this most gracious being actually bestowed the saving power of her salutation, I do not say

that Love as an intermediary could dim for me such unendurable bliss but, almost by excess of sweetness, his influence was such that my body, which was then utterly given over to his governance, often moved like a heavy, inanimate object. So it is plain that in her greeting resided all my joy, which often exceeded and overflowed my capacity.

La Vita Nuova XI

As with so many soulmates, Dante remembered the exact details and time of that meeting throughout his life. That following night he had had a powerful dream that was the inspiration for *La Vita Nuova*, written late in his life. Dante was inconsolable when Beatrice died aged only 24, but her memory and her muse stayed with him. His idealised love for her was the inspiration for his work and a deeply spiritual philosophy of divine love. That was her soulmate gift to him and it may well be that they are now united as twinflames – or could be moving on to new, separate relationships.

Like Dante and Beatrice, our present lifetime may not always be the point at which we are destined to be together again. This may be where we have to break off the contact to go on to new things. We may be seeing the 'negative face of love' and repeating what we have sown but still we yearn for our soulmate, or we may reject a soulmate for various reasons.

Our 'soulmate' may be a 'psychic vampire' who has been feeding on our energy for centuries and will continue to do so, if we allow it. This is negative symbiosis, parasitically draining. A gothic horror tale may not be the first thing that comes to mind when thinking about soulmates, but in the film of Bram Stoker's *Dracula*, Dracula loved his wife more than life itself. They were soulmates. On being told false rumours of his demise she threw herself into the castle moat.

Given the news, Dracula vowed to overcome death – to live until he could be with her again. He became, by sheer force of will, a vampire that fed off the blood of living beings, taking their lives to sustain his own. It was his way of taking revenge on God and on humanity for allowing such a thing to happen, and of sustaining his soul until he could be reunited with her.

When she is reincarnated again, Dracula moves to England to be near her. He tries to lure her into his world. Fascinated with her old love, who she recognises at a soul level, but torn between him and her new love, only Dracula's death can save her. To live, she has to be party to his release from this world. But it is a painful choice. It is no wonder the Dracula story has proved so popular down the years and been reworked time and again. It embodies a profound psychic truth: the undead can prey on the living, just as the living can. An old soulmate contact can suck the life out of someone. But equally, an ancient desire for revenge can keep someone, or something, alive. One day we too may have to let go of the past for the sake of our soul.

The search for a soulmate, or the memory of a previous life association, can wreck ordinary relationships. The search for perfection is a lonely, loveless road. Those who spend their whole life searching for their soulmate, and rejecting other relationships in the process, should perhaps bear in mind that Plato, in his explanation of twin souls, says that one being split in two and ever the twain shall wander seeking each other. He does not say they will necessarily be united again, only that something will impel them across lifetimes to search for each other and, as we shall see, if they do become reunited they may perish from inertia.

Love thine enemy

> The trick is to be able to express the hate, then return to love.
>
> Nancy Friday

As we have seen, soulmates come in many shapes and sizes according to what we need to learn in order to grow. Meeting your soulmate is not always a pleasant experience, nor does it necessarily occur within a love relationship. Soul growth may entail some extremely hard lessons indeed, as we shall see, and our soulmate may just be the person with whom we go to hell and back – not as a punishment but as a learning process. As one of my clients said: "Our soulmate is the person who is here to teach us the hardest lesson".

I prefer to look on it as helping us to learn, rather than being taught, a difficult lesson. And, I would add that our soulmate is the person who loves us enough at a soul level to put us through some painful situations – and to be with us through some difficult times.

Several soulmates I have known have found their 'other half' just in time to see them through, or be accompanied to the end of, a terminal illness. It is clear from regressions to the 'planning stage' before incarnation that such lessons are frequently, but not always, knowingly sought. It is also clear that members of our soul group agree to participate with us – we all have many such soulmates. But we may forget all this when we come into incarnation. It is, however, also apparent that other people can become caught up in our soul dramas unknowingly, and play their part accordingly. They may appear to be a soulmate, but the recognition is spurious and premature. Finding a false soulmate can be a bit like feeding the endorphin receptors in your brain with chocolate, valium or heroin. For a time the 'fit' is good and the body is fooled, but gradually it becomes obvious that the substance/false soulmate is addictive and deadening rather than life-giving and consciousness-enhancing.

Our own inner expectations play their part too. We attract what we expect, and it feels comfortable even though it hurts like hell. As fear, hatred, rage and old resentments are powerful magnets in mutual attraction, they draw us together again to complete the unfinished stories of our former lives. No one soulmate is enough to fulfil all these needs. Nor is a soulmate relationship necessarily 'forever'. It is for as long as it takes.

Learning from lack

Soulmates are not only partners, they may be parents, children, friends, mentors or pupils. One of the most powerful ways in which soulmates of all kinds help our evolution is through not providing us with something that we desperately seek or have lacked in other lives so that eventually we are forced inwards to find it for ourselves. This can apply, for instance, to the parent who provides a cold, lonely and unloving childhood but who on further examination is part of the soul group from which we originate or anyone who has loved us enough to help us with a hard lesson or to find a difficult gift.

A woman on the first day of one of my workshops told us about an extremely difficult relationship with her alcoholic, cold and abusive mother. She said, "I don't know why I chose her to be my mother, but I know I did". We talked at some length about people providing us with exactly the kind of environment – no matter how seemingly unlikely – that we needed. As part of the workshop we did a tie-cutting and she cut the cords with her mother and sent love and forgiveness to her. The next morning she told us that, on arriving home, she'd had a call to say her mother, whom she had not communicated with for many years, was in hospital dying. She said:

> I went to the hospital and sat by her bed. She was deeply unconscious and in a private room. So I took her hand and said out loud, "Well mother, if you were here to teach me about coldness and abuse and lack of love you certainly did a good job". And I went on in that way for about five minutes detailing everything that was missing from my childhood and what it had pushed me into finding for myself, all the gifts I'd found. I also told her that I forgave her and that I loved her no matter what. When I had finished she opened her eyes, smiled and said, "That's alright dear, that's what I was there for. I love you too". She closed her eyes and died peacefully. I sat with her awhile and then called a nurse.

Despite her bereavement, she had come in to the workshop to continue the work and explored her soul family and the past lives that had led up to the present. She wasn't surprised to find that, at the planning meeting before they reincarnated, the agreement had been that she would be given that cold and lonely childhood so that she could learn the self-love and forgiveness that she had lacked in her previous lives and also so that she could build her independence rather than being a dependent personality. In that respect her mother was a true soulmate.

2

How to Recognise a Soulmate

I looked up and into the room walked Linda. Our eyes met and something just went wham in both of us. . . She is the most caring, loving, supportive human being. . . She was, is, and will always be, the most wonderful friend and partner anyone could ask for. [1]

There are certain experiences that are ubiquitous where soulmate meetings are concerned.

- Did your eyes meet across a crowded room?
- Did your heart pound?
- Did you feel a sense of instant recognition? Of overwhelming love?
- Did you feel great, inexplicable antipathy?
- Did you want to run, somewhere, anywhere?
- Did it feel like a large magnet was inexorably pulling you onwards?
- Did you feel a wave of lust? Or revulsion?
- Is someone in your thoughts all the time?
- When someone went away did you feel like a part of you had left too?
- Are you convinced you are meant to be with someone despite their marriage to someone else?
- Do you feel you will die if you have to part?
- Are you especially close to one of your parents?
- Do you feel like someone is punishing you deservedly?
- Do you have a compulsion to be with a person, no matter what?
- Did you dream of finding one true love and now you have?

---

1. In personal correspondence but later used in *In the Light of Experience*.

If you answer yes to more than two or three of these questions, the chances are you have found a soulmate even though it may be an illusory or spurious one. Typical scenarios include:

"I caught a glimpse of this man, just one look. I have spent the rest of my life trying to find him again. I know we are meant to be together".

"I saw the back of his head, just for a moment as he walked along the street. I knew this was the man I would marry. Eventually we met. We married almost immediately. The relationship has not been easy however".

"I was on holiday. I saw him sitting at a table at a cafe. I knew I would speak to him. Then I panicked. What if I was mistaken? Just to make sure, I went for a long walk to give him time to leave, then I went back, he came straight up to me. We talked for hours and have never been apart since".

"All my life I had been looking for someone, my ideal woman. When I met my wife, I knew I had found her. But now she wants a divorce. Why?"

"1 went out with her when 1 was in my teens. Somehow, 1 could never forget her. Then one day I met her in the street. I grabbed her hand. That was it, I just could not let go. We began a passionate affair. I left my wife, but she would not leave her husband. I still cannot let her go. We meet when we can. I love her so much. Why does my soulmate treat me like this?"

"The first time I saw him my heart pounded, I felt sick and my legs shook. I was terrified of this man, and yet I had never seen him before in my life. I found myself married to him. I was never quite sure how it happened. It was like I was hypnotised".

"No matter how hard 1 tried, no man could ever match up to my father. My mother was very jealous of our relationship. I felt she hated me. In a regression, I discovered I had once been married to the man who was now my father. I had had him first, no wonder she was so jealous".

So often the 'love at first sight' scenario includes feeling like I have known him, or her, forever. We may pause, take a step back, try to rationalise or escape. But inevitably we find ourselves in a relationship. And equally often, it is followed by difficulties in the relationship as we get to grips with the lessons we have come together to learn, or we replay out old patterns. Equally we may find ourselves compulsively attracted to someone we know is bad for us. When we first met we may have felt inexplicable fear or rage. But somehow we find ourselves together in relationship. Our soulmates are not only those people who love us the most. We may have to learn forgiveness and compassion through interaction with an old soulmate who has reason to hate us, or whom we have reason to fear.

We may also find ourselves going through these same lessons or patterns with someone who is not our lover. It may be a friend, an employer, a family member, a lodger. Yet, when we met, it felt so right. How is it that we can replay the same power struggles, parental patterns, emotional games and so on in so many contexts? The answer may well lie in the past, in our previous contacts, or in the expectations we bring to our present life, or to the ingrained patterns that are, unbeknown to us, running our lives.

It is the intensity of the experience, coupled with the fact that the memory never fades, that is the key to recognising a true soulmate experience – but even then it may not be an a relationship that is destined to continue.

A meeting of twin souls

Two souls who recognise themselves as half of a whole meeting again is well illustrated by the story of Gordon Craig and Isadora Duncan, the exotic dancer. When Gordon met his soulmate in 1904 his description of her, like so many others, echoed Plato's perfect whole that had been sundered and then reunited:

> Our meeting first of all was... a marvellous coming together... Suppose one had been in a world with one's other half – once – and that world so wonderfully perfect, and then suppose that world had dissolved and time had passed over one, and one had woken up in another world – but one's other half was not there. One would have taken to the new existence as cheerfully as possible. . . Then, suddenly, the marvellous happens – that other half is standing beside one, she has found her way, after all these centuries and over all those hills and rivers and seas – and here she is – and here am I. Is that not marvellous? With what a cry we come together.[2]

---

2. Steegmuller, Francis, *Your Isadora*, (New York: Random House, 1974) p. 279.

Isadora said of that meeting with Craig in Berlin that she had been aware of him all evening (he was sitting in the front row of the audience). When the performance was over, "there came. . . a beautiful being". But he was angry, accusing her of stealing his ideas and scenery. Nevertheless, he said she was the "living realisation of all my dreams". Isadora responded that they were in fact her designs, which she had invented when she was five years old. But Craig insisted they were his and that she was the embodiment of the being he had created them for. The mystery, apparently, was solved when she found out that he was the son of Ellen Terry, one of Isadora's great childhood heroes – her ideal of womanhood. Craig wanted to spirit Isadora away from her family, so that she could be with him. "Like one hypnotised", she allowed him to put on her cape and take her away. When they eventually reached his studio, she said:

> All inflamed with sudden love, I flew into his arms with all the magnetic willingness of a temperament which. . . waited to spring forth. . . In him I had met the flesh of my flesh, the blood of my blood. . . Hardly were my eyes ravished by his beauty than I was drawn toward him, entwined, melted. As flame meets flame, we burned in one bright fire. Here, at last, was my mate, my love, my self – for we were not two, but one, that one amazing being of whom Plato tells in the Phaedrus [sic], two halves of the same soul. . . This was the meeting of twin souls.

This is the most usual view of soulmates: one soul, and one soul only, who makes us feel complete 'forever'. A couple who are bonded for eternity, an ideal – or should it be idealised – relationship. Within a few weeks of meeting Gordon Craig, Isadora Duncan found it was her "fate to endeavour to reconcile the continuing of my own career with his love" – an impossible combination. When she found she was pregnant, she was ecstatic. Craig was unhappy, "My work, my work", he would despair. The baby brought her great joy, him deep gloom. Isadora knew, despite the great love she had for him, that they would separate. Some soulmates find it impossible to live together and others were never destined to.

Dangerous Liaisons

> The soulmate experience may well not be the marvellous experience everyone yearns for.[3]

---

3.   Richard Bach.

She looked like Aphrodite: tall, willowy and blonde – exuding sex and promising passion. Every man on the small Greek island was hot and panting for her. The lust was palpable, it hung in the air. You could almost touch it. She had just been told her soulmate was coming, so she put out 'vibes' to attract *him*. When a goddess puts out with all her will, it is powerful stuff, nothing can resist. Unfortunately for the lesser mortals around her, she was only interested in him – the one and only. Dejected and rejected men fell like flies. Aphrodite is ruthless in pursuit of her passion.

Desperate for her soulmate, when she returned to England, Aphrodite, for we can call her so, met several men who might just be. . . But no, one by one they too fell away. Then it happened. A friend said, "I've met this man. I know he's the one for you. Come to dinner and I'll introduce you".

She stood in the doorway, unable to move. There he was. The archetypal tall dark, handsome and frighteningly intelligent man she had sought for so long. Their eyes met. That was all it took. Later that night, as though in a dream, she heard herself saying, "Why don't you stay the night?" Inside herself though, a voice whispered, "Don't do it, you'll live to regret this. Don't you know what he did to you?"

Six weeks later she gave a newspaper interview on 'Love at First Sight'. "I just knew", she said, "I could do nothing else. I had to be with him no matter what it cost. This was my soulmate from way back. We had shared many lives. We are fated to be together". A typically charming Gemini, he had much in common with Mercury, the adroit messenger of the gods and one of Aphrodite's many lovers. However, as he was half Finnish and seemed to belong in another myth altogether, we will call him Loki after the northern trickster god.

Six months later there was a white wedding, an enormous turnout of friends and family wishing her well. As she walked up the aisle, that still small voice inside screamed, "It's not too late, turn around and leave NOW!" As she walked back on her husband's arm, the voice asked, "What have you done?" And, unbeknown to her, he was having the same feelings but thrust them aside.

Apart from one incident on their honeymoon, they were blissfully happy. But the small incident stayed with her. She had gone out onto the balcony and sung the 'Chicken Song' complete with actions and clucking noises, to a group of hens in the olive grove below. He had closed the balcony door, shutting her out. Were they really on the same wavelength? She asked this question again sometime later when she cooked a romantic gourmet dinner, dressed only in her sexiest underwear. To which he gravely said, "Fantasy has no place in marriage".

All went well for six months. They shared many interests in common, and both believed they had a deep soul connection. They wrote for a New Age magazine on spiritual and occult topics. Then they joined a meditation group. It was guided by a channelled entity who supposedly communicated through a word processor. She was unimpressed. He took in every word. Two weeks later the group went off on a weekend together. Aphrodite and Loki were invited up to the room of one of the women, whom we will call Athene. When they got there, it was to find the room set out for two with roses, champagne and candlelight. Aphrodite found herself drinking champagne out of a toothmug. "Odd", she thought, "I feel like an intruder here."

The voice inside, which had been quite eloquent over the past months, was strangely silent. Waking later in the night, she found herself alone. Going to the door, she was just in time to see Loki emerging from Athene's room, looking flushed and dishevelled. But, rather than listen to her instincts, she preferred to believe her handsome, wonderful husband when he said he thought he'd heard Athene cry out and had gone to her in case she was in trouble.

As the weeks passed, relations in the marriage suddenly became more and more strained. He was absent much of the time, usually without explanation, and touchy when questioned. "Don't interrogate me", he thundered. She complained that she couldn't reach him, he seemed to have switched off from her. Their sex life, which had been passionate and inventive, dwindled away to nothing. Later she found out that the word processor had supposedly channelled that Loki and Athene were true soulmates who were destined to be together, to live and work as one. Athene left her husband and children to be with him. She was due to give a lecture tour in Australia. Loki went along too – but forgot to tell Aphrodite. Ironically the media at that time were promoting Athene as a happy, loving wife and mother: an expert on relationships. A closer look would have revealed her cavorting round Australia with her 'soulmate', but that would have destroyed her image.

While all this was going on, there was a pressing problem for Aphrodite. She and Loki had bought a house, for which she paid. He had mortgaged it to his family bank – who had insisted that Aphrodite sign the mortgage too. The mortgage money had been intended to renovate the house. Instead, Loki used it for his Australian trip. Now, the money was due for repayment.

When he returned, he moved out of the house but stored his belongings in the cellar. As Aphrodite said, "I couldn't be free of him while all these things were festering beneath me". He also cut off all contact with Athene, who then came to Aphrodite for comfort. But the biggest shock of all came when his family bank demanded from Aphrodite the return of the mortgage money. After all, they said, you are no longer living with a member of the family and he has no money. You will have to sell the house and repay us. We can push this through the courts. Her efforts to contact Loki were to no avail, he had gone to ground. Soon she would be both homeless and penniless.

At this point, Aphrodite had a complete breakdown. The experience had wreaked emotional havoc. All her hopes were shattered. Her dreams for the future gone. She felt totally betrayed. Her so-wonderful soulmate had been exposed as a sham. Physically, emotionally and mentally she was at an all time low. Spiritually, she had nowhere to go. She was suicidal and desperate – and furious. She finally understood 'Hell hath no fury like a woman scorned'. She was immensely angry: this was primal rage. She plotted to kill him. The anger rebounded into her body. She almost died from the complications of an illness more usual in childhood – which her doctor diagnosed as a psychosomatic disorder. During the high fever that accompanied the illness, she experienced herself as roasting in hell. The devil wielding the pitchfork was, naturally, her husband, an image that embodied a psychic truth. The bitter experience propelled her into therapy. That she emerged from it a new and stronger person was the treasure at the heart of the experience.

When she was in the depths of despair, she asked why it had happened and was shown a vision. She was before the witch finders in Scotland. She was found guilty and burnt as a witch (something she had seen over and over again all through her life). Before being executed, however, she was presented with a bill for her stay in prison, her trial and even her inquisition to exhort a confession. All her assets had been confiscated when she was found guilty, so she did not know how she would pay. Not surprisingly, in the vision the chief witch finder was none other than her husband, Loki. She had cursed him as she died, a curse that brought them back together. She assumed the vision embodied a psychological rather than psychic truth.

Notwithstanding, 'coincidentally', she was asked to do some research work on the witch finders in Scotland. There, on the page before her was a picture of her husband but it was the chief witch finder for Edinburgh some centuries earlier. Her present life husband had lived most of his life in Edinburgh and had always wanted to take her there for a visit. She, uncharacteristically, had refused. Scotland was the only part of the British Isles to burn its 'witches'. Elsewhere they were hung or drowned – burning was reserved for 'heretics'. "The bastard did it again", was her comment. "Not only did he roast me alive in this life too, but once again he made me pay for the privilege!"

This is not a unique story. So many of my clients have a similar tale to tell. Not all of them come out of it as well as Aphrodite did. Her therapy enabled her to take a long, hard look at her deepest patterns. One of Aphrodite's major lessons was to break her old emotional responses. Love and the emotional games attached to it had ruled her life. She had spent so long searching for her soulmate, and tended to assume that every man with whom she 'fell in lust' was the one, an illusion she had seemed unable to break out of. Now she had to detach from that old emotional reaction and learn to respond in a new way.

When she had finished this emotional transformation work, she did a ritual to contact the goddess Aphrodite. She wanted to heal her relationship with love, to find forgiveness in her heart. Not exactly one of the goddess Aphrodite's strong points, she was known to murder her rivals. However, after the ritual, the mortal Aphrodite was able to negotiate a divorce settlement that left her home intact. She also insisted that Loki remove all his belongings, after which she felt free. Possessions and photographs hold the 'vibrations' of the person associated with them. It can sometimes be cleansing to have a ritual burning of such items, or to give them away. Aphrodite certainly found it so when she burnt his love letters and gave his gifts to a charity shop.

Much as she had wanted to kill him, she had also recognised that retaliation would start the karmic round again. Although it was hard, she did not want to carry any karma forward into another life, and so she let go of the past and forgave Loki. In forgiving him, she recognised it was his nature. She could not blame him for that. The god Loki too was an untrustworthy husband, and his mortal counterpart a natural imitator. After the marriage broke down, she found he had left three other women in similar circumstances. He was a con man par excellence. Once the illusion was shattered, she could not only see him for himself but also recognised her own part in it.

Wanting to clear as much of the past as possible, she invited Athene to dinner. Before the Loki incident, they had been friends. She recognised that Athene had been as deeply hurt as she had. Now she was able to extend forgiveness here as well. She finally exorcised the whole tale by writing a novel – and Athene too wrote the story of her affair with him. In doing so Aphrodite found a deep well of creativity within her. One of her projects was so apt, a new way of looking at love and what it would bring, that it found instant success. But, of course, if I identified that, it would reveal who she is. So, we must now draw a veil over Aphrodite except to say that in the intervening years, she has refrained from serious relationships and still lives alone.

3

The Mythic Explanation

So God created man in his own image, in the image of God he created
them: male and female he created them. And God blessed them and
God said unto them: Be fruitful and multiply, and replenish the earth.

Genesis I:27-28

Have you ever wondered why, in Genesis, there are two stories of the
creation of man and woman closely following each other?

We are first told that God creates male and female in his own image.
Although not mentioned by name in the Bible, tradition tells us that
this first woman was Lilith, Adam's first wife who was created equal
to him. She refused to be dominated sexually and flew out of paradise
to live by the shores of the Red Sea and was later portrayed as a kind
of psychic sexual vampire who preyed upon men, especially celibate
monks. Whereupon the more familiar Eve was created because:

For Adam there was not found an [sic] help meet [mate] for him.
And the Lord caused a deep sleep to fall upon Adam, and he slept; and
he took one of his ribs, and closed up the flesh instead thereof.
And the rib, which the Lord God had taken from man, made he a
woman, and brought her unto the man.
And Adam said: This is now bone of my bone and flesh of my flesh: She
shall be called Woman, because she was taken out of man.
Therefore a man shall leave his father and his mother, and shall cleave
unto his wife; and they shall be one flesh.

Genesis 2:20-25

So here we have two versions of the creation myth, one of which
suggests that there may be unfinished business with a beautiful but
independently created soulmate who is her own person, and the other
that a soulmate is a pliant, dependent 'other half'. The mythic Jewish
tradition suggests that Adam was bereft without his first soulmate,

who was a spirit or goddess rather than a physical being. Indeed he was left soul-less and the first man needed spirit release therapy and a soul infusion before he could find his other half:

> Come and see: There is a female, a spirit of all spirits, and her name is Lilith, and she was at first with Adam. And in the hour when Adam was created and his body became completed, a thousand spirits from the left [evil] side clung to that body until the Holy One, blessed be He, shouted at them and drove them away. And Adam was lying, a body without a spirit, and his appearance was green, and all those spirits surrounded him. In that hour a cloud descended and pushed away all those spirits. And when Adam stood up, his female was attached to his side. And that holy spirit which was in him spread out to this side and that side, and grew here and there, and thus became complete. Thereafter the Holy One, blessed be He, sawed Adam into two, and made the female. And He brought her to Adam in her perfection like a bride to the canopy. When Lilith saw this, she fled. And she is in the cities of the sea, and she is still trying to harm the sons of the world.
>
> Zohar 3:190

It was Lilith that medieval monks blamed for their nocturnal emissions, she was said to visit them in their sleep and torment them, drinking them dry with her sexual wiles. She represents the demonised, rejected dark feminine aspect of these celibate men and the other half of their soul.

The Mesopotamian myth

> Let one god be slaughtered…
> Let Nintu mix clay,
> That god and man
> May be thoroughly mixed in the clay,
> So that we may hear the drum for the rest of time
> Let there be a spirit from the god's flesh.
>
> Atra-Hasis

In early Mesopotamian myth, man is created partially from a sky god and partially from the earth, uniting above and below. In a continuation of the Lilith story from ancient Sumeria (otherwise known as Mesopotamia, a land where the Jews had been taken into exile just before books of the Old Testament were first attested), Lilith was a consort of the goddess

Inanna. She was said to hold tantric secrets that she taught to followers of the goddess. Through this sexual mysticism, the inner masculine and feminine were united. In one of the earliest Sumerian myths (preceding Genesis by at least one thousand years and probably more), the Epic of Gilgamesh, there is mention of Lilith as a highly independent spirit who has to be vanquished from a place that Inanna, her bright soul-sister goddess, more familiar to us under the name Venus, coveted for herself:

After heaven and earth had been separated
　and mankind had been created,
after Anûm, Enlil and Ereskigal had taken possession
　　of heaven, earth and the underworld;
after Enki had set sail for the underworld
　and the sea ebbed and flowed in honour of its lord;
on this day, a huluppu tree
　which had been planted on the banks of the Euphrates
　and nourished by its waters
was uprooted by the south wind
　and carried away by the Euphrates.
A goddess who was wandering among the banks
　seized the swaying tree
And – at the behest of Anu and Enlil –
　brought it to Inanna's garden in Uruk.
Inanna tended the tree carefully and lovingly
　she hoped to have a throne and a bed
　made for herself from its wood.
After ten years, the tree had matured.
But in the meantime, she found to her dismay
　that her hopes could not be fulfilled.
because during that time
　a serpent who could not be charmed
　made its nest in the roots of the tree,
The Anzu bird set his young in the branches of the tree,
　And the dark maid Lilith built her home in the trunk.
But Gilgamesh, who had heard of Inanna's plight,
　came to her rescue.
He took his heavy shield
　killed the dragon with his heavy bronze axe,
　which weighed seven talents and seven minas.

Then the Zu-bird flew into the mountains with its young,
while Lilith, petrified with fear,
tore down her house and fled into the wilderness.

Prologue to *Gilgamesh*

This can, amongst many other interpretations, be looked upon as the conquest and subjugation of the dark feminine that has lodged itself in a bright soul. Lilith represents Inanna's shadow energies but shadow energies are complementary and hold great gifts although all too often the shadow is seen as undesirable and suppressed. If she had been able to integrate the dark feminine and find wholeness rather than having them vanquished, Inanna might have been able to avoid her own descent into the underworld and subsequent dismemberment. But this initiation was forced upon her by a dark twin the Queen of the Underworld, her sister Ereshkigal.

The story is a potent soulmate myth and, amongst other allegories, one of the great, and earliest, rebirth sagas dating back to before 3000BCE. Inanna's journey can also be looked on as the initiatory journey of the soul as it sets out from its 'heavenly abode' and goes down into the dark world of emotion and pain:

From the Great Above She opened Her ears to the Great Below
From the Great Above the Goddess opened Her ears to the Great Below
From the Great Above Inanna opened Her ears to the Great Below
My Lady abandoned heaven and earth to descend to the Underworld...
She abandoned Her office of Holy Priestess to descend to the Underworld
She gathered together the Measures of Heavenly and Earthly Powers
She took them into Her hands
With the Measures of Heavenly and Earthly Powers
She prepared Her Self...
Inanna set out to the Underworld.

Her journey is to visit her sister-goddess Ereshkigal whose husband has just died. Ereshkigal is in anguish, showing that even goddesses are not immune to the searing grief the loss of a soulmate or twinflame can bring, and she turns that pain onto her sister, forces her to become 'naked and bowed low', and eventually kills her and hangs her on a peg for three days. When Inanna is resurrected and returns to her throne, she finds her husband Dumuzi partying rather than being in mourning. Angry, she sends him to take her place in the underworld but Dumuzi's sister offers herself in his stead. Moved by the sister's devotion, Ereshkigal accepts a compromise: each will spend six months in the underworld and six above ground. This early saga has many aspects of soulmates: dismemberment, pain and anguish, sacrifice and transformation.

The Egyptian myth

> O Nut!
> O Great One who has become the sky!
> You have mastery, you have filled every place with your beauty.
> The whole earth lies beneath you, you have taken possession thereof,
> you have enclosed the whole earth and everything therein within your arms
> As Geb, I shall impregnate you in your name of sky,
> I shall join the whole earth to you in every place.
>
> Pyramid Texts

In an Egyptian myth that is at least as old as the Descent of Inanna, when Ra created the first god-beings, Shu and Tefnut 'without recourse to woman', from a cosmic orgasm, they were a divine pair. Their children Geb and Nut were the earth god and goddess of the sky. Originally these two had been closely united, like conjoined twins, both brother and sister and husband and wife. Indeed, in one version of the tale they had sexual congress in their mother's womb. But Shu, on the orders of Ra, tore them violently apart and fixed Nut high in the sky as the heavenly vault and Geb was flung down to form the earth.

Ever afterwards, so the myth tells us, Geb was inconsolable and his lamentations were heard day and night – the text above is a love poem to his wife. He is usually pictured with a huge penis reaching up towards his sister-wife. His longing for her is acute. Ra, who, according to one version, had separated them when they married without his consent, forbade them to have children. In another version their father separates them because Nut eats her children: the stars and the sun (an early eclipse myth). Thoth, the tricky god of wisdom, gave them five 'dark' days that did not belong to the official calendar. During these days Nut was able to bear five children and Geb's longing was assuaged. During the remaining 360 days of the year, they were parted.

An even earlier Egyptian myth tells the story of the creation of humans by the potter god Khnum whose name means 'unite', 'join' or 'build'. A fertility deity, Khnum at their conception created children from the silt of the Nile. He is usually depicted as a ram-headed god sitting at a potter's wheel where he moulds twins: the child and its ka or animating soul, looking exactly like twin souls so the longing for a soulmate may be for that part of yourself which is not in incarnation, you are really longing for union with your soul.

The Greek myth

> It is from this distant epoch then that we may date the innate love which human beings feel for one another, the love which restores us to our ancient state by attempting to weld two beings into one and to heal the wounds which humanity suffered.
>
> Plato

Plato's *Symposium*, which sets out a picture of soulmate origins that perhaps explains and certainly reflects the universal longing for a soulmate, seems to owe something to both the Mesopotamian and Egyptian myths. In it, Aristophanes explains that human beings were originally two persons in one body, with two heads and four arms and legs. In their completeness and self-satisfaction, they rolled along in ecstasy, ready and able to do almost anything. They had formidable strength and vigour and overweening pride that led them to attack the gods. Not wanting to kill them outright, Zeus, the Head God, split them in half, thus diminishing both their powers and their happiness, and forcing them to spend their lives yearning for the missing half and, if they did meet again, the outcome was not a happy one:

> Each half yearned for the half from which it had been severed. When they met they threw their arms around one another and embraced, in their longing to grow together again, and they perished of hunger and general neglect of their concerns, because they would not do anything apart. When one member of a pair died and the other was left, the latter sought and embraced another partner, which might be the half either of a female whole (which is now called a woman) or a male.[1]

---

1. Plato, *Symposium* (London: Penguin 1951) p.6.

Plato also tells us that there were originally three sexes: male, female and bisexual hermaphrodites. Each male was split into two male halves, each female into two female halves, and each hermaphrodite into a male half and a female half. The male halves then sought their twin in another man, the females in another woman, and the parts from the hermaphrodite in heterosexual union. So, in this view, a soulmate does not necessarily have to be of a different gender. We have just as much chance of finding our soulmate in homosexual relationships as in heterosexual ones.

We can see in Plato's description of what happened when the two parts of one soul found each other again one of the major pitfalls of the soulmate experience. The two halves became so enamoured of, and reliant on, each other they would perish from hunger. In a way, this is what happened to author Arthur Koestler and his wife who committed suicide together because she could not go on without him when he decided to end his life due to ill health. This kind of 'total union' can, contrary to popular belief, sometimes be totally disempowering and, as we shall see, it may be necessary for one half to get out of the relationship in order to survive.

Years ago, I met a woman at a party. She knew nothing about me, but spent a long time telling me about her problems in relationships. A couple of days later she knocked on my door. "I don't know what you do," she said, "But whatever it is, I know I need it, right now". When I explained that I sometimes took people back into other lives in order to find out the meaning of what was happening in the present life, she said, "That's it! Do it!" She didn't want to tell me why in case it influenced what I did, so we went straight ahead with the regression. One of the inductions I use is to open a door and step through into the other life. As soon as she stepped through, she gave a great sigh of contentment:

Mmmm... I'm in the most beautiful garden. It is so peaceful and tranquil here. I can hear the bees humming in the flowers and there are birds singing. I am sitting on a seat under an apple tree, just looking at the garden. In the distance I can see a small house. This is my home. It is so beautiful. Quite perfect. I am so happy with my life.

Now I am waiting for my husband to come home. We have only been married a year. Here he comes [great excitement in her voice]. He is so dear to me. We are so happy. I love him so much. He is here, he is kissing me. We sit in the garden and take tea. Life is so perfect.

Being a bit of a cynic even in those early days and thinking this regression was all too perfect – an illusion maybe? – I asked her to move forward in time:

> As the years pass we grow more and more in love. We are so happy, so content with each other. We do not have children, but we don't need them. We have each other.

Eventually I took her forward to her death:

> I am in bed. I know 1 will die soon. He sits and holds my hand. He wants me to be with him forever, but I know it is my time to go. He kisses me and I fall asleep. I never wake.

I asked her if she needed to do anything else, "No," she said, "I know what I came to find out". When I brought her out of the regression her comment was:

> It was all so perfect, so wonderful, and so very very boring. I didn't learn anything, I didn't grow. I didn't do anything with my life. I thought at the time love was enough. But it wasn't. And now I'll tell you why I wanted to do that regression. I have met a man. He seems to be perfect. We get on so well. He wants to marry me and spend the rest of our lives together. We seem to be soulmates. But somehow I don't want to. I couldn't think why. It was what I had been looking for all my life. But now I know. He is the man from that other life. I would be bored and I couldn't stand that again. I want a relationship that helps me to grow.

A past-life regression may not be to an actual, factually true, lifetime. But it nevertheless is a symbolic and psychic truth – it is the way our soul communicates to us what our psyche has experienced and is still experiencing at some level. This woman had experienced 'true love' with a soulmate but it was not enough. Deep down inside, she knew that the soulmate experience she so longed for could only take place through her own inner integration, not from someone outside herself.

But, in time she forgot that. Her need for companionship became so strong that she married that man, who looked after her to the extent that he hung up her clothes for her as she took them off, and even took the top off her boiled egg before she ate it. He had retired and they did everything together. At first they were blissfully happy, soulmates – she said. After a few months of marriage she was going up the wall. "I just can't stand it. I feel stifled, I have no life of my own. I have to get out. This is not what my life should be about". She needed to get back onto her soul's path and so they parted.

We all have different needs and expectations around love. Let us go back to those explanations of how soulmates arose. In Plato, yes, there are two souls seeking to merge back into the wholeness they once knew. You might be one of those souls. In which case, you are desperately looking for your idyllic partner who accepts, loves, cherishes and understands, as no one else can. But say you are one of the satellites of the Hindu oversoul (see Chapter 5), expected to take all your experience back into the group, so that the whole can learn and grow. How will you then become whole unless you merge back into the oversoul from which you came? Can you find completeness in another soul? Is that what you are here for? Unlikely. And how about those of us who came out of the soul group of Western esotericism. Do we have to merge with each and every part of the soul group before we can find lasting love? Do we need to redefine our view of relationship, to open it up to a much wider meaning, including everyone with whom we interact? Should we perhaps be seeking completeness in our self, in our inner union, so that through our learning the greater self can expand? This is the experience of those who grow through their soulmate contacts.

4

The Psychological Scenario

Human nature displays a strong tendency to attribute to others
the attitudes, impulses, feelings and ideas present within us.

Robert Assagioli

Psychology has various answers to the riddle of soulmates. In at least one psychological view, there is an inner being – named by Jung as the *anima* or *animus* depending on whether you are male or female although I would argue that we all have both genders within our inner being due to our experiences during reincarnation. This inner being was historically regarded as the opposite gender to the body you inhabit but it is now being recognised that our inner being contains both masculine and feminine principles. This inner being contains all the 'ideals' we have internalised – and quite a few less desirable qualities too. When we meet someone who embodies exactly these qualities, we recognise them. We say, "Here is my other half" and do not recognise ourselves. In other words, that kind of soulmate is a projection of our deepest desires, fantasies and expectations – our dream lover incarnate in flesh. This is, of course, a deeply unconscious process divorced from the everyday mind.

In the psychological view, so long as the projection of the ideal continues, and the other person does not intrude themselves into the picture, we will be satisfied. But as soon as they become an individual to us, or as soon as we begin to get glimpses of our own part in the interaction and they become someone other, disillusionment sets in. They are no longer perfect, simply because they are no longer reflecting our ideal back to us. With a nice twist, they then reflect back to us the undesirable, or unacknowledged, qualities in ourselves that we have been trying to hide from all this time. Whilst this kind of soulmate may offer us an irresistible opportunity to know our self, we may nevertheless resist with all our might. We feel that they have let us down rather than recognising that what we sought was the result of an unconscious 'fantasy'.

As we shall see, the anima or animus often wears the, unrecognised, face of a parent. As we begin to understand these projections, so we begin to know our self at a deeper level as the true Self, the eternal – and I would say divine – part of our being emerges.

The Mirror of our Being

> We are mirrors of stellar light and we cast this light outward as. . .
> magnetic attraction, characterizations, desires.
>
> W B. Yeats

The kind of soulmates we have been examining are the mirror of our being. As I have asked before, if we lived in isolation would we ever come to know our self fully? This seems to be a task for our soulmate: bringing to us face to face with all the issues that need our attention, all our karmic lessons and ingrained patterns, all those unrecognised and unloved aspects of our self that we have been avoiding for so long and all our undiscovered potential, offering us the opportunity to love ourselves unconditionally and totally – not a selfish action but a self-enhancing process. And also potentially bringing to us the love we seek.

This love may not always be apparent at an everyday level of being, it may have become warped and twisted, but it is there at the level of the soul, at the place where we make our deepest connection. If we seek love conditionally, if we limit it, put 'oughts' and 'buts' onto it, try to hedge it around with cast-iron guarantees, then what we get back will be conditional love. If we approach love with the view, "If you are right, then I must be wrong", or "You are doing this to me", then we will never resolve the duality of an I-and-You position. If we always see what we are seeking 'out there' in someone other, we can never be whole. But, if we seek love unconditionally, open to whatever is, then we will receive unconditional love.

As we will see throughout this book, many relationships, karmic or not, embody at least some element of projection or mirroring. Projection occurs when someone sees something which belongs 'in here' out there in the world or in another person. It is as though one, but usually both, partners in a relationship are reading from scripts, but each script is for a different play that they themselves have written from their unique viewpoint, based on past experience. Partners may believe that they are taking part in the same play, but in reality each is playing out a role assigned by the other person in his or her head, in his or her play. It is not a shared reality. Such projection is rarely spoken about and, even when it is, as we shall see, it is difficult for either person to recognise their particular projections. And when it is spoken, it is frequently rejected by the other person.

Projection in relationships can manifest on many levels – including the physical, emotional, mental and spiritual planes. A soul may project back into the past, bringing forward 'what has always been' to show this is how it should be now, or can introject 'what I want to happen' into the future. There are many varieties of projection:

- ♥ The soul sees what it expects to see – conditioning from the past produces a preconceived image that may be far from true.
- ♥ The soul sees what it wants to see and disregards the rest.
- ♥ The soul projects an idealised or demonised picture onto someone else.
- ♥ The soul expects a partner to behave as they did in another life.
- ♥ Expectations that the soul has brought from another life are mirrored by a partner.
- ♥ Behaviour by a partner mirrors issues from the soul's own unrecognised behaviour.
- ♥ Something unpalatable that the soul cannot own as mine is projected out onto another person.
- ♥ The soul sees its own unrecognised strengths in someone else.
- ♥ The soul projects past life behaviour and expectations by a partner into the present life.
- ♥ The soul recognises a spiritual connection and acts from the belief that it will be perfected in the present life.

Projections can change as a relationship progresses. What starts out as 'ideal' quickly becomes the exact opposite if the projection is not owned. In a 'negative projection' all the soul's worst fears appear to be confirmed in a relationship by the partner's behaviour. In the stages of relationship (see page 51) souls may successfully negotiate the shadow projections and power struggles of the early stages – where many relationships flounder – only to face them again at a much deeper level which I call spiritual relationship, when chronic soul problems are encountered and healed.

What do I see in you?

> Relationship is surely the mirror in which you discover yourself.
>
> Krishnamurti

So, as we can see, the simple answer to the question, "What do I see in you?" over and above karmic considerations, is: "myself". At a deep and fundamental level, like attracts like. The qualities that we seek in others in order to make us feel complete are precisely those that our soul has set us the task of discovering in our own self. The things we dislike in our partners are exactly those things we dislike in ourselves.

As Steve and Sharon Biddulph put it, "We have trouble living with our partner because we have trouble living with ourself".[1] They too believe that we attract a partner that embodies what we most need to learn, or relearn, about ourselves. If we can turn our attention inwards, and withdraw our projections, then we can recognise within ourselves the qualities we have been seeking 'out there'. This can take enormous pressure off partners and allow them to be themselves. After all, few people want to be idealised, or demonised, or pressured in any way, especially to change or to live out someone else's expectations. Nor do most people necessarily want to know what makes them tick. Many people who try to share karmic insights with a partner are met with indifference, or even hostility. In a letter written in 1951, Carl Jung said:

> In the end people don't want to know what secrets are slumbering in their souls. If you struggle too much to penetrate into another person, you find that you have thrust him into a defensive position.[2]

All we can do is work on our own soul growth and recognise what our relationships are trying to tell us – rather than our partners. If we take responsibility for our own feelings, then we can make the changes our soul is calling for – and neutralise relationship karma.

I use Christie and Tyrell's story to illustrate this point because he has a psychotherapy background. I had particularly wanted to include in *Hands Across Time* an experience told by both partners and preferably by someone who had a psychotherapy background with the insights that

---

1. Biddulph, Steve and Sharon, *How Love Works*. (Thorsons, London 2000).
2. Jung, C.G. *Letters Vol.2* Gerhard Adler with Aniela Jaffe, eds, trans. R.F.C.Hull (Princeton, Bollingen Series XCV, Princeton University Press, 1973) p.27.

could give. The couple I choose, Christie and Tyrell, had extremely interesting synastry between their astrological charts, particularly the deceptive and illusory Neptune-South Node contact that so often feels like 'Here is my soulmate at last' and which can be oh so right, or oh so very deluded and find it extremely difficult to tell the difference. I knew then they were finding it difficult to work their way through what was proving to be a problematic relationship, even though it had seemed so 'right' when it began. In their case, it was made more difficult through living in different countries and having to maintain very different lifestyles and yet there appeared to be deep love between them. One of the reasons I had asked for their story was that I felt the objectivity of looking at it from outside, of asking, "How do I really perceive this relationship?" might help to throw new light on the relationship – in other words, for them to look into the mirror of their being.

When I had examined their astrological connections two years previously, it had seemed to me that they truly were mirrors for each other. There was a powerful sexual attraction, but also a sense of "knowing each other from before". However they approached life, and relationships, in totally different directions. Communication was important for Tyrell, for him closeness involved shared thoughts and feelings rather than physical contact. For the much more tactile Christie, shared sensual and sexual experiences would lead to emotional closeness. Each had the astrological indicators of the problems the other was encountering. Each had a huge difficulty with intimacy and a desire to run away from it all. Both had the expectation that they were unlovable, and that what love they could get would be cold and distant, and in addition Christie had a 'Love hurts' scenario. Tyrell, on the other hand, had the ingrained expectation that he would not be heard. He had a deep communication wound. They shared a freedom-commitment dilemma, but Tyrell's love-planet Venus in particular wanted to be free. Christie played out this part of the relationship because she commuted between countries, leaving Tyrell alone for months at a time. So he felt abandoned where he would otherwise have felt trapped. She, on the other hand, felt trapped where she needed to be free.

Her Descendant (one of the major relationship indicators) was in the same sign as his Sun – authoritarian Capricorn. He represented what she was expecting from relationships, and we see what we expect rather than what actually is. His Moon and Venus were in the sign that made up most of her seventh house – the relationship house. He had qualities she, knowingly or unknowingly, sought in a man. But it would be like a mirror image, and, as with most people in this position, it was doubtful if she would recognise him as that mirror or see herself in it. Due to the astrological configurations, he, on the other hand, had more opportunity to recognise, "This is me, that is you". But it would be difficult to find the mutuality they sought. Anything that activated her Venus also pressed her 'I can't be loved' button. Anything that activated his Venus pressed his 'I want to be free' urge. He perceived her as taking his freedom, while she experienced him as cold and unloving. The placement of the Nodes suggested that she was trying to move out of losing herself in relationships to find her independence, he was seeking to merge, to find union with a partner – but each saw that in the other.

In the first draft I received from Christie, I got a 'There isn't any love there' saga. The second draft was cut in half by the fax machine (most symbolic). The third had the last page missing. Finally the full story arrived with its acknowledgement of the love they had shared. But, as she said later:

> This has kept me locked in a battle which had nothing to do with the relationship. It has kept me from recognising the love that is there. And yet, because I recognise the projection of the coldness and lack of love, how can I be sure the love I perceive isn't also a projection?
> – a difficult dilemma indeed.

Tyrell and Christie's story graphically illustrates what happens when one partner believes they have uncovered the past life reasons that lie behind a relationship and projects that 'understanding' – and all the boiling emotions and blame that go with it – onto the present life relationship regardless of how the other person resonates with the story. Past life 'knowing' is only beneficial when it is owned by the person who has the memory who uses it to understand his or her own story rather than projecting it onto a partner who may or may not be the person involved in the old tale.

Christie's story: The perils of a handsome French stranger

> This story represents a shard of my soul. . . a piece of the stream of consciousness which inhibits my ability to experience ordinary human

affection and love on an ongoing basis. A memory or feeling of love lost has haunted me since my first sweetheart at fifteen, with whom I had my first child. I used to cry and not understand what the tears were about. Writing this story makes my heart both ache and pound with anxiety.

Each man I've been with in this life has reflected a bittersweet sorrow along with the deep love I yearn to share with a partner. I have always had a man around to share my life with and, with only one exception, have fond memories of each one. Somewhere inside me there's been a caution. . . a feeling that the person is not the right man for me. That transparent layer of indecision affected my self esteem and peace.

This all changed twelve years ago when I realised how this sense of caution was diluting the quality of the relationship I had with my then partner. I allowed myself the privilege of loving one man deeply and fully and our spiritual connection is very strong today even though our physical relationship ended in 1990. He and I used to talk about things concerning the soul, Aquarian things. He challenged me to communicate love from the ache in the heart, and we taught one another volumes about our humanity. I was once told we would stick with the relationship until spirit moved to end it, my diamond inside would be polished.

I went to Egypt in April of 1990 and the first night encountered a male spirit who came to me in a vision and took me to a beautiful chamber where we were both wearing long, flowing white gowns. I was overjoyed to see him and remember a warm feeling inside filling me with anticipation. Then my mother opened a door and came into the room. I pulled back and withdrew my affection towards the man, at which point my mother smiled and gave me permission to be with him. After she left the room and closed the door behind her, he picked me up and laid me back on a chaise-longue couch. I thought we would make love, but instead he told me it was not time, kissed me gently on the forehead and disappeared.

I was in Egypt a month and barely slept for the joy I felt in having met him once again. During a later ceremony at Sakkara I knew that I would sell my home of eighteen years upon my return from the journey, the six-year relationship would end by Christmas (no signs at that point), and I had to give up over-mothering my daughter. All three things happened and I set out on a new course in life. I chose not to date, knowing I would remember the feeling of the man when I met him. I immersed myself in my work and began to write.

In December of 1993 I had a dream that the man from Egypt was coming into my life. I usually wore a ring on my left hand wedding finger to deter suitors in general and in the dream I took the ring off. The next morning I physically took the ring off and tucked it away. I felt the same deep joy and clarity I had felt in Egypt. Friends started asking me if I had met someone and fallen in love. I just smiled to myself in anticipation.

A couple of months passed and in early February of 1994 I was warned by an intuitive that I would meet a man and want to run away, but not to – because this would be an important relationship. I said I knew my partner was coming and left it at that.

The next morning, a lazy Monday, I met Tyrell, a man with whom I immediately felt a strong attraction. He rang me that night and we had tea on Tuesday at 11am. I soon noticed a clear, thick wall between us causing us to have a difficult time communicating.

On Wednesday I received a two-page 'sorry I'm not interested' letter – "You're a Leo and I've done that!" I wrote him back that day. Thursday I rang him at work to say I respected his opinion, yet I thought there might be value in our getting to know one another. Although he was polite, he was steadfast that he wasn't interested, and I hung up the phone with tears running down my cheeks. This was odd given the brief time we'd spent together. Also I wasn't that keen on anything getting in the way of my work. I went away for the weekend and walked along the country roads trying to make sense of the brief encounter and the deep feelings stirring in me.

He called me Monday afternoon and asked if I wanted to go out for a meal. I said yes. We were comfortable together and got on well. He called me the next evening and asked me if I believed in monogamy. I said I believe in being true to myself and that includes being loyal in partnership. We spent that weekend together. We laughed, lay belly to belly snuggling for hours, hugged continuously. Seven months later we had a private wedding ceremony with no family or relations – his choice of marriage, which began our nightmare. The communication broke down completely and I felt he wanted me to go.

Life with Tyrell was chaotic and exhausting. He's a psychotherapist and was constantly on about how I was "projecting on him". I'm not a therapist and found being a patient rather than lover and wife quite a shock. He enjoys words and presents to express love and I enjoy physical touching to express my deep feelings. It was obvious that neither of us had our needs met. I said I would go, which made him feel insecure. What a waste of energy.

I went away on business early each day and when I returned he was distant, not wearing his wedding ring, and constantly telling me how much I'd hurt him. I wanted to leave and get on with my life. Instead I stayed with him to see what I could learn. I had recurrent bladder infections and was unable to reach orgasm. A few months later I saw a Chinese medicine doctor-homeopath who prescribed essences and promised I would be able to orgasm in no time at all. He also detected a layer of depression. I took the remedies and I was finally able to relax and reach orgasm. . . Ah relief. Some months later my bladder symptoms cleared also.

Tyrell had been with his soulmate, his wife of twelve years, and they had parted years before we met. Later, after rethinking his concept of soulmates, he felt his sister was the closest thing he had to a soulmate. This didn't surprise me because they were very close. I told him I thought our family dog Max was my soulmate! I wondered whether either of us was even remotely available for this exercise in love.

I remembered a past life clearly in which my partner was a French trader and I was a native American woman. I called Tyrell 'Pierre', which he didn't like, being British, so I stopped. I always also had a strong sense that there was a spell to keep us apart. He dismissed my memories since he had no sense of them himself and said I was projecting.

The strange energies continued between us, and Tyrell mentioned his distress to his therapy supervisor, who recommended a shaman "who would straighten out my unhealthy projections". When we finally got to see him, the first words he said were, "There's no love here". He then proceeded to describe the Indian life I remembered and confirmed there was a spell designed to keep us apart forever. I trembled and wept as the memories swamped my senses. Pierre had asked me to leave my people and go with him. I loved him and agreed. My people refused to let me go. I thought about what they said and one night crept out to tell him I would not go with him. When I got to him, he was having sex with another woman. I was heartbroken. Within seconds a spell-laced arrow pierced his heart and he lay dead before me. There was a second arrow which would have taken my life. Instead I was left with the sight of the man I loved betraying me in a way which I had not imagined. It was not the way of my people. Heartbroken, I was taken back to my people, married the man I had been promised to before the French man came, and had several children.

During the session, I remember looking across the room at Tyrell, who kept saying as if to expose me, "See, she is projecting! She does this all the time! She's the problem". There was no mutuality in the memory or any compassion from my husband for the grief I was experiencing – nothing to remember together.

The shaman stopped time and pointed to my husband's dialogue, and warned me that staying in the relationship could be hazardous to my spiritual health. Remember, this is the therapist Tyrell forced me (my victim/authority issue) to see because he thought I was projecting something which had nothing to do with him. On his side, it was to sort out the shadow, so we could find out what was happening with the energies. Coincidentally, he did go along to see the shaman later and had the spell removed – just in case; but he has no memory of the experience and still believes I am projecting something that has nothing to do with him. The shaman warned me that once the spell was removed there might be no connection left between this man and me. What a relief after all the heartache.

Within a couple of weeks we went to see a European doctor who looks at blood cells and diagnoses what the cells in the body are up to. After meeting with my husband, the doctor said my husband did not trust me, and when there is no trust, there is no love. This confirmed what the shaman said. I left the office saddened and determined to clear this matter up. To me that means taking responsibility for identifying the emptiness in my heart in the light of day. It has been a difficult year to integrate the depths of consequences following from the chaos of the infatuation I felt for the Frenchman. The spell was meant to scatter the energies and keep us apart forever.

Tyrell and I don't laugh. We don't sleep well together. We barely touch one another. We are strangers once again. This reflects our communication breakdown. We are both looking deeply within ourselves for clues to continuing to spend time learning from one another. But living without the tenderness and affection of the remembered love with a group of people haunts me. I ache because I do remember. This is the journey of my soul and I will continue to follow my yearning.

We can see just how different Christie's approach to life is and glimpse some of the difficulties she and Tyrell encountered in entering into each other's reality when we read her, now ex, husband's account of the same relationship:

Tyrell's story: Perseus meets the Medusa:

I was once married to someone I perceived as my 'soulmate'. We had much in common and an intuitive knowing of each other. After twelve years the marriage ended, causing me to examine many things, including what a soulmate was. My resulting belief was that there was no such thing: if we had all evolved from an original point of being, then we were all equally connected to each other and therefore equally capable of loving and being loved by anyone. It was simply down to choosing whom we wanted to be with. I filed the concept of soulmates under 'romantic notions' until I had further evidence.

Over the following years my sister, Sara, and I spent more time together than we ever had done. We shared the joys and pains we were experiencing as we moved in and out of relationships, and noticed that we were constantly being faced by the same learning challenges. We would have similar 'ahas!' of realisation at the same time, similar thoughts, similar relationships. We also noticed that the degree to which we were able to support each other, and feel supported, far exceeded that of any other relationship we had. There was something 'twin-like' happening, as though we were taking our learnings back to a shared point of being. There was a sense of working for the same goal through parallel experiences. Even now, we both stand bewildered in our separate relationships, confused as to 'what the right thing is', awaiting the mutual 'aha!'

One evening we played around with the 'what if' of our being some sort of soulmates. The next day, Sara came across the writings she had made a few years before at a 'write-in', where hours are spent in endless writing without any purpose other than to clear creative blocks to the unconscious. Sara had never bothered to read what she had written until that day. Among the many things that she had absolutely no recall of writing was the sentence: 'Your brother is your soulmate.' This provided a comforting thought that there may be a special relationship in the world, helping with the feelings of existential aloneness, but not a belief that it was so.

My first words on meeting Christie were, "I know you!" And somehow, I did. I was immediately attracted to her but inside part of me was shouting "Keep away!" There was something in her that was too challenging. Having 'suffered' in the den of a Leo a year before, I was unwilling to be drawn in by the kitten aspect and initially resisted, yet here was something totally dissimilar to any previous relationship I had had. I saw Christie as a woman, not as a girl.

The differences between us were many. I was quiet, reflective and fairly solitary [Capricorn Sun and Aquarius Moon]. Christie was loud, expressive and very sociable [Leo Sun and Moon]. We were from different countries and cultures. And though I believed differences were important for a relationship to be 'active' and growth promoting, there seemed to be too much to deal with, with her. I not only saw the beauty of who she was, but also saw the shadow in her that she was not owning. In previous relationships I had considered it was part of the process to draw this part out but somehow knew it would not be easy with Christie. I didn't realise at that time how distorted that belief was!

Christie, however, gently pushed to get to know each other better – and I agreed. Seven months later, we were married. The seven months had been an intense and romantic time, much of it spent apart in our respective countries communicating through long letters and phone calls. Our commitment to each other was total and surprising. Neither of us believed we would ever marry again.

We chose the date and time of the ceremony astrologically in order to face as much of ourselves as we could within the relationship. I'm not sure that with hindsight we would make the same choice.

The conflicts began immediately – and we were both shocked. For my part, I couldn't believe this was the person I had fallen in love with. Where she had initially seemed the woman I would most like to be with if I were a woman, she was quickly becoming the opposite. I was training as a psychotherapist at the time, but my skills of objectivity were swept aside in the onslaught of feelings.

I was well aware of the stages of relationship and did not expect the romantic phase to last forever, but I felt overwhelmed by the power of what was happening. All I could do was hold onto the belief, 'There must be a reason'. The inability to communicate was the biggest factor. I had always put communication at the top of my list of 'absolute necessities' in a relationship. Suddenly I found myself unable to make any impression on Christie with my thoughts and feelings. It was as though I didn't exist. All my issues of not being seen or heard flooded forward. Frustration grew. She expressed similar feelings. I felt steam-rollered, manipulated, misunderstood, misquoted, mistreated and powerless in the relationship. I reached a point where I actually believed there was something seriously wrong with my perception of Christie. . . and the world, to be in such a chaotic state. My reality was being thrown up for examination [reflecting my Moon sign, Aquarius and much else besides]. The knowledge that I loved this person was consistently present. The other consistency was the sense of being in a relationship, yet very alone.

I slowly began to come to terms with the fact that I was 'out of control'. Everything I saw Christie 'doing to me' I had done in previous relationships. Everything negative I had felt about myself I now felt in a magnified form. Here was the perfect mirror for me to gaze at. Here was 'instant karma'. Whether Christie really was 'doing it to me' began to dwindle in significance. The importance was in how I dealt with it. Do I really want to feel hurt, rejected, angry? Or can I move into that more adult place of acceptance? And do I want to even bother?

One day I requested guidance and selected a book at random from the bookshelves. Equally at random I selected a page. It was the myth of Perseus. In the flush of manhood he accepts the king's challenge to go and cut off the head of Medusa. Any man who looked upon the horrendous face of Medusa, framed by writhing snakes, became paralysed with shock. Medusa is the image for the 'negative feminine' – the dark shadow aspect. Perseus took with him a burnished shield – not to protect himself in the usual way, but to use as a mirror, so that he did not look at Medusa directly but through the reflection instead. He manages to slay Medusa and from her head flies Pegasus, potent with the positive feminine qualities of creativity and spirituality. Perseus then went on to free Andromeda from being sacrificed – another metaphor for the freeing of the anima, the feminine aspect. This was the perfect summary of what was happening. In the past I would encourage the Medusa to come forward in relationships and my male part would become transfixed by her darkness. I would use the 'niceness' of my feminine to try to change her – and, of course, it didn't work. I would be constantly disappointed by my partner and never feel potently male. All of this I also experienced as a child in relationship to my parents.

With Christie, everything seemed exaggerated. I would often say to her that I was 'shocked', 'horrified' and 'appalled' by things she did or said, and I don't use these words lightly. My whole being would experience absolute horror. I was still trying to deal with the dark feminine by 'looking to her' and becoming transfixed. When Perseus held up his shield as a mirror, he was looking at his own dark feminine instead of someone else. But without Medusa's existence he would never have had cause to look in the mirror.

The sword that Perseus used to slay Medusa was given to him by Hermes, the 'crosser of boundaries', who is connected to moving between the conscious and unconscious. It was clear that the challenge was to face, and accept, my own unconscious aspects of the dark feminine in order to free the positive. Presumably Medusa's death results then from natural causes!

I feel this is where I am now, working to slay my horror of Medusa by 'allowing' the feminine in all her forms to come through, and learning how to use my masculine to hold the form of my life for it all to happen. At the same time, all this affects my relationship with Christie through a progressive acceptance of her.

For as long as I can remember, my interpretation of the word 'love' has been 'complete and unconditional acceptance'. When I react to my partner, I am not accepting, and the only path to acceptance of something in others is to first find it in ourselves and accept that.

Anyone who helps us on that road of self-investigation and self-acceptance has to be a messenger from God. Yet that messenger can only ever be perceived as someone to run as far away from as possible – or be destroyed, which is surely why 'soulmates' is not a term usually applied to such relationships. We like comfort, not confrontation!

Would I prefer a warm, cosy, supportive relationship? Yes, and yes again, but it's a bit like the mountain that has to be climbed because it's there – I just hope there's a good view from the top.

Whether my own story will transpire as beautifully as Perseus is yet to be seen. By its nature, mythology describes the ideal rather than the norm and it may be that I am not a 'hero'.

I still don't believe in soulmates, but I do believe that the gift Christie has given me, forcing me to look deep inside, is every bit as valuable as that of the more conventionally accepted version of mutuality. And who knows, perhaps one day we may have that too – if we manage to stay together. . .

Notwithstanding their apparent differences, these were two people who at that time still seemed so right together. Despite the cultural differences, they were so alike in many ways that they could almost be twins. When my daughter met Tyrell she said, "I just knew he had to be Christie's husband. He couldn't be with anyone else. They are so alike". Before they separated, I had hoped that when Christie had recovered her heart from that handsome French stranger (whether or not this had been

Tyrell in a previous life) she would be able to make her own inner marriage with the 'Egyptian' who was waiting. With Tyrell having faced his own dark feminine, the relationship would inevitably change – potentially for the better. But it was not to be. In an update Christie wrote:

> That was a year ago and I have learned much since that time. I am grateful for the confirmation. Grateful for the deep healing and release, and the connection I feel with all people has deepened. I travelled to the Yucatan on my own, keenly aware that there is no longer a man 'out there' for me. I have stayed with myself and the sweetness of the heartfelt memories intact before this man (the Frenchman) crossed my path so long ago.
>
> The greatest gifts of this marriage are that I have got my heart back from the Frenchman, released the energies of the spell, and have freedom to begin again. I was also able to grieve deeply for the sense of loss from 'giving my heart' to a French stranger in another time. I identified the emptiness of living without welcome, the darkness of losing the love and acceptance of a community for a stranger.
>
> According to a recent meeting with an astrologer, our charts are such that we are opposed in every way – leaving us to 'agree to disagree' and struggle to meet in the middle on most issues. This information was tremendously liberating.
>
> Tyrell has offered a good lesson for my heart, one which I'm still learning. I do love him and somehow always have.

And as Tyrell later wrote to me:

> Eighteen months ago, I told Christie I wanted a divorce.
>
> Five months later we were separated.
>
> Unsurprisingly to me, I was exhausted – emotionally, mentally and physically. However, six months after our separation, instead of recuperating, I seemed to be getting worse.
>
> Three people, two of whom knew nothing about me, told me I was under serious psychic attack – no prizes for guessing where it was coming from. One added that I was also being vampirised by my mother. I am tempted to say that is another story, but it's not, it's the same story. By the end of the marriage, I was virtually penniless, I had M.E. and I was told I was pre-cancerous. At every level, my energy had been utterly drained and I was spiralling downwards. And the draining was to the dark feminine.

In the original text for *Hands Across Time*, I wrote 'presumably Medusa's death results from natural causes!' I felt vague when I wrote it. What I have discovered since is that it is not possible to remain in the cave of Medusa without a clear purpose. She does not die of natural causes, her darkness dies through her being clearly seen in the mirror (in myself) brought forward and then integrated. I was reminded of this quotation:

If you bring forth what is within you, what you bring forth will save you. If you do not bring forth what is within you, what you do not bring forth will destroy you.

The Gnostic Gospel of Thomas

I had to make a choice, either to give up on a world that could not provide the partner who would love me and make me feel whole, or bring my unacknowledged feminine forward and work toward an inner marriage. It's too early to say for sure if I have made the second choice, though I feel I have.

I had been co-authoring a book, but it was not a book that sprang purely from the heart and pleasure of my own creativity. When I did begin work on such a project, energy began to return. This continues to fit in with the myth of Perseus, as Pegasus (creativity and spirituality) is released.

The dark feminine is merely the unrecognised. I am learning how to welcome that part of me. My work as a therapist is far more intuitively led. My writing is beginning to flow again. More and more I connect to and am fed by Nature. And for the first time in my life, I am very consciously staying out of relationship. (As is my sister!)

I no longer see happiness 'out there' but rather through the integration of the healthy inner masculine and feminine. It has been an understanding that I spouted forth to clients, but never before did I know it so well as now.

There was another gift of learning from all of this. I realised I had spent much of the marriage (and my life) protesting my truth – wanting for it, and therefore me, to be acknowledged. In this way I was externalising my need to be validated. This was bigger than just relationships, I had a great desire to change the world – to make it better (in my view!).

It took a judge's mocking cry in the divorce court, "Truth! What is truth?!" for me to see he was right. What is truth? It really doesn't matter. But I knew this issue was very old for me. It was time to validate myself.

Christie unwittingly brought me to that awareness.

Our primary responsibility has to be to ourselves – to take ourselves to the limit of our potential, and if another person offers to help us on that path, no matter how they do that, then that person deserves thanks.

Thank you, Christie.

The good news is that Tyrell, having validated himself and learned how to be intimate with both himself and another, is now in a relationship with someone he had loved from afar as a young man and re-met many years later after his marriage to Christie broke down. Despite initial difficulties including the logistics of his partner having lived in another country for most of those lost years and her having to relocate and adjust not only to a new country but to a new love, the relationship is blossoming. Whether they are twinflames or not remains to be seen.

The Stages of Relationship

Relationships are the juice of life. If you do not experience them as an elixir, then they have probably become a poison.

Chuck Spezzano[3]

According to Chuck Spezzano, who has worked with many couples, the development of a relationship falls into clearly defined sequential stages, during which certain issues will come up and various states of mind will be encountered. Clearly Tyrell and Christie whose story we have just heard moved rapidly through the initial stages until they became mired in what Spezzano calls 'the Dead Zone', but they could have got stuck in other places too. 'Stuckness' doesn't only occur in the present life, it is possible for a relationship to pick up at any point where it left off in a past life, or to repeat the stages from the beginning. Although Spezzano uses this cycle for a couple, it can also occur with myriad soulmates as souls interweave into and out of incarnation.

♥ **Romance:** This is the stage where potential becomes visible and the promise is held out of a wonderful relationship to come. The couple have fallen in love – possibly with each other and most definitely with the idea of being in love. A romantic relationship fulfils the soul's need

---

3.   Spezzano, Chuck, *Wholeheartedness*, Hodder and Stoughton, London, 2000.

to be special to someone. It is a time when the ideal man or woman is projected onto the prospective partner, and may, or may not, be fulfilled. In this phase it is 'sameness' that is perceived, similarities to the ideal or behaviour and looks that feel familiar and comfortable.

♥ **Power Struggle**: This is the time when past life tensions, power struggles and ego conflicts surface. It is also the phase where differences become apparent as fears arise and each partner struggles to get their needs met. For some partners, that fear is of stepping into their own power. They prefer to remain in powerlessness and open to victimization because that is what is known and familiar – and therefore safe. For other partners, the fear is of 'giving away their power' in an equal relationship. Yet other fears include that of intimacy and trust, or commitment.

Within 'Power Struggle' there are different stages. In 'the Shadow', the worst case scenario from past experience, childhood and split-off parts of the self are introjected into the relationship and issues arise around the personal shadow and negative expectations. The partner may be demonised – or demoralised – as each struggles to get their needs met and to feel in control. This stage was clearly demonstrated by Christie and Tyrell's story. The challenge here is to forgive and integrate all the qualities of the split-off self that are perceived in the partner into oneself.

The 'Independence and Dependence' phase is where the partners learn to balance out the conflicts. At this stage each partner will take on a role – which can switch – and play that out for a time as they negotiate to have emotional needs and expectations met. If the soul can value the partner more than the need to have its own way, then healing takes place and the relationship progresses.

In the 'Positive and Negative' phase each partner usually plays out one of these roles – which are simply different ways of seeing and interacting with the world. 'Positive' goes for the bigger picture and solves problems, whilst 'negative' identifies problems and attends to the details. If the two can work together in partnership, they are complementary styles and lead to a successful relationship.

♥ **'The Dead Zone'**: The Dead Zone is that plateau most relationships hit when the excitement and initial challenge have gone and boredom sets in. It is where many past life issues will be replayed and, potentially, worked through to resolution. The soul's ingrained expectations from childhood and past lives will arise as well as deep-seated needs that demand satisfaction. It is where Tyrell and Christie in the previous case history very quickly found themselves.

'The Dead Zone' can be characterized by a sense of being trapped, and one soul then struggles to be free whilst the other holds on or tries to merge. There can also be withdrawal due to fear of relating or commitment, so one partner holds back and the other partner either tries to give them the space they need or presses forward to fill the space as they withdraw. When this occurs, the soul who is holding back either feels abandoned as the partner withdraws, or feels overwhelmed if the partner advances: all the fears seem to be coming true.

In the Dead Zone fusion or 'counterfeit bonding' can take place. It is characterized by diffuse boundaries and co-dependency, or by one person being swallowed up by the other in a powerfully symbiotic relationship. For a time fusion may feel very comfortable. The souls believe, falsely as it turns out, that they have achieved exactly what they set out to find: union and togetherness. When they recognise consciously or unconsciously that the partnership is without heart or shared soul purpose, then the problems begin again and the soul will use various strategies to feel comfortable once more. Partners caught up in fusion may become 'heroic givers' out of guilt, or act out the needy demanding role that causes the other partner to fear being swallowed alive or dried out by psychic vampirism. One partner may well go into self-destruct mode or create an illness in an attempt to get the attention and care he or she so desires, or to break free from the situation.

This is also the plateau where over-compensation for perceived failures takes place. The ego is at work here. It will be 'over-good' and sugary sweet as one partner tries to cover feelings of inadequacy or self-hatred. It may cause one soul to sacrifice his or herself to compensate for what is perceived to be a lack of love given. Whilst the partner may not fully recognise what is going on, at a subtle level the lack of congruency between the inner feelings and the outer behaviour will be picked up, which forms a block to continuing relationship until the two can align and become authentic.

Partners can also play on each other's weakness and create chironic pain or wounds as retaliation for perceived hurt. The ingrained patterns to which people are still attached make themselves felt. People play out roles or take on burdens – or stay in a relationship because of duty or guilt. They may, for instance, replay childhood trauma or unfinished parental business with a partner. They could also do the right things for all the wrong reasons – to make themselves feel better, for example, rather than coming from the heart or in order to be thought good and caring rather than genuinely expressing compassion and interconnectedness.

If the souls can successful negotiate the pitfalls and traps of the Dead Zone, the relationship can continue into a more positive phase:

♥ **Partnership Stage**: By the time the partners get to this stage they have become comfortable with each other. They will probably have incarnated together many times and taken on a number of different relationship roles. They now truly recognise each other and value what they see. Two people have become one not in the sense of merging into each other but in the reality of having created a relationship that functions creatively and well. But it does not do to get complacent. Souls have an impetus towards growth and deep issues may well arise which need healing or reconciliation so that the souls can move on into the next phase.

♥ **Spiritual Relationship**: Spezzano terms this stage 'leadership' but I find this term difficult and prefer to call this the 'spiritual relationship' or twinflame stage. This is where the day to day struggles have dropped away and ego needs have been left behind. It is 'transformational, inspirational and intimate'. The souls know each other very well indeed and offer support at all levels. They honour and respect each other's individuality and yet are closely bonded. This is where sexual alchemy begins to subtly transform the partners and their soul energy in the spiritual dimension. They commence the journey of reunification with the divine. At this stage, where the souls totally trust and have limitless compassion for each other, deep 'soul fractures' can be brought to the surface for healing. These are the chronic problems that have dogged the soul for many lifetimes and when these are released, spiritual peace is achieved. This is the place from which a twinflame or soul companion relationship (see Chapter 17) operates.

Beyond this is what Chuck Spezzano refers to as 'Vision, mastery, tantra and union', stages that take place at the level of the spirit rather than the psyche or the ego. Souls have to have cleared all their issues around relationships and be practising truly unconditional love for themselves and others to enter these levels of partnership. When they do, they step off the wheel of relationship karma and into an entirely different space.

Seeking the Twin

> Each of us then is the mere broken tally of a man, and each of us is perpetually in search of his corresponding tally.
>
> Plato

Soulmates are often referred to as twin souls – something different to a twinflame. Twin souls are someone's 'other half' or twin. Soul splitting can occur during the soul essence fragmentation and regrouping as a group soul incarnates (see Chapter 5). But another explanation for this yearning for a twin soul, which comes close to what Plato had to say, occurred to me sometime ago whilst listening to a programme on twins. The researcher said that as many as sixty percent of pregnancies are 'twin' pregnancies in their early trimester. That is to say, a fertilised egg splits and two foetuses share the womb together for a few weeks. Then, one twin is absorbed by the other so the bodies become one again. This may be why, traditionally, in esoteric thinking the soul only joins the body fully when the quickening occurs. One foetus may also be lost by miscarriage or by stillbirth but the other thrives physically but perhaps not psychically, whilst the other may remain psychically attached but have no physical life. As only one soul generally inhabits a body, one has to leave and find another home. If that soul returns to another body and the two souls meet, it will feel like 'here is my other half'.

This loss of a twin in the womb can leave a lifelong sense of incompleteness and longing, an experience for which a client of mine, Tim, seemed to find confirmation, during a shamanic experience in South America.

Tim is an extremely psychic and sensitive Pisces with the Sun and North Node conjunct the wounded healer planet Chiron in the seventh house of relationships and a deeply constricted Venus-Saturn contact at the head of a Finger of Fate with mystical Neptune on one side and Pluto-Jupiter-Uranus on the other, which meant that he had a deep soul wound in need of healing, an intense desire to return to 'oneness', and just about every negative karmic script it is possible to have about love.

He undertook a classic shamanic journey. The drugs shattered him, took him apart so that he had to put himself back together again. Then, when Tim was at the Temple of the Moon with a shaman called Augustine, he was given San Pedro cactus before going into a cave:

> I knew it was going into the womb… I lay in the foetal position with my head over this circular hole that felt very, very deep…
>
> I started to connect to my birth into this present life… I was conscious of being a twin, and then the experience of miscarriage [of his twin] and the pain of that. It was really heart wrenching. It was like losing someone, a relationship breaking up.
>
> I connected to the fact that whenever a relationship was breaking up, I would go right down into the worst pain of loss, and that the loss was coming from losing my twin. I was shown that birth sets you up for your whole life. The energy that you are born into is important and very special. Whatever that energy is, you're implanted with that dynamic. Like your birth chart, that is your energy.
>
> I also felt the pain of losing the other half, of how I have carried that pain all my life, in everyday life it has always been there. It affects how I do things. I also felt how I did not want to be born because of that loss. I wanted to stay in the womb because it was a safe space, and nearer to where I had come from.
>
> Then the healing of the birth started. By being shown everything, it was transmuted at the same time.

Tim went into a powerful healing memory of a past life during his birth in a tepee as a native American. The child was welcomed by the whole community, which was closely involved in the birth. Drumming was used to stimulate the baby into birth:

> The drumming became more erotic, began to move around more, like a swaying and sensual dance…. It was wonderful to be born with that feeling instead of being induced with drugs as happened in my present life.

When Tim left the cave it was dusk, exactly the time he had been born the first time in this present incarnation. But now he has been reborn. He is convinced that the miscarriage his mother suffered, apparently just before his conception, was actually of his twin and that he himself stayed in the womb and was born ten months later. Throughout his life, he had felt incomplete but after the shamanic healing, he was whole in himself. He then entered, for the first time in his present life, a committed, long-term relationship.

5

The Esoteric Explanation

> The *self* is the creator. The person, the physical, material manifestation
> is only one half of the true being. The other half has remained behind
> in the unconscious, unmanifested state… When a person has made both
> halves of his being conscious, and experienced them consciously, he has
> become identical with his self, and he carries within himself both the
> male and female principles in complete equilibrium.[1]

The esoteric answer to where soulmates began can only be symbolically
described at best. I find words limit our understanding when trying to
get our heads around such an esoteric concept. They do not add to it.
But I have to try to explain so that we know what I'm talking about, so
here goes.

In certain schools of Hinduism, there is the concept of an 'oversoul',
which has several facets in incarnation at once. These facets are rather
like puppets controlled by an oversoul, so that they gather the experience
it is seeking. When two of these facets meet, they are attracted to each
other and feel like twin souls. When the facets move out of incarnation,
they take back to the oversoul all they have learnt. So, meeting any
one of those 'puppets' will feel like meeting another part of yourself, a
soulmate, and their experience will feel like your own. There is a similar
Sufi teaching in which souls that are departing the earth hand over their
experience to souls coming into incarnation so that they can benefit
from what has been learned.

In Buddhism there is no one soul or self, indivisible or divisible, only
consciousness and qualities that split, combine and recombine through
endless rebirths – until liberation is reached. If we all partake of the same
consciousness, then anyone can be, or feel like, a soulmate, especially if
they carry experiences or expectations with which we resonate.

---

1. Haich, Elisabeth *Initiation* (London: Unwin Paperbacks 1965) p.477.

In the Western Mystery Tradition view that I learnt from my mentor Christine Hartley, which is loosely based on Theosophy, a pool of spiritual essence contains the whole (see Figure 1). A piece of this 'breaks off' – the soul group – and then continues to subdivide into individual souls. However, the parts can come together again to unite, fragment and reunite, sharing all that has been learned. This is the interweaving web of soul connections. Each part of this web will feel like a soulmate, some more strongly than others depending on how far from the original branching the souls have moved and on the experiences they have had together in former lives. So, souls A and B will probably recognise each other, and may feel like soulmates. G and H will be 'soul companions', one in incarnation and the other guiding from another dimension. E and F will probably feel like soulmates if they meet. But will C and D? They have come a long way from the original split. From experiences in other lives, they may feel like powerful enemies. Love and hate are two sides of the same coin. In this picture, there are souls that will never incarnate on earth at all. They act as 'guides' or soul companions. I have since realised that the lines of descent from point B could result in twin flames if they reincarnate at the same time. Other lines of descent would be

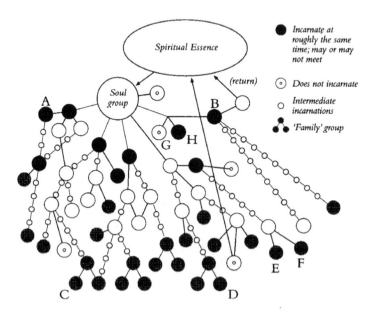

Figure 1. The Western Mystery Tradition soul group.

soulmates. This is the concept I personally find most helpful as it accords with my clients' experience during regression in the between life state.

Whilst not everyone we meet will be part of our soul group, it is likely that important contacts, whether they are fleeting or lifelong, will be with someone from 'our group', although some groups interweave with others and certain people stand at the interface between several soul groups acting as catalysts or movers and shakers for soul evolution. In this view, our parents or wider family, friends or partners, may or may not be from the soul group. It all depends on the impact they have on us.

It is possible to choose a family for the genetic, skill or emotional or attitudinal inheritance rather than a soul connection – although we usually find at least one member of our true soul group within the family to support us in our early years as, if not, life feels very lonely indeed. It is possible to be attracted to a partner because he or she embodies soul patterns and traits with which we are all too familiar within the soul group. They feel comfortable, and safe, even when they are far from being so. It is also obvious from regression work, that we can belong to more than one group, although if we trace the connections back far enough, we will find that the two apparently disparate groups are in fact one.

Sex and the chakras

> My backbone feels like a bridge of glowing embers, holding seven burning torches.
>
> Elisabeth Haich, *Initiation*

Chakra connections are an important part of the esoteric explanation of soulmates and karmic enmeshment can take place at an energetic level through chakra connections. The chakras are energy centres along the spine, rising from the base chakra at the bottom up to the crown chakra at the top of the head and on up through subtle chakras way above the head (an important part of energetic soul enmeshment). These energy centres form the link between our physical bodies and the more subtle levels of our being. They lie along the pathway that the kundalini takes as we open up our spiritual – and our sexual – energies. Kundalini is our 'inner fire', both raw sexual energy and a spiritual force that resides, until awoken, in our base chakra. Eastern yogis have always stressed the importance of right preparation before kundalini is awoken, as otherwise the consequences can be dire.

In the book *Initiation*, Elisabeth Haich connects the potential for spiritual union, at a soul level, with the desire for sexual intercourse and says that it is the unsatisfied longing of the soul for 'paradisical union' that lies at the heart of the dissatisfaction and fatigue that many people feel after sexual intercourse. I would, however, suggest that it can also be because of energy depletion through the chakras as one partner energetically or emotionally 'feeds off' the other. Haich also points out that the higher someone rises in their spiritual evolution, the higher their vibrations are, and the more irresistible their emanations become to other people – and such an attraction may be misused by false gurus. She highlights the need to control the flow of spiritual energies through the body as otherwise the nerve centres (what I would call the chakras) can be damaged by the flow of untransformed energies into the lower centres. In her book, the High Priest tries to warn the initiate of the result of such an unrestrained act. But, with deep feeling with which I am sure many people would be in total accord, the initiate points out that:

> The best advice cannot change inexperience into experience, and my inner lack of balance and self-control had to be brought back into equilibrium through painful experience.

While I was researching the story of the poet Dante and Beatrice – whom we have already met – for another project, I was interested to see a website that offered the view that the kind of idealised, unrequited love that Dante felt was actually part of his pathway to enlightenment. Peter Y. Chou points out that:

> Images of enlightened masters and sages usually show a single person in meditation, alone in a cave, desert, or mountain. On the other hand, images of romance show couples embracing, dancing, kissing, closely together.

Chou goes on to point out that:

> At first glance, romance and enlightenment appear exclusive of each other – the first mostly physical and emotional, the second mostly mental and emotionless. But the path of romance need not be stuck on

the lower three chakras (energy centers of survival, sex, and food). If we learn to rise to the fourth chakra (heart), true love enters and we become compassionate to all sentient beings. Dante's love for Beatrice enables him to glow 'with a flame of charity' (as exemplified in *La Vita Nuova XI*). From here on, his spirit would rise to the fifth chakra (throat) – the voice of poetry, then ascend to the sixth chakra (third eye) – celestial vision, and finally soar to the seventh chakra (thousand-petal lotus) – spiritual awakening and bliss. The spirit of romance is also a valid path to enlightenment. Dante Alighieri [did] it when his love for Beatrice enabled him to experience the soul's ascent to paradise, then toiled to write *The Divine Comedy* for us to drink.

Chou goes on to say:

May we be worthy of these celestial gifts when we bestow our heart on those whom we love.[2]

The chakras play an important part in soulmate relationships. The base and second chakra are closely connected to our sexual organs and to the sacrum or 'sacred bone', and can be opened through sexual intercourse. With the right partner, all the chakras will open and the kundalini flow during sexual congress, leading to a true union on the physical, emotional, mental and spiritual levels of our being – the mystic marriage or twinflame experience. With a past-life sexual partner, or with a false soulmate, the bottom chakras only will light up but the kundalini can still ignite – sometimes with dire consequences. One treatise on Tantra says that the kundalini is likely to be stimulated and awakened by sexual contact as the life energies merge. This is an unmistakable experience. There is a rising tide of 'liquid fire' that is both hot and cold, lightening and liberating. It is an electric feeling that almost paralyses as it takes the breath away and opens up the whole being.[3]

Despite all that the Christian church – and others – have taught about the value of celibacy over the last 2000 years, such sexual energy has its place in spiritual work and may be why soulmates seek each other so assiduously. Whilst celibacy may be one way of attaining a spiritual peak experience, sexual experience is equally valid. Millennia ago, sexual

2. Chou, Peter Y. http://www.wisdomportal.com/Romance/Dante-Beatrice.html
3. Douglas, Nik & Penny Slinger, *Sexual Secrets*, (Destiny Books, 1979).

energy was recognised, and utilised, for spiritual growth. The kundalini force, when approached with proper reverence for its power, could take one to the spiritual heights – instantly. Tantra is one of the remnants of this age old teaching. However, in the hands of the inexperienced, the kundalini force could blow someone apart, physically, emotionally, mentally and spiritually. So, the unfolding of this power was in the hands of those who were trained to understand it. Knowledge was withheld from the inexperienced, not to gain control, but to prevent harm.

Sexual magick was a part of the esoteric teachings revived at the beginning of this century by metaphysical organisations such as the Order of the Golden Dawn. (We will look at the experiences of two initiates later). For the most part, although there are genuine masters trying to revive this knowledge, these highly trained beings are no longer easily available, especially in the West – but many false gurus have tried to take their place. So, humankind is now left to find its own way. But the old forces are still there.

Powerful, and often inappropriate, sexual attraction is one of the pitfalls of the spiritual and soulmate path. Men and women who are developing their intuitive and spiritual faculties find themselves compulsively attracted to, or attracting, sexual encounters of a destructive kind – especially when control over this force has not been mastered. Some people have a magnetic sexual charge, a sexual frisson that touches everyone around them – look at some of the great actors or actresses and some of the more enduring pop stars.

A past soulmate can have this same effect on a previous partner. So often, the first meeting with a soulmate is accompanied by a wave of lust as our lower chakras burst open under an irresistible force. The challenge is to transform the energy, to bring it to a different way of functioning, to be truly creative on the level of the spirit, coming into union with the self. We may not be meant to jump into bed to immediately discharge this energy nor should we just ignore it. So often the energy is repressed, only to rise again even more strongly.

One only has to read the early desert-dwelling church fathers to see how obsessively they dreamed of sexual temptation, and, today, some priests and guru-figures hold a particular aura of sexual magnetism for certain women – and men. Sexual charisma exudes an aura of power, and power is open to abuse. Contact between priests and choirboys regularly features on the front page of the tabloids, as do bishops and their love affairs. Gurus and their disciples make the news less often, but the attraction, or the abuse, can be the same as my postbag attests. It can be an irresistible, inextricable mix of the sacred with the profane, the forbidden with the greatest temptation. One does not have to be a priest or guru to carry this air of 'forbidden fruit'.

Over and over again, when people describe their first meeting with their soulmate, the common thread is overwhelming sexual desire. When I began my work with Christine Hartley many years ago, she explained this kind of soulmate attraction as the result of the opening of the chakras and the rise of the kundalini energy. It literally results in a magnetic attraction to the powerful emanations of the kundalini force, and, because the soul is involved, it feels like the highest spiritual experience. In some cases this is so, and the sexual interaction is appropriate.

Unfortunately, many people find themselves pulled into this kind of pseudo-spiritual sexual attraction and try to justify it by saying that it is spiritual – the instructions being received 'from a higher plane' when in fact it is the repressed and denied side of their own sexuality. Like so many things, it is difficult to judge from the earth perspective exactly when such an interaction is appropriate and when it is not.

Chakra disconnection

When we have a sexual relationship with someone, they leave an energetic imprint in the chakras that can be 'felt' or sensed which is why tie cutting on the subtle as well as physical levels can be required to completely end a relationship (see Chapter 13). In cases where people come together purely for self-gratification, or to exert power over another person, it would seem that future karma can accrue and the passage will be even rougher, and it is even more essential that the chakra connection is dissolved and disconnected.

If it is possible to do this exercise with an ex-partner or present partner with whom you want to move to the next level of spiritual connection, then do so, if not then picture in your mind standing in front of him or her to perform the ritual or use a photograph.

Chakra disconnection ritual[4]

Place your hand on your crown chakra at the top of your head and then lightly on your partner's crown chakra while your partner does the same: Both say out loud, "I know you in all your fullness and accept what I know of you with love". Then remove the hands and say, "I release you and our connection at this level and at any higher level". Picture a white light healing and sealing the chakra as the connection is dissolved.

Place your hand over your third eye (just above your eyebrows) and then lightly over your partner's third eye while your partner does the same. Say out loud, "I see you in all your fullness and accept what I see at every level with love". Then remove the hands and say, "I release you and our connection at this level". Picture a white light healing and sealing the chakra as the connection is dissolved.

Place your hand over your throat and then lightly over your partner's throat while your partner does the same. Say out loud, "I speak to you in all your fullness and accept what is said in truth and love". Then remove the hands and say, "I release you and our connection at this level". Picture a white light healing and sealing the chakra as the connection is dissolved.

Place your hand over your heart and then over your partner's heart while your partner does the same. Say out loud, "I love you in all your fullness and accept your love". Then remove the hands and say, "I release you and our connection at this level and at the higher heart level". Picture a white light healing and sealing the chakra as the connection is dissolved.

Place your hand on your solar plexus and then on your partner's solar plexus while your partner does the same. Say out loud, "I feel you in all your fullness and accept what I feel with love". Then remove the hands and say, "I release you and our connection at this level". Picture a white light healing and sealing the chakra as the connection is dissolved.

Place your hand over your sacral chakra and then on your partner's sacral chakra while your partner does the same: Say out loud, "I honour you in all your fullness and creativity and create love with you". Then remove the hands and say, "I release you and our connection at this level". Picture a white light healing and sealing the chakra as the connection is dissolved.

Place your hand over your base chakra and then on your partner's base chakra while your partner does the same. Say out loud, "I share my fullness

---

4. Taken from Judy Hall *Good Vibrations* (Flying Horse Publications 2008).

with you in love". Then remove the hands and say, "I release you and our connection at this level". Picture a white light healing and sealing the chakra as the connection is dissolved.

Take your attention down to your feet and say out loud, "My grounding is my grounding and your grounding is your grounding. May we walk the earth separate and apart from henceforth".

Walk away knowing that you are now separated and on your own pathway.

If you are non-visual: place your hands on your own body and that of your partner if present. If your partner is not present, use a photograph and touch the appropriate parts as you speak the ritual. Place a piece of clear Quartz, Rose Quartz or Selenite over each site before moving on. When you have finished the ritual, clap your hands loudly to signify the end. Stamp your feet, walk a few steps and feel yourself firmly on your own path.

6

The Karmic Scenario

The shackles of an old love staiten'd him,
His Honour rooted in dishonour stood,
And faith unfaithful kept him falsely true.
                                Alfred, Lord Tennyson[1]

In many ways, we bring our relationship disasters or joys upon ourselves. This may be a positive, constructive choice because we have recognised that we need to learn specific lessons or change certain ingrained patterns of behaviour – although it rarely feels positive whilst we are going through the lesson! So often, we can only appreciate what we learnt in these situations with the value of hindsight, and that may have to wait until we move on from the present body. On the other hand, we may be so caught up in that old ingrained pattern that we unconsciously re-create it time and time again. Abuse, misuse of power, abandonment, rejection, domination-submission, and many other such scenarios have a powerful hold over us simply because they are known and familiar. In other words, they are compulsive and obsessive. They are rarely conscious and we may agonise over where we went wrong, how we came to be caught up in such scenes.

But go back to another life, then another, and another, and the chain of events becomes plain. It is only by compressing and intensifying this experience, bringing it to a point past bearing that we break out of the pattern – or away from the person – and find a way to move on. When this happens, we may go into a similar relationship for a short time, recognise it for what it is, and move on. When next the possibility arises, we will avoid it altogether. We have tested that we have truly learned the lesson and will not face that kind of relationship again.

---

1. Quoted in Viederman p.1.

A variation on this theme also comes up rather frequently: one life one way, the next life the opposite way. In other words, swinging between two poles of the same experience. Somewhere, somehow we have to stop and find the point of balance. We may also be getting back what we put out. If we abused, we become abused, if we were abused, we become the abuser. If we manipulated, we become manipulated, if we were passive, we become dominant. If we persecuted or ridiculed, we become the persecuted and the ridiculed. If we abandoned, we are rejected, and so on. It is rarely black and white. The person we treated so badly may either come back to us in the role of abuser, or we may find that we have to care for them. They could be our child, for instance. We may also find ourselves having to care for a child who, in another life, murdered us, abused us, made our life hell. We could also find ourselves married to that person. The confusion comes in when, despite all this, this person could still feel like our soulmate. Indeed we may have been attracted for this very reason. Our lesson is to change the pattern of interaction, to forgive, to let go, to love in a truly unconditional way.

The varieties of karmic relationship

> The heart has its own reasons which reason knows nothing of.
>
> Blaise Pascal

As we have seen, relationships are a fruitful, exciting and sometimes painful way of learning and growing and our present-life experience is seldom enough to fully explain our relationships. We can look to other lives for the roots of our relationship patterns. For convenience sake I call these past or previous lives, but these should not be looked at as strung out in a long line behind us. Our 'past' lives are all around us. We meet them everyday and it is these hidden influences that draw us to a soulmate.

From the karmic perspective, our soulmate comes to work with us on the karma that exists between us or which we individually carry. Karma is all that has gone before. It is action and reaction, credits and deficits. It is also potential, where we can grow. Whilst there is positive and 'good' relationship karma, it is the destructive, negative patterns that create most of the problems people encounter in their relationships, especially on a soulmate level. Part of our reason for being here is to recognise and reverse these patterns. Once a pattern becomes consciously acknowledged, it can be changed. Rather than blindly reacting in the same old way, we can chose to respond differently. We can become proactive instead of reactive. It is our soulmate (or mates) who are most likely to help us in this endeavour.

Earth is the place where we work on our emotions. It is the only level of existence where we can 'hide' our emotions. Communications from other levels, especially that 'closest' to the earth in vibrational terms, describe emotions as instantly visible by colour, emanation etc. So, the earth is where we may fool ourselves, and try to fool others, about our emotional state. It is also the place where we can gain emotional equilibrium. Relationships, or lack of them, are of course the vehicle for much of our emotional experience. Karmic relationships fall into two distinct types:

♥ Relationships based on a prior soul contact where themes or experiences are carried over and continued in the present life, and where our 'worst enemy' may well turn out to be someone with whom we have a strong and loving soul link or are on a karmic treadmill of disaster. This is the soulmate contact. Here the karma is personal to the two people concerned. These relationships fall within our 'soul group' – a group with whom we have had long connections and within which all relationship interactions have been experienced. Soul links can bring people together to undertake a specific task, to deal with unfinished business or to repay debts and obligations, to act as a catalyst, to learn soul lessons or to spend a lifetime together.

♥ Relationships in which we have no prior contact with the person concerned but where we are both working on a particular theme or pattern, and so we come together to try to resolve it or fulfil the potential of the contact. This is where we might feel we have met a soulmate because the contact feels so right, but it is more likely to be a spurious soulmate contact. It is plugging into all our old comfortable 'relationship receptors' and the other person is mirroring our most intimate self back to us through their innate patterns. But, the connection is rarely there at a deep soul level. We may sometimes create it through our relationship, but it is not an inherent factor in that relationship.

Reasons for reincarnating together

> Fear and hatred are the most powerful magnets in drawing souls
> together to complete unfinished business.[2]

The major reasons for two or more people coming back into relationship
together are:

- Spiritual bonds
- Previous relationship(s) carried over
- A soulmate connection
- Unfinished business
- Habit or inertia
- Dependence and symbiosis
- Lessons to be learned
- Attitudes to be transformed
- Debt or duty
- Attachment to mutual unhappiness or happiness
- Pacts or promises
- Love or hatred
- The desire for revenge
- Specific tasks
- Catalyst
- Positive service
- Enmeshment
- Guilt
- Holding onto the heart
- Illusions
- Karmic bonds
- Compulsive emotions
- A between-life decision to let go

---

2. Pauline Stone p.189.

♥ To be soul companions or twinflames

♥ To facilitate soul lessons

These reasons may well overlap and a relationship can include elements of several themes being played out.

♥ **Spiritual bonds**: Many people incarnating together will either originate in the same soul group or have built up powerful spiritual connections over many lifetimes. Some may have been specifically trained to connect at a soul level, such as making a 'mystic marriage' in which they were joined at the physical, emotional, mental and spiritual levels; or through several incarnations together as priest and priestess, monks or nuns within a religion where the emphasis was on spiritual oneness. Spiritual bonds can underpin relationships that flourish within the most difficult circumstances and may well support a couple through many incarnations. They often feel like 'soulmate' connections and may well be twinflame or soul companions.

♥ **Previous relationship**: A previous relationship that has carried over may play itself out again and again pulling the two people back into incarnation together in the process. This is particularly so when a pattern of dependency or abuse has developed but it can occur in families and marriages as well as other interactions. Such a relationship can be experienced as 'good' or 'bad' depending on how it is played out and the pattern behind it.

♥ **Soulmate connection**: as we have seen, soulmates feel as though they are made for each other, to the extent of being 'two halves making a whole'. Two people may well be soulmates, although this does not necessarily mean they are destined for a sexual relationship this time around or that it will be blissfully happy experience. Soulmate connections can occur between parents and children as well as friends and mentors.

♥ **Unfinished business**: Unfinished business is one of the most powerful factors in returning to earth together. If a lesson or task is incomplete, or not yet begun, or if a pattern has been strongly established and not broken, then the souls are pulled back time after time to resolve or fulfil matters. One soul may have to learn forgiveness, or to let go, to be independent, or to assert its own needs and so on. The other soul provides the opportunity for this to occur. Unfinished business may also be positive, the souls will have an on-going plan or purpose they are in the process of completing or they may be evolving together towards a specific aim.

♥ **Habit or inertia**: If the souls have not been moving forward, growing and evolving together or separately, then habit or inertia has set in. They may well return together simply because it has always been that way. Habit may also show itself in how one person treats the other – as a slave, for example. The habit may not be personal to the two people concerned. The present incarnation may well be an opportunity to change.

♥ **Dependence and symbiosis**: If one person is used to relying on, or 'feeding off', another person they may well return time and again in the same mode. 'Psychic vampirism', where one person draws energy off the other is often found in relationships and the partner whose energy is sapped may be trying to break away. People caught in a symbiotic partnership often feel they will die if the relationship comes to an end and they may need to learn that this is not so.

♥ **Lessons to be learned**: Many souls plan in the between-life state scenarios in which lessons will be learned, qualities cultivated and skills enhanced. One soul may act as teacher or mentor to the other, or be the 'victim' or 'perpetrator' through whom the other soul experiences whatever is required for soul growth.

♥ **Attitudes to be transformed**: The attitudes may be personal ones that change through the association, or repeating patterns that show themselves within a relationship. So, for example, if one person has always felt superior to the other it may result in a relationship in which the other person takes an 'inferior part' until the attitude is transformed. On the other hand, a soul may need to undergo a lifetime where it feels inferior, simply to understand what it is like and to overcome previous arrogance and then to recognise and respect the equality and difference of every soul.

♥ **Debt or duty**: A soul may feel that it owes a debt or duty to another soul. This may arise from promises made, either in another life or in the between-life state, or from events that have taken place. One of the souls may have saved the other's life, for instance, made a sacrifice, or performed a service in the past.

💜 **Attachment to mutual unhappiness or happiness**: Two souls may be held together by an attachment of one or both of the parties to the status quo, or to the desire of one party to make the other party happy – or miserable. This attachment may be to unhappiness just as much as happiness. If, for example, a couple are unhappy, one of the parties may feel 'if I can't be happy, he can't either', or 'well, if I can't have him, no one else will' and, therefore, refuse to divorce or let go. The depth of the attachment pulls the couple back time and again until detachment is reached. This is really an underlying control issue and cannot be solved until the dominant partner surrenders control of the other person's life into their own hands, or the submissive partner assertively takes back that control.

💜 **Pacts and promises**: Pacts, vows, promises and soul contracts hold people together across lives (see Chapter 13). These may be intentional or unintentional – saying such things as "of course I'll always be there for you", can create a powerful bond as can vows of fealty or obedience. They can occur between lovers, parent and child, or strangers. Declarations that, "I'll never have another relationship", "there'll never be anyone else for me" or "I will always love/hate you", can have a powerful effect through many lives. It can pull couples, or parents and children, into relationship time after time until a way is found to heal the interaction and change. Even decisions to "always love you" can be karmically blocking. It may be more appropriate for spiritual growth to let go.

💜 **Love or hatred**: The love and hatred in this interaction is not necessarily personal, although it can be. One person may feel great love and loyalty for someone he, or she, deems to be far beyond them on the social scale and similarly the hatred may be on a collective level – for a tribe or race for instance. At the personal level, however, 'love' or 'hate' holds many couples together and this may be constructive or destructive depending on whether it aids their mutual evolution or holds it back. Not everything that masquerades as love is a positive experience, it can be smothering or symbiotic for instance. Similarly, hatred may actually be the spur that helps a soul to grow. Nevertheless, hatred does create an exceedingly strong bond between two people and the lesson involved may be forgiveness and letting go.

Spite is a lesser version of hatred, although malice can itself be lethal. In a fictional tale, author Robert Goddard has described 'the secret ecstasy of spite rewarded'.[3] In the story, the sister-in-law of the Home Secretary is concerned that her own place in the family will be jeopardised by his forthcoming marriage because his bride-to-be is so much more attractive and outgoing than she – and younger. She ferrets out a secret of his bride-to-be – membership of the women's suffrage movement – and tells the government whips who are horrified. In real life, such an action could tie the souls together into another life, maybe in the guise of soulmates because they would be so well remembered, although had not been well loved.

- **The desire for revenge:** The desire to be avenged or to 'get even' with someone can pull two people back into incarnation, but the attitude may be transferred onto people other than the original perpetrator of whatever set off the desire for revenge if there is a resonance in the circumstances, attitudes etc. Here again, the soul is challenged to forgive and move on, or to do something constructive to transform the karma embedded within the situation.

- **Specific tasks:** Two or more souls may incarnate having agreed to take on a specific task together. This can range from creating the latest weapon of mass destruction to finding a cure for a rare disease. It is often concerned with healing or transforming earth life, for better or worse. Once the task is completed, the two souls may well go their separate ways. Many people who incarnate with a 'task' tend to forget as they become immersed in the incarnation. Meeting the other person again may be misconstrued as an opportunity for sexual contact as the attraction, or reaction, can be powerful.

- **Catalyst:** One soul may well incarnate to be the catalyst for another's growth or to bring about change. From outside, this may appear to be through destructive as well as constructive events or attitudes. For instance, if someone has always been clinging and dependent or if a relationship has simply run out of steam, the soul acting as a catalyst may well leave the relationship abruptly, precipitating the other soul into finding his or her own inner resources to deal with the crisis.

---

3.   Goddard, Robert, *Past Caring*, (London: Corgi Books, 1993 p.82).

Alternatively, an outside person may intrude into the relationship, causing it to split.

- **Positive Service**: Positive service can occur in friendship, families, love relationships or work situations. One person takes on caring for another or performs a task specifically to help the soul growth of the other which can occur in surprising ways such as a disabled child who offers his parents the opportunity to develop compassionate unconditional love. This is the positive manifestation of service; inappropriate service can occur if the parties become stuck in the helping or enabling scenario. Positive service may also include the opportunity to develop unconditional love through one soul playing an extremely difficult role.

- **Enmeshment**: Enmeshment is a situation where two souls are strongly intertwined due to karmic experiences. The souls incarnate together again and again in an effort to clear the situation. Enmeshment occurs:

  - where relationship karma is unfulfilled or unresolved.

  - if the obligations to a soul for whom one is responsible (as in parent and child) are not fulfilled or are opted out of.

  - where too much responsibility is taken for someone else.

  - where someone who seeks their freedom is held onto.

  - when someone else is blamed for the soul's own limitations or inability to move forward.

  - in situations where old promises remain.

To hold others culpable for the limitations a soul puts on itself creates a situation where the souls are drawn back time and again as one struggles to become free from the other. One soul may have to learn to stop blaming the other and take responsibility. Another scenario that invites karmic enmeshment is where one person feeds off the other: in other words, psychic vampirism which can be energetic, emotional and monetary, particularly where the vampire demands support at every level. Symbiotic, dependent relationships and situations such as master/slave or marriage where one person owns the other body and soul also create the same problem. The lesson is to let go, even when it is passing for love.

Enmeshment can occur when a soul takes on too much responsibility for another – especially for their wellbeing or their feelings. But equally, if one soul has failed to take appropriate responsibility for another – as in a situation where a child is abandoned for instance – then releasing the enmeshment may first involve appropriate parenting or care (possibly to the extent of caring for someone for an entire life if they are ill or disabled). At the right time, the soul must then be allowed the freedom to make its own journey.

- **Guilt**: Guilt is one of the strongest factors involved in drawing people back together who would perhaps be better served by letting go and moving on. People become 'heroic givers' out of guilt. Quite often the guilt is out of all proportion to what provoked it in the first place but guilt grows – and may be stoked by the other person as a form of manipulation. Unnecessary guilt can also fuel relationships. The challenge is to forgive and forget, and to let go (see page 159).

- **Holding on to the heart**: Popular songs from all ages include lines like: 'That kiss you stole held my heart and soul'. The heart has always been associated with love and we speak of a broken-hearted lover. However, it is clear from regression to other lives – and to earlier events in the present one – that 'giving away the heart' or 'someone taking a piece of my heart', are all too common experiences. This may be done intentionally or, seemingly, by accident or as a 'game'. If the event took place in another life and was not resolved, it brings the two parties together again so that the heart can be reclaimed (see Chapter 15).

- **Illusions**: as we will see, illusions in another life can create a situation where souls are pulled back together, apparently as soulmates although this may not actually be so.

- **Karmic bonds**: can include, but are not limited to, many of the above, and various examples are given throughout this book.

- **Compulsive emotions**: anger, grief and obsession or other powerful emotions draw souls back into incarnation together until they are let go of or healed.

- **An opportunity to let go**: letting go is an enormous karmic challenge. People hang on to what passes for love, or to the way they feel things should be; and to hopes, dreams and illusions. Letting go sets all the parties free and allows new possibilities but does not rule out the old. If it really is true love, if things really should be that way, then it will happen. But if it is not, then the soul is freed by letting go, stepping out of the karma, and moving on.

- ♥ **Soul companions or twinflames**: incarnate to mutually support each other with unconditional love – see Chapter 17.

- ♥ **To facilitate soul lessons**: as we have already seen and will continue to see, the most unlikely scenarios are organised by souls prior to incarnation so that one soul can learn from a lack of rather than from being given everything it needs or so that a soul will recognise that it is indeed stuck in an old pattern from which it needs to break free.

The Influence of the Past

In all the endless lives I was able to remember... I was always seeking the same voice and the same eyes in all the voices that spoke to me.

Elisabeth Haich, *Initiation*

An incarnating soul's emotional experience in previous lives colours its relationships in the present. Everyone goes into relationship, whether karmic or present life, carrying the weight of the past, projecting old experience forward into 'what might be' – unless they have come to recognise the inbuilt reaction and changed it into a more positive response. The different themes of previous lives usually appear as warring factions that battle for domination. The incarnating soul's behaviour at any one time depends upon which faction is in ascendancy over the others, but the overall behaviour patterns will present all the underlying themes.

The soul attracts relationships and situations that mirror the expectations around love carried forward from other lives. We create what is familiar and known. If our relationships in the past have been painful, we attract pain in an effort to exorcise it. If we have experienced positive loving, we expect to repeat the experience. Childhood experiences strengthen and reiterate these karmic patterns, which are then carried forward into adult relationships. Most adults unconsciously desire love to make up for any lack of love not only in childhood but in other lives and suppose that a partner will 'make my life better'. However, as Ben Renshaw explains:

A relationship can encourage you to be fulfilled, but it cannot make you fulfilled. No relationship can match your expectations because that is not the purpose of a relationship.[4]

It is not only in 'love' relationships that karmic expectations intervene. If there has been a tendency in the past to project power onto other people, the soul may attract a powerful mentor or employer who holds the power. Work-related issues are really those of personal relationship in a different setting. The major expectations are:

Negative expectations around love

- Love is all there is/all consuming
- Love has to be perfect
- If it isn't hurting, it isn't love
- Love hurts
- Love leads to heartbreak
- I don't deserve love
- I don't need love
- There will never be enough love
- Love is a power trip
- Sexual love is sinful
- Need equals love
- Love is manipulative
- Love will be taken away
- Love costs
- A partner will save me
- My partner is responsible for/will take care of my needs and feelings

Positive expectations around love

- I grow through relationships

---

4. Renshaw, Ben *Successful But Something Missing*, (London: Rider 2000) [hereinafter Ben Renshaw] p.111.

- ♥ Love heals
- ♥ Love sets you free
- ♥ The more you love, the more it comes back
- ♥ I deserve love
- ♥ Love knows no boundaries
- ♥ There is an abundance of love[5]

Also see the section 'Adult Relationships' later in this chapter for a further explanation of these 'Love Scripts'.

Karmic themes

In our intimate relationships we tend to act out certain themes over and over again and which may well feel like soulmate connections. Typical karmic themes include:

- ♥ **Father/mother/child**: roles that are rarely anything to do with the actual family relationship and which carry over from the past into other interactions. We all know the woman who is her husband's 'little girl' – or his mother, the father who flirts with his daughter whilst relegating his wife to 'mother', the mother who cannot let her son go, the child who has to parent a parent. We see marriages where the two people concerned are more like brother and sister; somehow the sexual element is missing or weak. The personal assistant who mothers her boss and the employee who expects to be parented are familiar themes – and can be played out by men as well as women. As these roles are so known and familiar and so often form part of our previous soul group connection, it is easy to slip into them inappropriately. They often form part of the spurious soulmate experience.

- ♥ **Victim/martyr/persecutor/rescuer**: frequently the rescuer ends up as the victim or martyr. Abuse and misuse of power, sometimes in an extremely covert way, is fundamental to this type of karmic interaction. In a family, one child may be made the family scapegoat, picked on by everyone. The rescuer/victim role is common in families where

---

5. Hall, Judy *Hands Across Time*, and Ben Renshaw p.132.

addiction of any kind is a problem and one or both parents or siblings take on the 'helper' role, but it happens in so-called love relationships too. As one need matches the other, it can so easily feel like a soulmate contact. Co-dependent relationships of all kinds are based on this pattern. They cannot function without one person feeling inferior or superior to the other. But need is strong on both sides. A victim needs a persecutor, a rescuer needs someone who – apparently – cannot help themselves. If someone is continually helped, 'rescued' or persecuted for being 'weak' they can never find their strength and the pattern endlessly repeats – often down through generations.

♥ **Dominance and submission**: a power and control issue. It may literally re-create an old 'master-slave' type of interaction or be a metaphor for power trips of all kinds. It is based on the need of one partner to be dominated, and the desire of the other to dominate. If the scenario is played out unconsciously, then there may well be considerable violence – emotional and mental if not physical – within the relationship, especially where the person with the need to be dominated unwitting evokes the domination, or where the formerly submissive partner begins to assert his or her own power. Common in parent-child interaction, the parties may be drawn back together to re-enact an old dance that has become a set piece. This is why so many abused partners find it difficult to leave situations of domestic violence: like it or not, they crave the security of the known and familiar domination. It is important to recognise that it is not only the dominant who abuse, the 'meek and mild' too may be tyrants in their own way and skilled at pressing the buttons that erupt into violence. Of course, it is well recognised that the children of abusive relationships often go on to abuse as the wheel turns and they experience the opposite polarity.

The healing in such relationships comes when the dynamics are recognised and each makes a conscious effort to incorporate the other end of the polarity rather than simply reacting blindly. Role play or role reversal may be needed to fully understand what is going on – and this may be experienced through another life. Learning mutual trust is also an essential ingredient as is hearing the other person's needs and finding a creative outlet for the mutual power play.

- **Dependence and collusion v. unconditional love:** two ends of the same axis. So often collusion and dependence masquerade as 'helping' or being helped. People believe they are practising unconditional love when they give someone whatever they appear to need or want. It may, however, be better for their spiritual growth to practice 'tough love', stand back and let them find the way, or to say no and mean it. Such 'helping' tends to disempower or enable, rather than facilitating someone taking hold of their own power.

    Unconditional love means accepting someone totally, warts and all, honouring their unique way of growing, letting them be what and who they need to be. Equally, unconditional love means knowing when to say no – and stick to it. It does not mean allowing someone else to walk all over us in the name of 'love' or growth. It does not mean allowing them to abuse or misuse us – or abusing or misusing them in the name of 'love' – patterns which can entwine down through a family, or a soul group. Loving someone unconditionally may also mean challenging the way they are, their assumptions, their actions. They may need to be brought up short, to face consequences – but with love. This is the hard and rocky path of the soulmate.

- **The betrayer and the betrayed:** so many promises made, so few kept. This theme is obvious in adult relationships where one of the parties takes a lover, often repeatedly. It is less obvious in family situations where a child is encouraged along a pathway only to have support abruptly withdrawn. So, for example, an only child may be the apple of his mother's eye, but when a new child is born, all interest is lost in the first child. He or she, bewildered and alone, finding that they are no longer the centre of the universe, then carries into adult relationships both a lack of trust and the desire to dump someone before there is a possibility of being dumped. If a child is continually promised something, only to be disappointed, it will set up the betrayer pattern in adulthood. If the pattern is carried over from other lives, the parties involved may interweave a tapestry of betrayal over many lifetimes. Nevertheless, one soul can feel deeply bound to another by promises made and broken.

- **The enabler and the enabled:** common in addictions of all kinds, this interaction is also found in many so-called soulmate relationships.

It feels like a soulmate relationship 'because he (or she) needs me so' and 'I can't do without him (or her)'. It is common in marriage partnerships where the wife puts all her energy into her husband's career rather than her own, or in parent-child relationships where the child follows a path of dependency, fuelled by the parent's money or need to be needed. One person inevitably puts in all the energy, or creates exactly the situation in which the other person can flourish or wither according to orientation – usually in a 'weakness' or dependence of some kind, thus keeping the enabler in power. Such a pattern has a tight hold over the parties, who believe they cannot survive separately. It can also be a covert relationship, the seeming enabler is just as likely to be the enabled when the relationship is subjected to the bright light of understanding.

♥ **The seducer and the seduced**: often based on a past love relationship, the soulmate connection can be abused and misused in friendship, love and family. Seduction is not always sexual. It is often intellectual or emotional and can be spiritual too. This pattern is also common in guru-pupil interaction. The guru (spiritual or otherwise) seduces the pupil by seeming to know, and keeps the control by parcelling out just enough of the knowledge the seduced is so desperately seeking. Of course, in so many guru-pupil relationships (and other types too), the emphasis then switches to a sexual sharing, all too frequently in the name of passing on power but in reality to binding the seduced ever closer. This again is a theme that travels across centuries and which can subtly underlie soulmate meetings.

♥ **The freedom-commitment dilemma**: the 'can't live with him, can't live without him' theme played out over many lifetimes. Some relationships are sporadic, exciting, highly passionate – so intense that they could not possibly be sustained for a whole lifetime but when the parties meet again, it feels exactly like a soulmate. If left together for too long, the partners become bored with each other, the relationship burns out, or one partner may run out on the other, unable to take on full responsibility in the relationship. The two partners concerned may have chosen to have a life together where they learn how to commit fully. To do this, they need to give each other space: space to grow, to be, to do whatever they need but within the framework of a committed relationship. The urge is to flee, to fly into freedom, but the soul says, "No, wait". Or, they may come together to learn to live apart, to finally let each other go. If partners have always been heavily committed to each other, symbiotically entwined and karmically enmeshed, or dutifully bound, then the lesson may be to let go, to find freedom – to learn to love another, or in a different way.

- **Positive service:** a strong feature of both soulmate and twinflame relationships. The parties have agreed before incarnation that one of them will perform a particular service. This may entail looking after someone who needs an illness or disability in order to learn compassion and empathy, for instance, but it may also be the ill or 'disabled' person who is performing the service. Rudolph Steiner says people with a disability may have taken it on not as a learning experience for themselves but as a gift to others, so that they might learn. If someone has a particularly hard task ahead in the outside world, then a soulmate might take on the role of support, offering a loving relationship within the home, or a parent might prepare a child as well as possible for adulthood.

- **Reparation:** may be made or received. Guilt can be a powerful force in repeating karmic interaction, but reparation can also be made in a positive fashion. It entails repaying past debts or honouring agreements made in other lives. So, for example, if someone has offered us an opportunity to learn and grow in a past life, we may put our own development on hold for a while to support them. Equally, if we have harmed them in some way whilst learning our lessons, then we may want to make things better for them in the present life. This can lie behind parent-child or mentor-pupil and many soulmate relationships.

The family

> We live and breathe in the energy field that our parents create
> through their relationship with each other.
>
> Stephen Arroyo[6]

Our earliest relationship is with the family and it is within the family that many soulmate and karmic connections are to be found. We choose

---

6. Arroyo, Stephen *Astrology, Karma and Transformation*, (Vancouver: CRCS, 1978).

our family for the genetic and emotional inheritance they offer us and for talents they may pass on. We may have prior contact or old karma with individual members of the family. One or more of our old soulmates may well now be our parent or sibling. The whole family may be part of our soul group but this is not necessarily so:

> Your true family is a soul group who are linked not by blood but by respect and joy in being in each other's life.[7]

It is not necessarily the case that members of such a soul family live under the same roof and meeting a family member may feel like a soulmate connection.

The family relationship reiterates and reinforces our deepest expectations and beliefs – positive and negative – carried over from previous lives. We may well be continuing an old pattern into which we have become locked. For instance, if we expect bad parenting, this is what we will notice, even if we have perfectly adequate parenting ninety percent of the time. On the other hand, if we have previously had and now expect good parenting, we can more easily cope with inadequate parenting (for a time). If we carry low self esteem, we will most likely attract parents that reinforce this by valuing us for what we achieve or conforming to their expectations rather than for who we are intrinsically. If we have high self-worth, we are much less likely to be damaged by difficult early relationships.

If we have incarnated expecting to have – or needing to have – a particularly difficult childhood, we often find that a grandparent is a soulmate who offers us support. We have that one person who seems to understand, even when everyone else does not. This can become a problem if the bonding is too tight. A woman consulted me because her granddaughter and she were so very close. The mother, her daughter, had split up with her partner just prior to the child's birth. Depressed and unable to cope, she handed her child over to her mother. Although the mother had kept in close contact with the child, it was four years before she was ready to take her home. In this time, she had found a new partner. The child, given no time to adjust, hated her 'new father'. She was uncomfortable with her mother, did not feel safe, and desperately wanted to stay with her grandmother. In a rage, the mother, jealous of

---

7. Bach, Richard *Illusions*, (London: Pan, 1979), p.121.

her mother's close relationship with her child, dragged the child away and then would not let them meet.

The grandmother was in despair. She really felt that a part of herself had been torn away She was in telepathic contact with the child, and I suggested that she use this ability to 'talk' to the child to reassure her that she had not abandoned her – that she would be with her on other levels, especially during sleep (children naturally accept such ideas), but that, for the time being, they would not be able to meet. We also did some tie cutting (see Chapter 15) so that the child would be set free from all the grandmother's expectations but would still be loved unconditionally. The grandmother used appropriate flower essences on a photograph of the child to help her adjust to the new situation (a useful technique when they cannot be given directly).

Eventually, she was able to talk to her daughter and reassure her that she did not want to take the child away, only to love and support her during this difficult transition. Gradually her daughter came round and in time allowed visits. With the new freedom, grandmother and granddaughter were able to spend their 'special time' together, and the child gradually began to enjoy family life with her mother and stepfather.

Family relationships can be complicated by previous-life sexual relationships between the parties. Mother and son, father and daughter, or siblings, may have been husband and wife in the 'past'. Recognising and accepting the old contact can go a long way towards explaining otherwise inexplicable interaction such as inappropriate 'love', emotional or incestuous abuse and attachment.

For instance, one of my clients was locked into a symbiotic, emotionally incestuous relationship with his mother. In his teens, his father had died and his mother told him he had to take his father's place. This he had struggled to do for many years, and it spilled over into his adult relationships. His mother broke up every relationship he had. She simply would not let go. She treated his girl friends as though they were adulterous relationships, which, of course, from her perspective they were. He had taken his father's place, therefore they were taking her rightful place as his partner. He, on the other hand, was terrified of his mother. He could not stand up to her.

In desperation he undertook a regression. Not surprisingly, he went into a life where he was married to his mother. In that life he had a mistress whom he loved more than anything. He did his duty, as he saw it, and stayed with his family, but his wife knew that he did not love her. She made his life hell and eventually forced him to give up his love, taking punitive measures against her over which he was powerless to intervene. After that, his wife was possessive in the extreme, never letting him out of her sight. At social gatherings she made his life miserable with her jealousy and accusations. Time and time again she made him promise, "You will love only me". As far as she was concerned, he was her soulmate and belonged to her. She had carried this expectation forward into their mother-son relationship. Family and ancestral patterns can affect soulmates in other ways too as will be seen.

Adult relationships

> Our intimate partners are deeply and knowingly chosen for the particular pains and joys that relating to them brings us.[8]

Despite all our romantic notions, our efforts to find a blissful soulmate, our adult relationships are often painful. It is hard to believe that we would willingly put ourselves through this but as Mavis Klein says:

> We attract pain in an attempt to exorcise it. We seek out a painful situation because it is familiar but this time we hope it will end differently. Pain in our intimate relationship challenges the fixity of our personalities, and joy in our intimate relationships is the fulfilment of our ideal self.[9]

We attract in our partnerships soulmates, and others, who resonate to our patterns, who slot into our particular receptors. These receptors relate to our expectations around love and hook into our lovescripts: expectations that have built up over many lifetimes and are deeply ingrained in our being. Themes that we may be dealing with include:

♥ **'Love has to be perfect'**: this theme often prevents relationships from beginning at all. In this search for perfection, there is such a high expectation, such impossible ideals to be met, that no one can meet these standards. A man in his forties told me of his increasingly desperate need to find his soulmate. But, he said, she had to meet

---

8. Klein, Mavis – source unknown, believed to be in an article but Mavis could not recall it when asked.

9. I made a note of this years ago from a article by Mavis but neither of us can remember where it appeared.

certain criteria in looks, dress, intelligence – and it all had to be immediately obvious. "If it isn't right at the start, it's no good. I just can't get interested". Not surprisingly, he never gets beyond the first date, if indeed he gets that far, so never gives himself time to get to know someone intimately or to let a relationship develop.

Within a relationship, the need for everything to be so special all the time creates an enormous strain on both parties. There is no room for the 'mistakes' that help us to learn, no room to be human even. Perfect love does not account for off days or PMT. I had a client who told me that he and his wife only made love about once every six months, "But everything was perfect. We went out for dinner, came back and played beautiful music, sensuously massaged each other, and then made love perfectly". He also told me that they had desperately wanted a child, so it was timed to her ovulation.

He said, "Somehow it didn't happen, and yet when she left me and went to live with someone else, she was pregnant immediately". When I suggested that maybe more frequent but slightly less perfect sex might have been the answer, he simply said, "I couldn't do it. It had to be perfect to work".

The way to heal this problem is to learn, little by little, to set more realistic expectations, to give oneself permission to experiment, even to make mistakes – and then to recognise that there are no such thing as mistakes, only learning experiences – to loosen up and allow for spontaneity and fun, to allow oneself and one's partner to be merely human, and to find that this in itself is a wonderful thing.

♥ **'I don't deserve to be loved'**: someone suffering from this pattern will settle for anything resembling a relationship. They will accept 'punishment' and abuse whether physical or psychological, or prostitute themselves for the housekeeping, for instance, because they do not feel they can be loved, they are not worth it. This pattern usually involves looking to other people for approval and validation. It can also be linked to lifescripts such as 'poor me', 'it is not my fault', 'I can't help it', 'I have no control over my life'. These scripts indicate victim mentality. One of the difficulties is that, offered love, such people cannot allow themselves to accept it because they think, 'If someone loves me, then they must be as desperate, useless and unworthy as me' – and so they reject the possibility of having a relationship that would heal this belief. Unfortunately, as with so many patterns, it is a self-fulfilling prophecy.

Learning to love oneself first, to find inner self-worth, and then to accept love from other people is the lesson here. Here too, connecting to our spiritual core reverses the destructive process. Also recognising that we create, and attract, exactly the relationship we expect at our deepest level.

♥ **'Love hurts'/'If it isn't hurting, it's not working'**: this is a treadmill. We create what we expect, our experience reinforces our expectations, and on and on we go – another self-fulfilling prophecy. If we expect love to hurt, then we either attract those with whom we have had painful relationships in the past, or we attract someone with the desire to hurt, and our expectations are reinforced once more. If we feel it must be hurting to be working, then again we attract someone who makes this so. Our soulmate may be only too happy to oblige, especially if we have been locked into this pattern for lifetimes together.

Breaking the pattern, recognising that you are entitled to, and capable of, fulfilling relationships is the only way to change this. Forgiveness, of self and others, helps as does letting go of the past.

♥ **'I don't need love'**: separation and isolation are a choice many people make in order to avoid the pain of loving or the possibility of rejection and abandonment. They are seemingly independent and strong, but may be running away from old pain that, because it has been suppressed, has a powerful hold. Unfortunately, even when someone with this pattern has at last ventured into love, at the least sign of any perceived slight or hurt, they will immediately run, or struggle and fight. It is a patient partner indeed that can introduce someone with this pattern to intimacy. Reconnection to the spiritual core and releasing the old pain helps here, but a basic need is to take the risk of connection with humanity as well, especially through a one-to-one contact. Old vows and declarations, such as celibacy, may need to be rescinded before love can flourish.

♥ **The madonna/whore dichotomy**: sacred versus profane love. Too many nights spent in a monastery or convent can underlie this difficulty. The fundamental problem here usually stems from a search for perfection, and incredibly high expectations of ourselves and others, and from seeing sexuality of any kind as 'bad'. The beloved is placed on a pedestal, idealised, idolised. When he or she behaves like a mere mortal fallible human being, total disillusionment sets in and the whole edifice comes crashing down. I so clearly remember one of my first clients telling me that marriage was for procreating children. Love was something different again: it did not involve sex. In her previous life she had been a nun who was sent into a convent for refusing to marry the man her parents had picked out for her. In her present life she had had a husband, whom she did not love, and, having had a child with him, she had refused him further sexual relations. She also had a 'beloved' whom she could neither marry nor make love with and a man with whom a relationship had been a possibility but frigidity on her part and impotence on his intervened. Sometimes, a person will settle on celibacy as a way of avoiding the issue of sex and sexuality altogether.

Unconditional love is the antidote to this pattern – as is seeing all love, sexual included, as healthy, natural and divine.

♥ **The emotional black hole:** that there will never be enough love is the greatest fear. There is usually a long history of manipulative, abusive relationships where anything that passes for love is accepted and held onto because of the great fear of loss or lack of love. A desperately needy and greedy desire for 'love' underlies this pattern. For many people, abuse and anger become internally confused with love. It may be the only attention they receive. So, 'if someone abuses me, they must love me' can be an underlying script. And, of course, abusers of all kinds so often use 'love' as an excuse for their actions. People with this pattern find it almost impossible to go back in time to a life where they were loved fully and unconditionally. They have become used to settling for second best, but the hunger for love intensifies, it does not lessen.

Learning to find love deep inside instead of seeking it from someone other – connecting to the divine or cosmic love that is within us all – and being able to give and receive love secure in the knowledge that the source will never run out reverses this pattern.

Nevertheless, wouldn't it be marvellous to have a lovescript that said: love can be wonderful, loving and supportive and life enhancing and we can still grow that way? Some people do have this and, as we shall see, it is possible to create such a script but it does help to understand the negative expectations so that they can be identified and cleared out.

The Karmic Treadmill

> I have discovered that many troubled couples were not lovers in their former lives but enemies. In extreme cases, one partner may have even murdered the other. The person who was killed is motivated by revenge, and by marrying their killer they are in a position to do the most damage.
>
> Dr Motoyama

Repetition creates a 'karmic treadmill'. The karmic treadmill is not necessarily negative. It is simply an ingrained habit, situation or type of interplay that no longer serves the soul's growth – which is why some seemingly idyllic relationships have to end. Whilst there are karmic associations that are life enhancing, productive and positive; others can be destructive and depleting. Things are not always what they seem and the soul may need to pass out of incarnation before all the ramifications of a relationship are understood.

At a personal level, your soul may have an agenda that you are totally unaware of. This is particularly so when it comes to qualities that need to be developed, and emotions and attitudes that have to be explored, or let go. If you are a woman who has incarnated with a desire to learn about tolerance and patience, for instance, that impossible man you are married to may be just the thing you need. Love it or hate it, he is giving you the opportunity to develop exactly those qualities. There's no point trying to change him, especially if you are the one for whom the lesson of acceptance or giving up control is intended. So the quicker you learn to accept, the sooner he can be set free to explore a new way of being or, if you really are intended to be together, he may make changes himself once you let go. You could well have planned things in advance and will, when you return to the between-life state, thank him for being such a good teacher. On the other hand, the lesson may have been to say enough is enough, and leave. And, of course, clarity is essential. Some people are so besotted that they don't even notice the flaws and foibles that are gnawing away at the relationship – and at their own souls. 'Not-seeing' and denial are very different to acceptance. Acceptance sees what is, who the person is, and loves regardless but without being eroded. It is a way of being. The problem in all these instances is that it is extremely difficult to recognise the difference and the lesson in the scenario.

There are factors that can hold you in non-productive, repetitive situations. If a vow has been made in the past to 'always be with you', for instance, then the soul finds itself pulled to the person to whom that promise was made. But! Without careful planning, the soul may find itself the parent or child of that person, or find 'true love' only to discover that the beloved is already married or that there is a vast age different or some other barrier exists to relationship. Even when careful planning has taken place, the souls forget as they come back into incarnation and it may take many years for the intention behind the connection to surface again.

At a joint soul level, not all 'love' relationships are intended to be 'happy ever after' fairy tales. A couple may have been together for many lifetimes and have decided that the time has come to pursue new contacts, and yet they get pulled back together either by habit or by a strong physical attraction. One half of such a couple may be helping the other to learn some difficult lessons such as independence and assertion. From the superficial view, the relationship may appear to be destructive although at a soul level it is beneficial.

Many people travel with their 'soul group', coming back into incarnation with the same people around them although the roles may change from incarnation to incarnation. Such soul groups may comprise a family but this is not necessarily so. Soul groups can tend to play out the certain scenarios over and over again, although the major players may take different stances. So, a present life husband and wife could have been parent and child, master and servant or other combination of dominant and submissive roles, and so on in other lives. Elements of these roles are inevitably drawn into, and reflected within, the present life interaction.

However, it is not necessary for there to have been a previous, personal connection between the people involved in a 'soulmate' relationship.

A soul may have had a repeating pattern of destructive relationships through several lives and is on a 'karmic treadmill'. It will be pulled back into the same old scenarios – and the actors in the drama can change or remain the same. It is rather like a long-running play that may use understudies from time to time, or find a new co-star, but the script remains.

Star-crossed lovers

> From forth the fatal loins of these two foes
> A pair of star-cross'd lovers take their life
>
> > William Shakespeare

One of the most painful of soulmate contacts comes when the two people concerned are from different sides of a fence: warring families or cultures. We are all familiar with Shakespeare's tragic tale of Romeo and Juliet. Their families held an old enmity, but this did not prevent the two young people from falling in love. Juliet recognises that, while the families feud, it is a doomed love. Their only hope is to move beyond the ancestral pattern. She begs Romeo:

> Deny thy father, and refuse thy name,
> Or, thou wilt not, be but sworn my love,
> And I'll no longer be a Capulet.

What the enmity did prevent was them living happily ever after. Tragedy inevitably piled upon tragedy as the ancient tale played itself out. The families ended more split than ever, they could not find it in their hearts to be reconciled despite the sacrificial deaths of their young. The curse is continued:

> A plague o' both your houses!
> They have made worms' meat of me.

It is a tale that has been played out many times over the centuries, both in literature and in real life. In *West Side Story* it is reworked and given a contemporary theme, but tragedy still triumphs. Over the years I have worked with many couples to try to understand what lies behind an attraction that pulled them across cultural and religious lines: Catholic and Protestant, Moslem and Christian, Hindu and Atheist, black and white, young and old. In every case (my sample is, of course, biased since these are the people who consult me), the relationship had, initially, split the families further apart. Despite the sincere wish and, in many cases, soul purpose of the couples concerned, they could not heal the breach. Each couple felt like soulmates, called across centuries to be reunited. Some defied their families and married, others succumbed to family pressure and parted.

I have heard a similar story from so many women who go to Egypt or the Mediterranean. Sadly such stories, no matter how deep the love may appear to be, rarely have a happy ending and, from the soul growth perspective, may not be meant to.

A couple had to leave their home, Ireland, in order to be together. He came from a militant Catholic background and she from an equally belligerent Protestant family. Both fathers and all the brothers were in paramilitary organisations, actively fighting. Neither family could possibly conceive of one of their own marrying the hated 'enemy'. The young man in question had already had a battle to break free from the family tradition of violence. He simply wanted to pursue his profession as a teacher in the hope, as he said, of bringing some sanity and peace into the situation by educating the young in a new way of being. She had felt the same. They met at an organisation that was trying to promote peace and reconciliation, and fell instantly and totally in love. Despite all family opposition, they married. It quickly became clear that his life was in danger from her family if they stayed in Ireland. They moved to England and cut off all contact with the families. Unfortunately, they also had to cut off from all their friends too, in case anyone inadvertently told their families. They simply did not know whom they could trust in that confused system of devout loyalties and religious bigotry.

When they looked at their soul purpose, it was to bring about harmony in a country in which both had incarnated on several occasions. One of these had been when 'the troubles' began. They had been parted by that, when one of them was killed, and vowed to be together again. They had also been married in much earlier times in the Ireland of the Dark Ages, paradoxically a time of much greater light. It was an ecstatic marriage with a deep spiritual connection. But it was clear that in the present life, under the then prevailing conditions, they could not return to Ireland

and follow their souls' purpose. In order to be together, they simply had to leave their country and find a new life independent of family and reliant upon each other for mutual support and comfort.

Letting go

> Is our determination to hang on at all costs really a measure of how much we love?
>
> Pauline Stone

As we have seen, one of our karmic major lessons can be that of letting go. Letting go is an enormous challenge because we have to let go of the notion that we know best. People do tend to hang on, to what passes for love, to the way they feel things should be; to hopes, dreams and illusions. Letting go sets everyone free to take their own path. If it really is true love, if things really should be that way, then it will happen. But if it is not, then the soul is freed by letting go, stepping out of the karma, and moving on. Letting go of a present life soulmate connection, especially one that has deep karmic bonds can dramatically alter your life.

Whether it is a person or a pattern, the past cannot be repeated endlessly. Stagnation and inertia are death to our soul. So, we find ourselves in the situation where we meet a beloved from the past, only to lose that person again. In this respect, death can be a great teacher. On the other hand, we may meet a soulmate who is already happily married, or who is a child, a teacher, a brute. Whatever the interaction, we are inextricably bound up within it. Until we let go, we experience hell on earth. When we finally let go, we blossom. As an Alcoholics Anonymous handout explains:

> To 'Let go' does not mean to stop caring, it means I can't do it for someone else.
> To 'Let go' is not to cut myself off, it's the realisation I cannot control another.
> To 'Let go' is not to enable but to allow learning from natural consequences.
> To 'Let go' is to admit powerlessness, which means the outcome is not in my hands.
> To 'Let go' is not to care for, but to care about.
> To 'Let go' is not to fix, but to be supportive.

To 'Let go' is not to be in the middle arranging all the outcomes but to allow others to effect their destinies.

To 'Let go' is not to be protective, it's to permit another to face reality.

To 'Let go' is not to adjust everything to my desires, but to take each day as it comes and cherish myself in it.

To 'Let go' is not to regret the past, but to grow and live for the future.

To 'Let go' is to fear less and love more.

Letting go of our illusions is another challenge. We may need to re-vision, to see the other person, or belief, in a different light. If we have been used to putting a partner on a pedestal, idealising and idolising, then we have to recognise that any other human being we encounter is also mortal and fallible, not a god. We have to let other people reveal their true nature, not assume that we know it. If we give them an heroic, idealised role, there is no way it can be fulfilled. We will inevitably find our illusions shattered. Just as when we entertain illusions about ourselves, eventually they must fall away so that we see ourselves clearly. This applies equally to where we see what other people, or ourselves, can be, rather than what is. If we invest in, or project onto, other people what we are not yet ready to own in ourselves, one day we will have to take it back. Such a taking back can be done in a positive fashion, or it can be through the painful breaking of the shell of our illusion – a brutal psychic rape that hurls us into the essence of what we are. In the depths of our despair, we can either clutch at someone else, or find our own strength.

All lessons can be learnt in a positive, constructive fashion, or we can fall back into a destructive pattern. A great deal depends on how much conscious planning we have done in advance. Say our soul lesson is to find greater independence. The positive experience would be through soul partners or parent-child, teacher-pupil type interactions that are supportive and encouraging of self-responsibility and self-reliance. Gentle urging into new ways of being offers no criticism, makes no judgements. We are allowed to develop at our own pace, knowing that we have loving support behind us. We can make our mistakes, and learn from them, without incurring wrath. We may be challenged when it is appropriate, but this will always be done with compassion. When we are ready to fly on our own, we are encouraged to go. We go out into the world confident and well prepared. This applies just as much to a partner as it does to a child. If partners are unafraid, confident in themselves, then they can encourage their partners to be their own person. If they are afraid, they will clutch on, trying to keep them as they were and restraining growth.

The destructive, negative approach to achieving independence is 'heavy', narrow-minded, critical and cold. Disapproval, fear and punishment are used to force a break – although a break is the last thing the cold, critical person wants. They want to maintain control over this downtrodden soul. We have to leave for our own survival. We have to listen to the urging of our soul. We may achieve self-sufficiency, but it is at the cost of liveslong, or lives long, resentment of authority figures, usually accompanied by a deep feeling of inferiority and lack of confidence. If this lesson is being learnt within a marriage, it is doubtful indeed that it will survive this controlling approach. If it is within a parent-child relationship, then the child may well leave home and never return.

We need to look at relationships in the widest possible sense of the word: interaction with another, as even the most fleeting contact may bring us a karmic lesson or present an opportunity to grow, especially in our letting go. Soulmate contacts tend to be catalytic. We may meet one of our soulmates just once, for a short time only, but the interaction will mark our soul forever. Sometimes a soulmate comes into our life for just one purpose to do whatever it takes to propel us into what we may be. Sometimes they point us to a lesson we need to learn. Such lessons may not be earth-shattering, but they can change our life. We will explore more of these karmic themes and experiences throughout the remainder of this book but first we need to look at a place where things easily go wrong: the planning department.

The planning department

> [People] were often surprised to learn that the seemingly inappropriate relationship or the person they were experiencing such problems with had actually been planned that way.[10]

One of the main causes of anguish and pain in relationships and life in general is shoddy pre-life planning or a deliberate decision that has been forgotten once in incarnation. Both are linked to the planning stage

---

10. Hall, Judy *Astrology of a Prophet* available from the author see www.judyhall.co.uk.

prior to incarnation, the 'in-between life'. The place to which we go after death depends so much on our expectations, and on the level of spiritual evolution we achieve, but eventually we are faced with the possibility or the need to come back to earth to work on issues that can only be completed here. Some people bounce back into incarnation – especially if they haven't travelled very far in terms of either understanding or the after-death levels of being. Others consider the matter very carefully indeed.

From regression, it is clear that some people spend a long time planning their next life and especially their relationships. They ask members of their soul group to take on certain roles – some of which can be painful or harsh in the extreme. One woman went back to this stage and found that she had asked one of her soulmates to teach her about pain and rejection, which she "needed to learn so that I could have empathy for others". He was an exceedingly good teacher. Having apparently fallen head over heals in love with her, he walked out the door with no explanation and she never saw him again.

Other people in a similar situation find that their lover leaves through death so that they might learn strength and self-reliance, or even to open the way for another relationship to flower. In the Lennon-Ono relationship, for instance, when John Lennon died it may have been time for Yoko to become an independent woman again instead of the symbiotic half of a seeming whole.

We certainly cannot know from the perspective of earth whether soulmate relationships are the result of carelessness or careful planning. Someone whose lover had been physically cruel and abusive found that she had asked him to do this, so that she could learn to assert herself and say "No, enough is enough", something she had not learned in her other lives. In the end, she was able to thank him for his part in her learning process.

Some people, for whatever reason, omit this planning stage or make it sketchy to say the least. They are simply pulled back into an old interaction, often by one of those vows that says, "I must be with him" or "I will always look after you". They rarely take the time to discuss with their soul group or spiritual advisers what would be the best way to grow.

That we get what we most desire is one of the karmic laws. This sounds great until we remember that decisions like "I want to be with him/her next time", especially when taken at the moment of death, are a powerful desire that gets manifested, but without some between-life planning as to exactly how and in what relationship, the consequence is likely to be disastrous. Life can be acted out in a very literal way. My favourite story in this regard is the woman who vowed during a regression, "He's going to marry me next time". She burst out laughing and said, "He did. But he was the vicar who performed the ceremony". She was lucky, most people find it's someone else's husband or wife, their child or that of a friend, or that their intended soulmate is of the same sex, or there is a huge age difference, and so on *ad infinitum*.

We may have made a promise to look after someone, to be with them, without really considering the long-term consequences. We may need to redefine the karmic contracts we made, to renegotiate the concept of 'forever'. One of my clients could not break free of looking after her alcoholic sister, who relied upon her for everything. For many years her sister took up all her time. Having eventually married and now in her early forties, my client felt that she wanted a child, but somehow her sister was her child and needed so much looking after she wondered if she would have the time and energy for a child of her own. They were caught in an enabler-enabled scenario from way back. She had to recognise a life where she had made a promise to look after her sister 'forever'. In that life, it had been appropriate that she should care for her, then child, sister. They were very close, soulmates even. But it was not appropriate in the present life. After she redefined the vow, her sister was able to go into treatment for her alcohol problems. My client found herself pregnant with a soul she knew had been waiting to come. "He is part of my soul", she declared.

Equally, we may have been with someone for many incarnations and now have decided on a change, but we forget once we are in incarnation. We yearn for the perfect love we know we have had before, the soulmate who must be out there. We get pulled back together, only to find we lose them. We have to let go of the past and that needs careful planning in the between-life state.

I once counselled a woman who had been in a soulmate relationship for many years, but had been unable to live with her lover because he was married. Eventually he left his wife and obtained a divorce. They were 'blissfully happy'. A Pisces, the zodiac sign that yearns for total union with the beloved, her only gripe was that she knew they could merge, become one, and he was resisting fiercely. Six weeks after she was finally able to marry her soulmate, he died. Deeply shocked, she was worried that it was a punishment for having taken him away from his wife. She was contemplating suicide because she felt so strongly that they were meant to be together. He then came to tell her that it would not have been possible for either of them to develop as they had to if they had stayed together. He had to move on, he could not merge and become one with her as she so longed for him to do. She, on the other hand, had her own pathway to follow. One day they would be reunited, but not until she had completed her own karmic purpose. The gift was that she had glimpsed perfect love but had to find it within herself as a whole being.

Moving on

> I knew you once, but in Paradise
> If we meet, I will pass and turn my face
>
> Robert Browning

In any one week, there are inevitably several letters about soulmates – or the lack of them – in my postbag. One of the most poignant pleas I hear is: 'Please tell me why my soulmate has moved on and left me behind'.

Lives are irrevocably changed by the loss of a soulmate. In such situations there are two choices: to carry on as before and repeat the pattern, or to change. To turn the loss to positive advantage, to make something new happen. Where people try to carry on as before, it is almost as though they are pretending nothing happened. They try to turn back the clock, to recreate the past – often with another soulmate. Or, they enshroud the past, so that it becomes a frozen moment in time devoted to that person's memory. Both responses are death-dealing rather than life-enhancing, nothing moves nor grows.

In two sycophantic books written just after John Lennon's murder,[11] still very much concerned with presenting an idealised picture of two

---

11. Brown, Peter and Steven Gains *The Love You Make*, (Pan Books, 1983), p.392. Ray Coleman, *John Lennon*, (Futura, 1985), p.458.

soulmates, Yoko Ono was portrayed as being in a deep depression, having 'a full-time job living with John's memory', speaking of John in the present tense as though he had just popped out of the room. She appeared not to have taken in the fact that he was dead. She enshrouded John's memory in song: the broken glasses he was wearing when he died became the front cover for her new album. At the time, she denied that she had a new partner. But later it was alleged that, having sent John away 'on holiday' to Bermuda (see Chapter 10), Yoko had been all set to divorce him and marry someone else.[12] However, when John returned with a solo album full of the first new songs he had written for five years (and with plans for the first album to be recorded without Yoko for a long time), she apparently hastily scrapped her intention and insisted on recording *Double Fantasy*, matching song for song with him. According to these authors, Yoko had always used John to further her own recording ambitions. They also revealed that her 'new man' moved in days after John's death, with Yoko immediately taking up the reins of promoting the album she and John had just recorded. No doubt the truth lies somewhere in between and we will never know for sure. But what is certain is that, thirteen years later, Yoko Ono was touring Britain on stage with her singer-son Sean: things had turned full circle. She was back on the road again.

The karmic mirror

> My greatest miseries have been Heathcliff's miseries, and I watched and felt each from the beginning. If all else perished and he remained, I should still continue to be.
>
> Emily Bronte

As we have seen, we can look at our relationships as mirroring our own inner psychic reality. We create the situations we need to play out our karmic scenarios, to meet our ingrained expectations. The actors in the drama have often been known to us in the past. But this is not always so. New characters can be drawn into our 'unfinished business'. Indeed, we may choose to work through something with someone with whom there is no 'karmic charge' from the past so that we may learn the lesson and

---

12. Seaman, Frederick *The Last Days of John Lennon*, (New York: Birch Lane Press, 1991). Albert Goldman *The Lives of John Lennon*, (Bantam Books, 1989).

then apply our new learning to a relationship where there is a karmic link. So in what appears to be a repeating past life situation, the cast may change from incarnation to incarnation but the underlying theme will be the same.

Our surroundings and companions react to us in a way that responds to what and where we are at any given moment. In other words they 'tune in' to us and respond consciously or unconsciously, to our frequencies just as they are at a particular moment in time. If we or they fail to understand and adjust to these frequencies but react to them instead, a further chain of reaction is set up. This chain of reaction then carries over into another lifetime. However, by going back into the past we can sever that connection and change the interaction – and we can also alter it by tie-cutting in the present life.

A prime example comes from the regression experience of one of my clients. She found that she had said, "I hope you rot in hell" in response to some particularly nasty behaviour towards her in a past life. However, as she said, she was surprised to find that she had to do another life with that person to watch and be part of that hell. She had thought the hell would be nothing to do with her. She was suffering by seeing this other person that she had once loved suffer – and whom she desperately wanted to leave but felt a duty towards – so how could she have set it in motion? But, as she realised during the regression, she had actually set this in motion by her thoughts and words in that other life. By forgiving that person in the other life and taking the words back and by bringing the forgiveness into the present life, she was able to set them both free. Although the person who was suffering would continue to do so – he was working through his own karma on this – she did not need to stay in the situation that had been exacerbating things. She moved out and he became much less bitter. Both of their lives improved. Things are rarely what they seem at first glance.

7

Kindred Spirits

One essential feature of love may be that there is more to it than we can comprehend.[1]

I wanted to include a positive case history here, partly to offset all the difficulties I am writing about, but also to show that it is possible to circumvent what might seem to be at first sight to be barriers to love – and that love takes different forms. I heard about this love affair when the person concerned asked anxiously, "Don't you believe in soulmates? I know they are true". Some weeks later he wrote to me saying that although he had found writing about a twenty-year relationship a somewhat daunting task, he wanted to do this to tell readers that really happy relationships can exist and that they did not need to be sexual for them to be a soulmate contact. So it seems appropriate to include Peter's story:

Across a Crowded Room

So often relationships are seen as a battleground and I wanted in some small measure to redress the balance.

We met in the autumn of 1975 when we were doing our training to be yoga teachers. It was a case of seeing a stranger across a crowded room, although there wasn't a defining moment. I do remember at some point something inside me saying, "That woman will be important in your life". At that time I was 41 and Ellen 56. Her husband, whom she married at 21, had been her first love and I had only had one love affair before – with a woman 23 years older. Looking back I seem to have been drawn to more mature wise women since my teens.

I offered to navigate for Ellen on a long drive to the Yoga Congress and found we had many interests in common, both of us having had

---

1. Viederman p.121

mystical experiences at a time when such things were seldom spoken about. The weekend of 2-4 April 1976 seems one of the most memorable in my life. I was ecstatically happy without really knowing why. It was more like – I believe in retrospect – a meeting up again in this lifetime. Ellen had been happily married for twenty six years and also had a father and mother in law to care for. While I, who had always lived at home, had an ailing mother to look after.

During the next few years Ellen and I went to many yoga and 'New Age' events but only met at weekends due to our commitments. My mother died in 1979 then, quite unexpectedly, in 1980 Ellen's husband left her for a younger woman, which devastated Ellen but, in time, allowed us to deepen our relationship.

The next fifteen years were not without incident. On the down side I lost my home and business to developers followed by a two years legal battle. I don't know how I would have survived without Ellen's support. And she had several medical problems. On the plus side, our lives opened up immensely. We travelled, and ran workshops in the far North West of Scotland for five years – many wonderful memories.

People remarked on how our partnership seemed to shine out from us, which was very flattering, and one friend suggested that one of the reasons was because I [Peter] had the mother he always wanted and Ellen had the child she had never had. There was some truth in that.

On a visit to Findhorn we were shown why we were brought together and what our job was in this lifetime. We were told that we had to be lightworkers and that we would achieve far more as a partnership than individually. We were to share our talents and knowledge with others but not under any particular 'flag' (i.e. guru or 'ism'). Advice that held true for the rest of our time together. We offered yoga and a wide knowledge of healing therapies.

In the winter of 1991 Ellen had a successful operation for colon cancer but in the autumn of 1995 the cancer resurfaced and she was told she had only months to live. As there was nobody to look after her, I stopped work and moved in until she died on 26 June 1996. We parted very much in love.

The story doesn't stop there as Ellen 'came through' to a clairaudient friend who she had never met and interesting communication and advice has come through periodically ever since.

When I saw Peter a few months ago he said Ellen continued to give him advice and wise counsel from the other side and he was very content in his new platonic relationship.

The Freedom to Be

If thou must love me, let it be for naught
Except for love's sake only

Elizabeth Barrett Browning

When I first began to look at soulmates, I felt I needed to identify what made a soulmate relationship work as I already had so many stories of painful meetings, unfinished business and tangled webs that I needed to talk to people who were in relationships that felt right and good. When working on this book I wanted to differentiate between difficult-but-still-together contacts and the growing-together-happily scenario. So I returned to Kate, an actress who seemed – certainly from outside the relationship – to belong to the latter group:

My husband, Anthony, and I have been together for seven and a half years. Our coming together was an incredible leap of faith as I had just got married and Anthony had just bought a flat with his partner. Our lives were set in one direction and with great struggle and pain and shock we realised we had a different journey to take together.

We were not propelled out of our previous relationships by lust but by kinship, a recognition of the other that went beyond words. A strong spiritual glue seemed to bond us together, for at any time in the early stages we could have abandoned the other in favour of the safety and familiarity we had with our ex-partners. But after our meeting we knew things could never go back to how they were, and our lives continue to be gently nudged forward.

This forward motion of growth and change is the cornerstone of the workings of our relationship today. Each of us provides the safety net for the other, enabling us to try new ventures unfettered by the other, but supported nonetheless. It is important to us that neither interferes in the other's individual work, but creative inspiration is always welcomed and received. The reading we had at our wedding from *The Prophet* encapsulates the way of being in relationship that works for us:

Give your hearts, but not into each other's keeping.
For only the hand of Life can contain your hearts.
And stand together yet not too near together:
For the pillars of the temple stand apart,
And the oak tree and the cypress grow
Not in each other's shadow.[2]

The life Anthony and I share flourishes through the many creative theatrical and writing projects we have together. It is a great joy for both of us to act together and to flow with ideas for screenplays and novels. Some friends can't understand how we manage to work together frequently and not 'fall out'. We answer that our creativity is vital to nurturing our love. We receive so much joy in discovering and sharing the other's gifts and talents. The times we 'fall out' occur during our periods of non-creativity.

In all of the satisfying family or personal relationships I have there is communication on a soul deep level, a reciprocal recognition of that person's essence. So this feeling has not been solely limited to my partnership with Anthony, but with him more than anyone else there is no desire to hide. We are unafraid to show and express our true colours to the other. There is a rainbow connection between us that was captured on our favourite wedding photo.

The freedom just to 'be' with the other means we enjoy a lot of time playfully bonding. Each day, when possible, we have an afternoon snuggle and doze. We make contact – check the other is okay.

The question of whether or not we are soulmates could make us complacent or burden us with false expectations, so we tend to shy away from such labels. For my partner and myself to be together is an unexpected joyful miracle. We have our challenges, but we face them together. There is an ebb and flow of love between us that brings creative fulfilment and fun. It can't be analysed, it just is. To be together is enough.

Kate was wise to be cautious in labelling them soulmates let alone twinflames. Like so many other couples, in the intervening ten years between books, this relationship too had broken up when her husband met another soulmate. Some couples are simply not meant to stay together for a lifetime. Kate blossomed after Anthony left becoming even more creative in her own right and finding another soulmate with

---

2. Gibran, Kahlil, *The Prophet* (London: Arcana, 1992).

whom she could develop her exceptional healing ability, but her story does demonstrate that relationships like this need time to mature before being labelled as a twinflame connection – as it would have been all to easy to do in this story's idyllic first seven years phase. It might perhaps be wise to allow eighteen years – astrologically speaking a whole nodal cycle – before saying for certain that a twinflame relationship exists, although as we will see, people do make that judgement far earlier than that.

Soul Companions

> An expanded concept of love may allow us to discover the unique pleasure in the sharing of pleasure; the abandonment of pleasure; the liberation from self-interest; or the fusing of one's own interests with that of others.[3]

Soul companions are people with whom you may have had other life connections but have not accrued karma, or who are coming to join you on your spiritual journey in the present life, and with whom you may have a specific purpose or a task to undertake, or simply a joyful friendship. Whilst there is an enormous well of unconditional love and huge support and encouragement, there are no lessons that have to be undergone although profound learning may take place. Nor is there is any physical, sexual pull to each other. The relationship is not complicated by sexual attraction, emotional games or unrequited love.

Soul companions may well be part of your overall soul group but can also be a link to other soul groups – a kind of junction box that passes on learning and brings information in. I have been fortunate to meet several soul companions and can honestly say that each has in his or her own way enhanced my life and my learning without the heaviness of a soulmate experience. Such a relationship is comfortable and easy, and very open with each other, sharing incredibly deep thoughts and feelings but rarely do the two people become partners in the usual sense of the word, although as the next case history shows, it may be so.

Soul buddies

Back in 1995 I spoke to two people who seemed to be soulmates or even twinflames. Everyone who knows them says they have the perfect

---

3. Viederman p.62.

relationship. They were – and still are – extremely loving and supportive of each other without being co-dependent and symbiotic. Bianca had said when I first mentioned soulmates, "I know Jack is only here on earth now because I asked him to be with me this time round". So, my question, "What makes you soulmates, why does your relationship work so well?" produced a surprising response:

I found it incredibly difficult to write or even speak into the tape about soulmates. It is only now, having just done an automatic writing session that I understand why that has been the case.

I was assuming that Jack and I were soulmates. Wrong. We do get on extraordinarily well, but that is from much practice in many different places, on many different missions and in many different times.

It is my understanding that soulmates come from the same soul group. Jack and I do not. We come from similar and complementary soul groups but if looked at from an earthly point of view, very far apart. It seems that it would be a waste as it were of the group's resources to double up souls in one situation, being that it is a group's goal to gain as many and varied experiences as possible. It is rare for two souls from the same group to incarnate together. Only when there is a particularly tricky situation to overcome and extra understanding and support is required, does that happen. It seems that is not the case where we are concerned.

I have in the past thought of Jack as a soulmate, and perhaps in a way he is. He is my buddy, but from a different soul group. These groups seem to get together and interact for mutual benefit, creating greater understanding over a wider area. In our case I suppose, having done many jobs together, we have an easy relationship that makes many people uncomfortable and sometimes jealous, but we are able to do a good job supporting each other now in this life. I do really believe that it was only because I asked him to come and help me that Jack is here now. You would understand if you knew him!

All this sounds rather pompous, I am afraid, but there we are, that is obviously one of the traits of my group. Also, of course, all of this is only my group's understanding from their (our) current place in the evolutionary scale. No doubt it will all change as more information comes in. Slippery lot, eh? You can never take anything as fact.

Looking back on the coincidences in our lives and all the people we know in common, it is fairly obvious in hindsight that Jack and I laid down many situations that would bring us together one way or another. I am glad we both had not closed down so much that we failed to take notice of the signs!

Bianca and Jack are one of the few couples I spoke to in 1995 who are still together and have no doubt that they will remain so, although she is still not quite sure where the relationship is going. They have weathered difficulties in their relationship that would have torn a lesser bond apart and yet she still maintains that he is definitely not her soulmate. Nor, she is adamant is he a twinflame but she agrees he could well be a soul companion.

Several times during the writing of this book, I have encountered people who have had to radically review their concept of soulmates in the light of their experiences. It was often a case of assuming they knew what soulmates were, and then looking at the evidence of their lives and finding it was something different. But Bianca was the only person who, on looking deeply into the matter, actually reached back to the original soul group and found that, contrary to expectation, she and Jack came from different groups. However, they have clearly travelled a path together over many lifetimes: they are truly kindred spirits or soul companions.

The power of 'if only'

Poor Catullus, drop your silly fancies, and if what you see is lost let it be lost.

Catullus

I also wanted to look at those times when, seemingly, a kindred spirit is met but no bond is visible whether in the past or present life. Occasionally what I call an 'if only' life will surface in past-life regression. It is characterised by a certain quality of yearning, a wistful sense of 'this is how it should be' rather than a gutsy, full-blown reliving. I have come to see these 'relivings' as the fantasy that was being played out in someone's mind at the time rather than an actual event. So, if a spinster had romantic dreams of her future husband and these were never realised, they can well become imprinted as 'memory', along with the promise to herself that 'I'll never forget him'. It was something I had already spotted when talking to elderly women about the First World War. So many of them nostalgically referred to 'my fiancé who was killed in the war, you know'. Of course, many men were killed then, but talking to other family members would often reveal that, far from an engagement, it had been a passing fling, or someone who had been admired from afar, or even the boy who lived down the road who had been idealized into the perfect partner-if-only.

Equally, if someone is in a 'bad marriage', they will often look back wistfully to another suitor, "If only I'd married him (or her)" they will say longingly, "It would all have been different". I'm not so sure it would: we tend to attract the same patterns to us. But this is not the point. It is the desire that imprints, the wishful thought, and, with the passing of time, it can be seen as fact. So, when I take someone back to look at the source of a soulmate contact, I bear in mind that it could have originated in the imagination. It might possibly be one-sided. Then again, it might not.

Forgiveness of yourself and letting the illusion go heals the 'if only scenario' and frees you to make a solid and substantial relationship firmly based in the present moment with your kindred spirit, whatever form that relationship may take.

8

Illusion, Delusion or Something Other?

The Master asked of his disciple, "What troubles you my son?"

"Ah! Well might you ask, oh! Master, I feel it is time that I moved on and searched for my beloved soulmate, the one who is to be my perfect partner, the most beautiful woman in the whole Universe".

"So be it my son, but, remember, when all your searching is over, do return here with her".

"Yes oh! Master that will surely be".

Many years later the disciple returned to the Ashram, alone and disconsolate. The Master welcomed him warmly and enquired of his search, "Did you find that whom you sought?"

"Beloved Master, yes indeed. I found her of whom I had dreamt. She was indeed the perfection of those dreams, the perfect woman".

"Well my Son, where is she?"

"Oh! Great sadness, my Master. She too was looking for her perfect man. It was not me".[1]

So often there is an element of illusion or delusion to soulmate meetings, a slippery quality that it is difficult to be certain about. Sometimes they do not take place in the body at all, and may seem to inhabit parallel universes. At other times the experience is an intimation of things to come. It is this elusive quality that makes the whole soulmate experience so difficult to judge or to pin down as the following stories show.

The dream lover

I've been labouring under the delusion that you and I were so in sympathy, so one, that you'd know without being asked what would make me happy.

Bette Davis' character in *Mr Deeds*

---

1. *All till my youth was gone*, A Sufi tale as told by Ron Cuthbertson.

The following case history was contributed by Sue Bose and shows how an 'ideal man' may apparently be foreshadowed in dreams but may in fact be being dreamed up – that is created by intense although subconscious longing. In preparing for such an illusion, much time and energy may be invested, but the purpose of the relationship may, once again, turn out to be entirely different:

Joanna began to dream of a mysterious lover. These dreams occurred night after night, becoming more acute as the weeks went on, until one morning she woke with the overwhelming desire to completely redecorate her bedroom. She literally became like a woman possessed. Previously her taste had leant towards plain, muted colours, but now she found herself drawn to dreamy white muslin curtain material covered with glittering golden stars, which she made and hung. She then became obsessed with the idea of buying a new duvet cover and pillowcases that had to be covered with bright pink roses. She also became addicted to the smell of rose and jasmine to the extent that she began spraying her bed with their scent and bathing in the oils. She spent a small fortune on new slinky underwear. Something was definitely up!

Joanna became filled with delicious unexplained feelings of anticipation at some moments, while at others she would find herself gazing into space, lost in a romantic dream. She became convinced that someone special was coming into her life. But how and when? A month went by with this knowing growing stronger by the day, yet nothing outwardly manifesting, until out of the blue an old work colleague rang to invite her to a birthday party. On the night of the party, while she was changing to go out, a voice inside told her that she would meet the person she had been waiting for that evening. Her immediate response was to tell herself not to be so silly. Yet she knew it was true.

Although it was dark by the time she arrived, due to the warm autumn evening, the guests had gathered in the garden. Joanna walked up to her host to say hello, whereupon he took hold of her and swept her directly into the arms of a friend who was standing on his own under a large maple tree. They took one look at each other and the magic happened.

It turned out that Peter had also been on his own for many years, hiding his loneliness under a mountain of work pressures. Several months previously he too had begun to feel that someone was coming into his life to the extent that he told a number of friends that he was thinking about getting married!

Peter and Joanna embarked on a powerfully healing relationship in which they both learnt to love and trust again. Yet, as time progressed, they reluctantly realised that, although they were extremely close, they were not destined for each other as life partners. Somehow they knew that they had been brought together to help each other overcome their loneliness and disappointment, and once that had happened they would go their separate ways. They parted the best of friends. She and Peter are in regular contact and enjoy a warmth and depth of understanding that neither has experienced with any other partner. They believe that they are true soulmates because they accept and know one another on an intensely intimate level, and accept unquestioningly that they are there for each other for the rest of their lives no matter what.

Joanna's need for perfect love was clearly a love theme she carried with her. The search for Mr One and Only so often precludes other relationships from growing. In attracting her dream lover, Joanna manifested exactly what she thought she needed. But, as she found out, whilst he was instrumental in her healing and an experience not to be missed, he was still not the lifetime partner she longed for.

Spurious Soulmates

Her lips suck forth my soul. [2]

I have heard many spurious soulmate stories over the years. Sometimes the instant feeling was, "here is my soulmate", only to turn to "oh no, it's not" a few days, weeks or months later. At other times it can feel so much like 'the one' initially but be completely unrecognised by the other person. Sometimes it is based on a subliminal recognition of a similarity to something (or someone) that is so known and familiar that it feels utterly comfortable and is assumed to be 'the one'.

The best example I have of this is from a client of mine who was married for twenty years to an international banker with high-functioning Aspurger's autism who was utterly charming and charismatic – especially in social situations although he was highly unpredictable within these – and totally incapable of emotional intimacy. But she was used to this.

---

2. Marlowe, Christopher, *Dr Faustus*.

Not having eye contact did not worry her, lack of emotional empathy did not phase her. She found him witty and stimulating and that was enough for her. She said life was never dull with him around and she "loved him with all her heart".

As he spent most of his time working in Amsterdam, the relationship did not grow stale. Not surprisingly she was devastated when he left her for one of his Dutch colleagues with whom he could "pursue a deeper working connection". Shortly afterwards she met a man through her own work who was equally charming and charismatic to her, although more socially inept and withdrawn, and quickly struck up a friendship with him. He was advising her on a computer installation and they worked very creatively together. But something was 'off'.

She said she "recognised him as a soulmate" – and felt a powerful response to him in her lower chakras – but the relationship never developed despite every appearance of interest on his part. Although outwardly he was very different to her husband, in his response to life and to emotional interaction he was so similar that he could well have had a mild degree of Aspurger's himself (the condition covers a wide spectrum of behaviours and responses and is characterised by difficulty in emotional appropriateness and intimacy).

With the benefit of hindsight, she began to see that what she had recognised was not his soul but his energy. It was resonated exactly like her ex-husband's and, therefore, felt very familiar – and safe – to her. The friendship lacked the emotional challenge that deep intimacy would have offered her but the benefit was that it carried her over a difficult period in her life and enabled her to finally recognise what had been missing from the relationship with her husband. She began to consciously reframe what she was seeking in a partner and specifically decided she wanted someone who could appreciate what she had to offer on all levels and with whom she could explore a bond of emotional intimacy. Shortly afterwards she began a much more intimate relationship. It may be that this recognition of 'energetic resonance' operates in other spurious soulmate situations and may go partly towards explaining why people have a series of relationships with alcoholics, 'victims', 'abusers', and so on. That so familiar feel is not a soulmate but simply a seductive pull towards something destructive and yet enticingly familiar.

Delusion can play an enormous part in a soulmate experience. We see what we want to see, especially when it agrees with preconceived notions, or when it supports us in destructive behaviour which is not in our best interests but to which we are addicted – and, more especially, when it might have a past-life component.

As many people find out, a spurious soulmate can be a very powerful attraction, especially when it allows you to live your life addicted to some form of escapism. A soulmate can be one such addiction, alcohol another. They both involve self-delusion and a removal from reality. From inside the relationship, *they appear to be* blissful experiences so long as they last, no matter how the relationship would appear to an outsider.

Debasement in love

> Where they love they do not desire and where they desire they cannot love.
>
> Freud

In a false soulmate experience, Gaynor certainly found a part of her soul group, someone with whom she had had many lives before, but this was a soul part that, in the present life, simply refused to grow. Such a soulmate may cause you great anguish because, although they may be available to you, they are not in accord with your soul's purpose.

Gaynor had joined a spiritual group. There she met Larry. Instantly attracted, he soon became part of both her business and social life. Within a year or so he was her business partner, as well as her lover. But, despite his protestations of eternal love, he refused to give up a promiscuous lifestyle – even though he made many promises to this effect. Gaynor was deeply hurt by this. She believed that lasting love called for eternal fidelity. The group to which they both belonged set great store by spiritual principles and taught that sexual encounters outside a soulmate relationship were bad for the health of one's soul. Larry, however, whilst paying lip service to the beliefs of the group, followed his own rules. He never really took his spiritual development seriously, pleasure took priority. He used Gaynor's past-life beliefs, and the fact that the leader of the group had told them they were soulmates to manipulate her if she appeared to be slipping out of his grasp.

Somehow the relationship struggled on for another two years before they parted. But by this time, she relied on him for much of her professional work, so she still saw him frequently. Then, on her birthday, they went out for a meal together and Gaynor had a spontaneous regression to a past life in which she had been very much loved – by Larry, or so she thought. They had been blissfully happy, true soulmates. At the same time, she was listening to Larry telling her all about the new relationship in his life. She said she felt the recall was so that she would know that she had been totally loved, something she had not had in her present life, and would recognise it again when it came. But Larry? How could he be her soulmate when he treated her so badly? What was she to do?

It did not occur to her that the lesson might well be that they had to separate as lovers, so that she could find that love again but with someone else this time. Nor had it occurred to her that they might have been intended to work together rather than become lovers in the first place. She had a pioneering business that brought help to many women. He had the marketing and financial expertise she needed. By mixing 'love' with business, with its resultant conflict, her business went inevitably downhill. She felt the spontaneous recall was confirmation that Larry was her one and only true soulmate. She took him home with her that night, and the night after. She believed in 'higher guidance' and consulted many mediums, as well as the leader of her spiritual group (who assured her Larry was her one true soulmate). The result was total confusion. Some said he was her soulmate, others that there was another soulmate waiting for her. Some said, "stay", others said: "go".

During this time, Larry was putting her through hell mentally and emotionally. Spiritually, they were not even close, but financially, she was totally reliant on him. Eventually she just could not take it any longer. She left the relationship and severed the business partnership. Her business soon picked up again and became extremely successful. She realised that her recognition of Larry as the character who loved her so much in her spontaneous regression was just wishful thinking, an illusion. She saw other, less idealised, contacts with Larry in the past. She began to find a more realistic picture of their interaction.

Soon she was being told that her true soulmate was just around the corner. In the meantime, she met a young man who was very gentle and loving. She knew it was not her ultimate soulmate but nevertheless, they got on very well. She contacted me to see what I thought. I encouraged her to go for it but to have no expectations, just to see where it led. I believed that this could be a healing relationship for her. She did not need the intensity of a one and only soulmate and was certainly not ready for a twinflame at this stage. She had to lick her wounds and give herself time to recover. A gentle, loving man would help her with this, providing she was honest with him. Sure enough, when she became involved with him it was so. For that short time it was good, and it ended well.

What had got in the way of all her relationships though was the desire for perfect love, instantly. First of all the unconscious memory and then the recall of that wonderful love in the past nagged in the back of her mind. She was not prepared to settle for less. By now she had one or two candidates in view for the position of chief soulmate, but could not make up her mind. While she dithered, one potential relationship after another slipped away. She was always living in the future, not the now. This was her great lesson in life, but one of which she was unwilling to grasp hold. When she eventually began to live in the present moment, she found rewarding friendships and some good companions around her. This, she decided, was what she would settle for until 'the one' came along. In the meantime, she would continue to work on her own spiritual development. That seemed to be as far as she could go at that stage.

As Gaynor found, a spurious soulmate, no matter how close the contact was in the past, coupled with the desire for perfect love can lead to many missed opportunities. Opportunities which, had she progressed with them, could have led to her learning new ways to love. For so long she had tried to fit Larry into what she knew he could be, rather than what he was. It is an enormous insight to realise that a past-life soulmate may have put on a totally new personality in the present life and therefore be incompatible. Truly unconditional love allows those we love, and have loved, to develop at their own pace in their own way. If this does not accord with our way, then we have to stand placidly aside while they take their own pathway. There is an old esoteric story that says if we hold a bird tightly in our hand, we will kill it. If we let it go and it flies away, it was never ours in the first place, but if it is meant to be with us, given freedom it will return. The same applies to love.

The Romance of the Knight

The pleasing sweets of spring and summer past,
The falling leaf flies in the sultry blast.

Thomas Chatterton

Years ago I met a woman who believed she was joined to Thomas Chatterton, a fairly obscure eighteenth century poet who had poisoned himself at the age of seventeen. For the English Romantic poets of the nineteenth century he was the epitome of neglected genius. In the twentieth century, English graduates sometimes studied him, but few other people had heard of him until his story was presented on British television. This woman's experience began long before this last event however. According to her, they had been together across the centuries. He was her one and only soulmate, but he was not in incarnation. He was manifesting through her from another level of being. Their experience of lovemaking was, however, at what felt like a particularly physical level. Eventually she came to believe that he manifested in her physically as well. She developed breast cancer and was convinced that the lump was Chatterton making his appearance, and therefore refused to have the lump removed. This was not a woman who would have been immediately diagnosed as schizophrenic or suffering from delusions. Apart from this one somewhat unorthodox belief, she was the epitome of upright English middle class suburbia. Unfortunately, I lost touch with her and have no idea of the outcome of her story. I do know, however, that she was longing to be reunited with her soulmate, so, presumably, she joined him in death.

Many discarnate souls make their appearance in regression and soul-healing work. They may be old soulmates, comrades in arms, chance acquaintances, children who were never born, or a myriad other connections – but they hover close. They are connected to our soul and may well feel like a soulmate or even a twinflame. Depending on how you look at it, the entity is loosely or tightly attached to the etheric or spiritual level of the person who is here on the earth. Some people see these entities as being rather like a psychic vampire who lives life through the incarnated person. Others see them as strongly influencing that person, or guiding them in some way. It is rather like the biblical concept of possession, although discarnate soulmate experiences usually feel rather more benevolent. What is clear is that the discarnate soul is held in attraction to the person on earth. To understand how this can be, we need to go back to previous lives and those vows we make, promises such as "Next time we will have a relationship no matter what" or "I'll never leave you". If we desire something strongly enough, or if we fail to free ourselves from our vows, we could well find ourselves in similar relationships. A true spirit attachment may require specialist assistance to detach the soul and send it on its way.[3]

The ghostly lover

> What I love shall come like visitant of air
> Safe in secret power from lurking human snare.
>
> Emily Bronte

In a 'dream lover' experience, a woman met her 'soulmate' every night in her dreams to make passionate love. Sexual magic is an ancient art and they had practised it before. She said it was a meeting on the astral plane. Both left their physical bodies behind and journeyed to this other place. In everyday life, he was married and she lived alone but they worked together. They never discussed their strange affair, but each knew how the other felt. She was convinced he was her soulmate and that somehow they would find a way to be together. Eventually, however, it became clear that he would not leave his wife. She broke off the affair but was desolated at the loss of her soulmate. Psychoanalysts may well categorise this as a fantasy separated from reality, a kind of wishful thinking deeply rooted in childhood experiences in the same way that some psychologists believe a near-death-experience is either imagination or a product of a chemically disordered brain. But, having had a near-death-experience and many instances of leaving my body during healing work, I keep a completely open mind on the out-of-body lover as, to me, it is perfectly feasible.

I have recently come across another phenomena in this ghostly or dream lover saga. Several clients have reported having very powerful, 'out-of-body' sexual relationships with someone who they know in their present life but who is celibate from inclination or religious training.

3. See Judy Hall, *Good Vibrations*.

Whilst the relationship feels very physical, and they are very much in their own physical body, there is literally no other body present although there is a strong feeling of love and all the physical responses. Maria's story is typical. Mitchell was someone who was celibate by choice as he belonged to a 'lay order' of monks, and with whom she worked in a refugee project. Although they enjoyed a friendly working relationship, there was no possibility, in her mind, that the relationship could develop and yet:

> I woke up to find Mitchell curled up beside me, quietly holding me in his arms. I was suffused with love. When he realised I was awake, he began to caress me all over and we soon progressed to gently making love. This experience was physically intense and deeply spiritual rather than passionate. My whole body was involved and it felt very tantric. It was the most earth shaking orgasm I had ever encountered. The strange thing was I knew all the time that Mitchell could not be physically present even though he felt immensely solid and real to me. Nor, had he been present, would we have been making love as he, from choice, lived that celibate lifestyle. But I know that I was not dreaming as I was wide awake with every sense heightened. This experience was repeated many times – and, indeed, continued after I left the project so that we were in different countries. Much as I would have liked to question him, I did not feel able to. We were friends but that was all, there has never been a hint of physical attraction between us. And yet I long for him at a soul level, the love that manifests between us is so strong and so unconditional that I really don't know how to live without it if he leaves me alone on that level.

In an effort to understand what was going on, she had a reading from a psychic who told her that she and Mitchell had been together from way back and that in the incarnation before the present one they had been monks who had an intense sexual attraction to each other that was sublimated into a deep intellectual friendship. The resulting mental bond was so strong that it carried over into their present life, along with the taboo against taking it any further. However, she felt that something else was going on and asked me to have a look. The answer was somewhat strange, even by my standards, and yet it fitted with what other clients and therapists have experienced.

It seemed that Mitchell had been celibate from choice even as a teenager because he was deeply afraid of his own intense sexual feelings – a fear he had brought over from previous lives and had then been reinforced when he was a teenager and which was instrumental in his eventually becoming a 'lay monk'. So he had split off from these feelings and in so doing he created an energetic 'desire body' that was capable of operating independently of him. A friend of his who had been killed when riding a motorbike as a teenager, and who felt that he had missed out on life, had taken over this desire body and was using it to have sexual experiences. Somehow, because the real owner of the 'body' was still in incarnation, this desire body was able to physicalise much more strongly than most discarnate etheric or astral bodies could. When the 'friend' was evicted from the desire body and sent off into the spirit realm so that he could reincarnate if he wished, the energy body returned to Mitchell. As Mitchell was not my client, I was unable to ascertain whether he had accepted this body as part of himself. But the experiences ceased for my client.

I suggested to Maria that she use this experience as a way into a mystic inner marriage (see Chapter 13), seeing 'Mitchell' not as the person he was externally, out there in the world, but as a personification of her own inner 'perfect lover' with whom she could merge to achieve an integration of her masculine and feminine energies, being very careful, however, to distinguish between the Mitchell-out-there and the inner figure. This brought about a change, although she confessed to missing the out-of-his-body experiences very much and it would appear that more work may be needed to set her free from the longing for Mitchell before she is ready to let go and find a physical partner in the everyday world.

To be or not to be

A friend who read this book in draft asked me to point out that from her experience – and indeed from that of other people – it is possible to be in a twinflame relationship for over forty years and yet still be tempted by an overpowering soulmate experience. In her case she met two 'soulmates' in quick succession. "There was an immediate recognition, a feeling of having known this person for ever". She described that ubiquitous base chakra lighting up sensation as they looked deep into each other's eyes. Something that has been the undoing of many a soulmate. She said that, in that moment, it would have been all too easy to throw away her marriage and the very deep and real soul companionship she and her twinflame have always enjoyed for the ephemeral, momentary passion aroused by these soulmates. But something held her back, a sense not only of loyalty to her twinflame but also an inner warning that 'soulmates may not be all they are cracked up to be'. How right she was and how wise to listen to that inner voice. It may well have been on her soul plan to meet and overcome such a temptation but equally it may have become one of those 'if only' memories that hold such power. They could also have turned out to be a spurious soulmate and she would have been left bereft.

Her experience brought up the question, 'is it on our soul's agenda that twinflames will part in the present life other than by death?' To which my answer has to be: rarely. If it is a real soul bonding, as in the twinflame marriage rather than the soulmate, then no matter how great a fleeting temptation may be, an inner sense of the rightness of the twinflame relationship will almost always prevail. There may be rare occasions when other soul contracts and obligations transcend the twinflame bond causing a couple to part or experience extended periods apart, but this is extremely unusual, especially in a marriage. Twinflames in other relationships such as family or friendships will, of course, differ.

9
Scouring the Soul

If grief for grief can touch thee,
If answering woe for woe,
If any truth can melt thee,
Come to me now!
I cannot be more lonely,
More drear I cannot be!
My worn heart throbs so wildly
'Twill break for thee.

Emily Bronte

As author Sue Minns says, soulmates can be spiritual brillo pads that scour us and polish our souls. The experience can be far from pleasant, but the consequences can be momentous and far wider than the purely personal level our experiences usually touch.

The following story is one in which I was involved because I had done considerable work with Lily-Ann during the years she had been with her 'soulmate' but it echoes the experience of several of my clients. This soulmate was a guy she had met while on holiday in Greece. She had been quietly meditating on a beach when a voice said to her, "Go. Now!"

Leaping up, she collided with a man. When they had picked themselves up, they started talking – and didn't stop for the next two weeks. When she had to return to British Columbia where she lived, she was devastated at the thought of never seeing him again. Within weeks however Dermott had followed her, found himself a job and moved in.

Whilst not exactly blissfully happy for the next ten years, they had muddled along with occasional rows and tantrums. She was adamant she didn't want to cut the ties or leave him. Eventually Lily-Ann came over to England for some further training and, before she left, she told him the relationship was over, she couldn't handle it any longer, and he was to leave. She was extremely angry to find, on her return, that Dermott had taken her at her word and moved in with someone else.

But it was one of those 'can't live with you, can't live without you' scenarios that are so common in soulmate situations. He moved back in with her but as a soul friend. They slept separately and she had a much younger boyfriend who was around much of the time.

One night I was awakened at about 3am by a feeling of being pulled out of my body and rushing very fast through the air. I landed at Lily-Ann's house (which I recognised from photographs) and Dermott was there, looking very confused. Realising he was dead, I suggested he should go with me to the light. He was extremely concerned about Lily-Ann and the intense grief he knew she would go into. He said that his soul had tried to leave a few months earlier but he had been too worried about her. I told him that if he went to the light he could then come back to see her but that if he stayed where he was he would become stuck and unable to help her.

We travelled a little way into the light, an easy process, and I later found out from Lily-Ann that he already believed that when a person died they went back to light. This seemed to help, although there was still considerable anxiety in him about how Lily-Ann was taking it. I said we could wrap Lily-Ann in light and love and have healing go to her heart. He was still unable to go fully into the light but I suggested he let himself move deeper into it when he was ready. I then emailed Lily-Ann to check on her. She confirmed Dermott had indeed died and said she had been able to feel him still around, very confused, but that it was more peaceful now although he was still close-by. She had talked to him, saying she would always be a part of him. That, of course, unwittingly held him back.

When I woke up the next morning, I went back to see how he was getting on. He was much calmer but still very concerned about Lily-Ann – her grief was holding him back from going fully into the light. I suggested he should go and talk to her, telling her whatever he needed to say. I left him doing this and checked in with him from time to time during the day. He had become much less confused but his concern for her was still pulling him back.

When I checked into why he had gone so suddenly, part of it was to give her the opportunity of learning about the effect of such intensive grief both on the departing spirit and on herself. The remainder was that his Higher Self had yanked him out of his body. Although an exceptionally talented person, he was working in a dead-end job with no fulfilment. Lily-Ann had said a couple of years previously that she could see him slowly dying inside. This process had accelerated. No further movement was possible. Although he had innate wisdom and awareness, he was not consciously pursuing a spiritual path and his material one was blocked. So, his Higher Self decided it was time for him to leave. When the autopsy was carried out, it was found that he had had a previous heart attack five months earlier – but told no one. So his soul had indeed tried to leave.

A day or two later I became aware of extreme agitation and anxiety, and tremendous outpouring of emotion and deep shock. I tuned into Dermott who kept saying how sorry he was. He was distraught and wanted to apologise to his family. It was almost as though he had committed suicide (which he hadn't), he felt so guilty about his death and the effect it was having. Telling him that everything was alright and that he had followed the timing he needed to, I took him to the light – and he went on into the deep light and was then at peace. I sent healing to Lily-Ann and the family as the tremendous outpouring of emotion and shock seemed to be connected to them.

It seemed, according to Lily-Ann, that Dermott's family had gone straight from their arrival at the airport to view his body. They had only seen one other dead body before and that had been in a funeral home where it had been made to look as lifelike as possible; they were extremely traumatised by the sight of his unprepared body in the morgue. I awoke in the middle of the night, feeling great panic, and only later found out that this was the moment when the coffin was being nailed down. One of Dermott's great fears – as with so many people – had been that he would be buried alive, a reflection of an earlier past life experience. I reminded him that he was now in the light, and he became calm once more.

A couple of days later I was overwhelmed by feelings of loneliness. 'How can I go on? What will I do now I'm all alone? How could this happen?' kept running through my head. There was enormous grief and sadness. At first I believed I was tuning into Lily-Ann's grief, which was indeed great. But this built up until I realised it was the collective grief of the American Indian nation. Dermott had been deeply involved with the native people and they had carried out their own funeral ceremony for him that day. I took Sturt Desert Pea flower essence and then homoeopathic Ignatia for several doses to heal not only Lily-Ann but also as a surrogate for the collective grief, and carried out a forgiveness ritual in which Lily-Ann joined.

So, what was achieved by this scouring of souls? Well, Lily-Ann had worked with the native people for thirty years and was aware of her and Dermott's deep connection to that culture in other lives. They had lived through the great purges carried out by the white man and still carried resonances of that grief in their souls. In their own healing and by offering forgiveness to everyone concerned throughout aeons, they helped the collective to heal. Dermott told me that this had been a spiritual task that they had agreed to undertake together, but he had also offered Lily-Ann the opportunity to learn to deal with grief at that very intense level and scour her own soul clean.

A Turkish adventure

> Will it alter my life altogether?
> O tell me the truth about love.
>
> W.H. Auden

Soul scouring can be a catalyst for the necessary changes to be made in your life as this next story from Jayn Lee-Miller shows. It also demonstrates how events, apparently, conspire to draw us into soulmate experiences that we need – and how difficult it is to distinguish astrologically between a soulmate or twinflame relationship and a wonderful illusion:

> My story really starts when I attended my first Angel Workshop with Doreen Virtue in 2003. During a meditation, Archangel Michael communicated with me saying, "If you give me permission, I will cut the cords in every area of your life and change your life completely. I must warn you though that this may cause some turbulence so I have to receive your permission before I can go ahead". I gave Archangel Michael permission to go ahead and get to work. Little did I know what was in store.
>
> My son had been one of the first babies in the UK to be born in a birth pool and I had founded Splashdown Water Birth Services as a result. I played a big part in promoting the use of especially designed pools for labour and birth. Nathan's father had left us when Nathan was a baby, which had been devastating for me. I had worked immensely

hard after he left to build myself up on all levels and had been tested to the roots in all areas of my life. Over the years I had built myself up to a level where things were going quite nicely with no real problems and was enjoying the success of a thriving business.

Nathan had always been a very easy child to raise and I have very supportive parents and a lovely home I work from. However, my home was very cluttered. After my Archangel Michael meditation, I kept bumping into a medium whom I had met at local Spiritualist Churches. She asked me if I could offer her any work with Splashdown and, as I wanted to concentrate on getting my house in order I asked her if she would like to help answering the phone. When she walked through the door, she said that Archangel Michael had sent her and that she was actually not here to answer the phone but to clear and completely redecorate the house. She had previously worked in a similar capacity for a Nigerian Prince and has amazingly good taste so I was very happy to leave everything in her capable hands. So with my home eventually looking beautiful and everything going so well in my life, the only thing missing was a lovely man to share my life with.

I had booked a week's holiday with my friend, Estelle, whom I had known since I was four years old. The travel agent advised us to go to Turkey and when we booked there was only one hotel available that could offer us a single room each at a good price and it seemed that it was 'meant to be'. I was aware that some Turkish men were out to con English women and was determined not to get involved with anyone.

The first night we arrived I noticed one of the waiters who was quiet and seemed shy. During my stay, there was an important Stargate astrological configuration and after doing a deep meditation for this, I went to have a late night snack in the Restaurant with Estelle. Ibis, the shy waiter I had noticed, was extremely attentive and would clear away our cutlery and crockery the moment we had finished with it as if he was very eager to finish his day's work. He caught us laughing at this and joined in on the joke. The next morning as I went down for breakfast he kissed my hand and asked if we would sit at the table where he would be serving that evening, which we did. That night there was a knock at my apartment door and Ibis stood there with a bottle of champagne – a sure way to my heart. I thanked him and sent him on his way.

On the last night of the holiday, he asked me out and I (foolishly?) consented. His English was very poor – supposedly. He was extremely charming, good-looking and a lot younger than me and although flattered, I did not take this date seriously at all.

When I arrived home, he emailed me after a week or so declaring love. I had booked to go back to the same hotel for a week in January by myself as I had got a cheap deal. It was definitely not because I wanted to see him again.

However, the turning point for me came when I had our astrology charts done for compatibility, mainly just to prove that this was NOT a serious relationship. This was done over the internet and the most important part of the interpretation, where it mentioned what the relationship was really all about, repeated three times that 'If we were not married already, then we would be'. According to this chart, we had a marriage made in heaven and this is what made me start to believe his declarations of love. Because of his charm, good looks and deeply romantic behaviour, it was easy to fall in love with Ibis.

After yet another visit to Turkey and a proposal of marriage, I asked a professional astrologer who specializes in events to work out the best date for a marriage for us. When he saw our charts he also said it was a textbook marriage and that we had obviously been married in the past and that we would be able to overcome anything life threw at us in during this incarnation because of our deep love for each other.

My parents and brother were devastated over this relationship and knew this would turn out to be a disaster. This unfortunately caused some horrible arguments but has since made me realise the deep extent of their love for me.

I took my son over to Turkey to meet Ibis with the intention of bringing him back with us to England. However, before I had left, I was beginning to have my doubts and the astrologer heard this in my voice. When I arrived back home with Ibis, there was a letter from him saying that he had done a progression chart for our relationship and warning me that the marriage did not actually take place. Everything was an illusion and, although we were extremely compatible, Ibis was actually out to deceive and con me – which turned out to be true. So, the computerised astrology chart had encouraged me to explore the relationship in more depth [it is never a good idea to have a computerised chart as computers cannot weigh up competing factors] but thanks to the progressed chart Ibis actually eventually confessed he had been 'bad' and I arranged a ticket for his return to Turkey after just one week of his stay. I treated him with great kindness even though he had deceived me and had also conned me out of money that I had given him in Turkey to buy a second-hand car.

So my life had gone from rock bottom when my ex-husband left in 1991 to gradually building everything up on all levels and then, when I met Ibis, I thought this is complete fulfilment. However, not only did the relationship go but I found myself in serious debt for the first time in my life. Then, as time went on, my son left home to live nearer his school. I had put on a lot of weight due to comfort eating so decided to address this and went on a special diet plan where you have just milkshakes. So here was I without a partner, without my son, seriously in debt and without food. As you can imagine, I asked and asked and asked for the angels to help. Although I had to wait a long while, they have eventually helped me to find fulfilment again.

My friend, Pattie, an Angel Artist, was due to do a demonstration of Guardian Angel drawings at our local Church and I asked her if I could talk about Angels as she worked. She agreed and the event was a great success. Our work seemed to go from strength to strength after that with lots of churches wanting to book us.

I attended an Angel Healing Practitioner Diploma Course and after the second day, the workshop leaders asked me if I would help them facilitate the next course as they could see I was really connected with this work. They then decided to train as Inter Faith Ministers and asked me to take over their work. Of course, I jumped at the chance and have since also become an Angelic Reiki Master and founded The Academy of Angelic Healing. I was 'discovered' at the Mind Body and Soul Exhibition at Olympia and now enjoy writing the 'Ask the Angels' pages every month for Take a Break's *Fate and Fortune* magazine.

So I thank Ibis for being such an important catalyst. No regrets!

So, Ibis fulfilled his soulmate function of a catalyst to move Jayn on and in being able to forgive him she was able to open at a new spiritual level. She now passes on the wisdom she has learned to others, fulfilling part of her own soul purpose.

10

Eternal Triangles

> I know we both agreed that if we ever felt the need
> to explore some karmic debt with a person that we met
> That we could sleep with them
> If there were dreams that we could lead with them
> Then we could sleep with them.[1]

Perhaps one of the most painful soulmate experiences is that of the eternal triangle. There are many stories and myths about this ubiquitous experience. Cleopatra, Mark Anthony and his wife Octavia played out the tale at the Romano-Egyptian Courts. Arthur, Guinevere and Lancelot repeated the drama in the Court of Camelot – Charles, Diana and Camilla at the modern Court of St James. Many people play it out in their everyday lives.

The triangle situation can carry over from past lives and, as we shall see, participants may well change sexual gender as the triangle forms and reforms, but the basic story remains the same. In this first triangle tale, the three people concerned came back into the present life as women and became involved in a complex lesbian relationship:

> Suzanne and I had been lovers for nearly two years. After three failed relationships, disillusionment had set in, and I felt emotionally weary. Consequently I welcomed Suzanne's decisive nature. It seemed natural to follow her saturnian lead. She had definite ideas about everything. She was upset if I read at the breakfast table, saying this was bad manners. She would make appointments with me if there was something we needed to talk about. She took my fading career in hand with real success.
>
> For several years I had spent two weeks in May on an island where I participated in an intensive yoga course. Whatever relationship I was

---

1. Felix, Julie *You Slept With Her* (© J. Felix 1986).

in, I had decided this was my solo time where I could share with other yoga participants, but not be entangled in personal interaction. When Suzanne suggested she join me after I had been there for ten days, I was hesitant, but then agreed. It was during the ten days before Suzanne arrived that I met Lisbet.

Lisbet and I both felt the strong link between us, but I knew I was playing with fire since Suzanne was due to come out in a few days. Lisbet is quite psychic and recognised that she and I were soulmates. When Suzanne arrived, I tried to act as if everything was normal, but, of course, it was not. I spent time with her, and yet it seemed my spirit was with Lisbet. I finally had to own up, admitting my attraction to Lisbet, but explaining that it was merely an attraction, and that I wished to continue my relationship with her. I certainly wasn't prepared for what followed. Suzanne completely freaked out and proceeded to punish me with the dedication of the 'wicked witch' in a fairy tale.

Lisbet's nature was much more mercurial than saturnian. Her sunny personality was an obvious contrast to that of Suzanne. One night I had a dream that threw an interesting light on the situation. It was a dream that I believe revealed a past life. In this past life I was female, and both Suzanne and Lisbet were male. I don't know when in the past it took place, but it was a Polynesian setting complete with palm trees and moonlit surf.

I was a young girl in what would be the equivalent of a 'respectable family'. Suzanne was a young man whose parents were friends of my parents. A marriage was arranged, and I married Suzanne (in her male form). He was an ambitious young man with strict rules as to what was acceptable and what was not. Lisbet was a young man whom I had grown up with. As children we swam together, climbed trees, and had secret places where we would play and create our own fantasies. He was a fisherman's son, and not considered a candidate for my husband. After my marriage to Suzanne, I became depressed and lonely. Then, eventually, I met this childhood friend (Lisbet) secretly. We would go for moonlight swims and we became lovers. After sometime, my husband (Suzanne) found out about my infidelity. He beat me, called me all kinds of names, and I was forbidden ever to see Lisbet again.

In this life, after several months of attempted reconciliation with Suzanne, we finally decided to separate. Shortly after that, Lisbet and I became lovers. Although we are no longer together, I still consider Lisbet to be my soulmate, my 'brother-sister' throughout eternity. We shall see!

And indeed their relationship was rekindled several times in the years that followed, although both had relationships with other people. The triangle aspect has never been resolved.

So many people had come to me with this kind of triangle story that I began to feel that something very real was being played out down through the ages. In a meditation I asked where it all began:

Triangles hung in the air. I was told that the event I was to see was the start of many 'eternal triangles'. This event appeared to take place on a planet far from earth. It was a barren place with strange, otherworldly colouring: slate blues and greys, pale sandstone and yellow ochre – like the Egyptian desert at twilight. The beings here were humanlike, but not so solid. They hung ethereal in the air or walked lightly on the earth. Reproduction was by means of binary fission. The being simply split in two (rather like Plato's soulmates). On sacred occasions, two beings could come together to make a body for a very special soul to incarnate into. This would be a 'holy being'. In other words, sexual union was a sacred act, reserved for a particular purpose. Procreation was a part of everyday life but that everyday life was far from earth-like.

There was some kind of catastrophe. It was hard to tell what happened. Many died. It looked like the devastation after a nuclear explosion, everything was laid to waste. From then on, instead of splitting into two, many of the beings split into three. This created a 'pair' and an 'outsider' who was forever trying to find a place to belong. The pairs would draw together naturally, shutting out the 'outsider'. The outsiders would try to form relationships together, but would always seek to return to their original triangle as this was the only place that felt like home. In this way the 'eternal triangle' was created. I was told that many souls lived this out on earth, with the three souls concerned taking on many different roles and genders in an effort to heal the split.

I assumed that this vision was allegorical rather than actual, but since then several other people have told me of the same vision and their belief that it took place on a planet far from earth. The jury is still out on that as far as I am concerned (even though more than a decade has passed, there has been no confirmation either way), but I did find it helpful in picturing why so many people get caught up in the, seemingly, eternal triangle. As far as I can tell, it is not always the original three parts of the one being that are attracted together. One of the three players in a triangle saga may well be an 'outsider' who is trying to find a place to belong – in which case the 'triangle' may form for one life only although the effects can carry over. This can affect the outcome depending on whether the existing partnership is one of soulmates or not. A quite usual scenario in the triangle situation is that two people marry, and then a soulmate of one of them comes along – or the third part of the original being arrives on the scene.

This is by no means a new phenomena and a number of spiritually-connected partnerships have found themselves in the same situation, quite a few of whom contacted me. In each case, it felt like an ancient contact being renewed, an old pattern closing up for resolution. In many cases it felt like fate. The relationship was torn apart by a third party. Often this third party acted as a catalyst, breaking down the relationship and then moving on, leaving pain and crisis behind but also the possibility of change and growth. Sometimes one of the partners left with the new partner, causing great anguish to the one left behind. Each threesome solved the dilemma in their own way, but for many it was an initiation into a new way of life. The vision I had did little to clarify individual cases, but more information was to come on these triangles.

Astrologer Pat Gillingham was receiving channelled astrological teachings at the time related to what her communicator called 'triad souls'. He told her that there were many threesomes (the triad soul) who had been created long ago. Such threesomes were drawn together down the ages and many were incarnated on earth at the present time because they had specific work to do. The relationship I had been examining appeared to be one of these triads. As David Icke wrote about triangles at important earth energy sites:

> One point of the triangle attracts positive energies, another negative, and the third point harmonizes the two together. It has a similar harmonizing role with spiritual and physical energies also.

In physical relationships, occasionally it will happen that the third party brings the other two more into harmony. But this is not always the case. Sometimes the adjustment means that fragmentation occurs. A soulmate comes into the relationship for a time, plays his or her part, and then leaves. In other cases, the original partnership either splits totally or the 'extra person' is accommodated into the relationship in some way. In some cases, for instance, they would live as two couples split between two homes, in others they lived together. For some people these threesomes have always existed. I remember reading the story of a woman who lived with identical twins. She simply could not decide between them, loving them equally. They in turn loved her and felt no jealousy between them. They lived together amicably, sharing a bedroom.

Pat Gillingham's communicator also told her that the triads were symbolised by the planets Neptune (love), Uranus (will) and Pluto (power). We all have these planetary 'gods' within us and they act out their archetypal dramas, sometimes with our conscious consent, sometimes not. According to Pat's source, the souls, each attuned to a particular planet, were playing out an archetypal love/will/power struggle which had to be resolved. A similar idea is found in esoteric astrology where a soul is aligned to a certain ray, each ruled by a planet. Particular rays interact and have to come into harmony.

From the symbolic picture I had been shown, it appeared that both twin souls and eternal triangles are relevant to relationships at the present time, with many people finding themselves in one role or another. I was told that the twin souls go back to the androgynous beings of early Atlantis and Lemuria that 'split' during catastrophes there. Whether this latter picture was symbolic, on not, hardly seemed to matter. It was a metaphor for a psychic truth. We are all busy searching 'out there' for what, in the end, must be recognised as a part of our inner being that has been split off, or projected 'out there' onto the outer world and has therefore remained unreachable. We can only find our twin soul, or the three parts of the triangle, in the integration of our own inner energies and our twinflame arrives in our life more readily when we have done the inner work.

The 'lost weekend'

> Learn what you need to learn.
>
>   Attributed to Yoko Ono

Ironically, when John Lennon and Yoko Ono separated it was apparently she who had sent him away, "To learn what he needed to learn".[2] This

---

2. Seaman, Frederick *The Last Days of John Lennon*, (New York: Birch Lane Press, 1991). Goldman, Albert *The Lives of John Lennon*, (Bantam Books, 1989).

resulted in his eighteen-month-long 'lost weekend' with her secretary May Pang. By the end of that time, John was writing and performing as a solo artist again. He had regained his creative strength. But, when his wife called, he returned to his 'other half'. "Mother [Yoko] has allowed me to come home", he allegedly told May Pang.

John returned to the symbiotic mother-child relationship that had become such a habit. Maybe in that time neither John nor Yoko had learned the lesson of living independently. After their reunion they became even more symbiotic and John stayed home for five years to look after their son, Sean, who was conceived after their reunion. Who knows what they had planned when in the between-life state?

That they were still together in the between-life state after John died, and while Yoko was still in incarnation, was suggested by an experience a client of mine had not long after his death. She had not been a fan of the Beatles, had taken little notice of John Lennon, and, apparently, had no reason to feel connected to him. But, when learning to draw, she had drawn his face from a photograph and felt powerfully pulled towards him. She began to 'dream' of him incessantly and to have powerful sexual experiences that felt absolutely real and very physical: a dream lover made manifest. Standing in the background was the shadowy figure of Yoko, who was encouraging him in his games, as the client later described them, and actively participating on occasion. This woman's mind – and body – were haunted by John and she was absolutely certain that she had had several past lives with him, a not uncommon experience (see Chapter 13).

Ancient herstory

May the Lord see justice done between you and me.

Genesis 16:5

The archetypal struggle between the different facets of the eternal triangle is one that has been recorded as long as history has existed. In an extremely karmic tale in the Old Testament, one that is still having repercussions today, the Patriarch Abraham was given a vision:

The word of the Lord came to Abram in a vision. He said,
"Do not be afraid Abram, I am giving you a very great reward".

Genesis 15:1-4

Abraham did not believe he deserved a reward. He was childless and therefore, under Jewish law of the time, had no standing in the community – this despite the fact that he clearly led a large and prosperous community. He was told that his descendants would be as numerous as the stars in the sky, something he could hardly believe. Abraham's wife, Sarah, was barren and suggested that an Egyptian slave-girl, Hagar, become a 'surrogate mother' and a second wife to Abraham. As Hagar then despised Sarah for allowing her to conceive, the story becomes deeply convoluted. Sarah says to Abraham:

> I have been wronged and you must answer for it. It was I who gave my slave-girl into your arms, but since she has known that she is with child, she has despised me.
>
> Genesis 16:5

Abraham tells her that her slave-girl is in her hands, "deal with her as you will". So Sarah mistreats Hagar, who runs away. An angel finds her and tells Hagar to return to Sarah and submit but promises her descendants will be too many to be counted. As to her child, he says the boy shall be called Ishmael and that "his hand [shall be] against every man, and every man's hand against him, and he shall live at odds with all his kinsmen". It appeared that Hagar could not escape her 'fate', or was it destiny, and neither could her child (ancestral karma passes down through the generations). She had to face up to the karma that came from lying with another woman's husband, even though that woman had herself suggested it. Her son Ishmael, however, although an outcast from Jewish society, became the patriarch from which Moslems claim descent and who, of course, practise submission to the will of God.

Eventually Sarah, despite her advanced years, also bore a son, Isaac. The father of many children and forefather of the Jewish race. However, this was not the start of this karmic tale. Some years previously, at a time of famine, Abraham and Sarah had journeyed to Egypt. Believing that if the Egyptians knew Sarah was his wife, they would kill him and take her – for she was very beautiful, Abraham said she was his sister. Pharaoh apparently took her to wife – more probably as a concubine as the Pharaohs did not marry outsiders. In retribution: 'the Lord struck Pharaoh and his household with grave diseases' (Genesis 12:17). Somewhat distressed, the Pharaoh asked Abraham why he had lied, and then sent them packing. Hardly surprising then, from a karmic point of view, that the Jews were later taken into so-called slavery in Egypt although this seems to have been much more like economic migration. If Genesis is to be believed, this is not the only time Abraham lied about Sarah being his sister and let another man take her to save his own skin, but this could be the same story (Genesis 20:2-18) with the details altered as it passed through the oral tradition.

Nor was the birth of the two sons to Abraham the end of the tale. We can trace the roots of the seemingly eternal conflict between the Jews (descended from Sarah's son) and the Moslems (descended from Hagar's son) back to this particular eternal triangle. The story repeats down through the ages as the archetype and collective karma continues to take hold. What happens in the collective, the many, also happens in the personal, the few. Eternal triangles recur throughout the ages.

The poet and his lady

> The triangle plays out to the end.
>
> William Butler Yeats

A different version of the eternal triangle occurs when someone loves someone who loves someone else. The poet William Butler Yeats suffered from unrequited love for well over twenty years. In a highly complex relationship, a triangle wove its way through his life and, 'took his youth'. It was not all bad, however. This was his creative muse, fuelling his greatest works and underpinning his life. The astrology between him and his great love was powerful, perfectly expressing a 'can't live with her, can't live without her' dilemma and the mystic merging that their souls eventually undertook.

The object of his affection, Maud Gonne, steadfastly refused to marry him but remained his close friend and magical colleague.[3] He was sure she was his soulmate. Both remembered past lives together. Maud dreamt that they had been sister and brother sold into slavery. They had been each other's sole support. Throughout Maud's life, she would always turn to Yeats at times of trouble.

---

3. See Greet, Mary K. *Women of the Golden Dawn*, (Rochester: Park Street Press, 1995).
    Jeffares, A. Norman *W.B. Yeats Man and Poet*, (London: Kyle Cathie, 1996).
    Yeats, W.B. *Memoirs*, (London: MacMillan, 1972).
    Jeffares, A. Norman *W.B. Yeats A Vision*, (London: Arena, 1990).
    Yeats, W.B. *Autobiographies*, (London: MacMillan, 1980).
    Ellman, Richard *Yeats – the Man and his Masks*, (London: Penguin, 1979).

On first meeting Maud, Yeats thought her 'a goddess'. He says in his memoirs that he had never seen a woman of such great beauty. She brought about in him 'an overwhelming tumult'. He proposed to her on several occasions, but she always said no. Almost ten years later they underwent a soul marriage. Both had a dream the same night. Yeats dreamed that she kissed him for the first time. Maud dreamt of a 'great spirit' who took her to a throng of spirits, amongst whom was Yeats. The Great Spirit put Yeats' hand into Maud's and said that they were married. When Maud related this dream to Yeats, she told him she could never be his wife in reality because there was someone else. However, commentators have seen this as a time when, if Yeats had pursued his quest, he could well have succeeded (Maud was at that time separated from her French soulmate). But, somehow, he preferred his woman to be unattainable (hardly surprising given the astrological synastry).

A few days later they did a silent meditation together. Maud found herself 'a great stone statue through which passed flame'. Yeats became 'flame mounting up through and looking out of the eyes of a great stone Minerva'. They both took this to confirm that they had made a spiritual and mental marriage. But once again Maud refused to marry him 'in the flesh', saying that she had an abhorrence of physical contact.

In 1908, almost ten years after their first spiritual joining, when exploring sexual magic on the astral plane (out-of-the-body tantric sex), they again shared a mutual experience, a 'renewing of their vows'. This followed on from Maud's separation from her husband whom she had married having, as Yeats saw it, forgotten the sacred vow between them. It was an experience that went far beyond the physical and the two do not appear to have been in close proximity at the time. Their second 'mystical marriage' extended over a period of several days. Yeats consciously evoked two red and green globes, a symbol of sexuality mingling together. He experienced a 'great union' with Maud. On the same night, Maud wrote to him about an experience she had just had. She had assumed a moth-like form, her own body travelling to the astral realms, and focused on Yeats. He appeared as a great serpent and they travelled somewhere in space. She looked into his eyes and they kissed. They melted into each other until they formed one being – a complete and total union. On reading this, Yeats immediately imaged himself as a great serpent, becoming one with Maud. At the same time, Maud felt him join her, so that they again became one being in ecstasy.

Following this experience, Yeats wrote to Maud, "I think today I could let you marry another... for I know the spiritual union between us will outlive this life, even if we never see each other in this world again".

When one of his biographers, Richard Ellman, interviewed Yeats' wife – who he had married towards the end of his long involvement with Maud – after his death, she was firmly of the opinion that her husband and Maud Gonne had been lovers in 1908. The question remains, however, as to whether it was a physical or spiritual affair. The magical working had been undertaken separately, but Richard Ellman had found reference to them staying together in France that year and letters from Maud saying she could not continue. Exactly what with was not specified, but it could just as well be with the astral working as with a physical relationship. With both Uranus and Neptune featuring strongly in the aspects between their charts, sexual magic was a natural outlet for the magnetic attraction between them. Uranus did not then have to worry about commitment or Neptune about holding back from being totally absorbed into the other person – for a time. The experiences they had during the magical working were far more powerful than anything that happened to them whilst anchored in the reality of bodily existence.

Maud, a priestess of the Hermetic Order of the Golden Dawn, was a striking figure. Six feet tall with copper coloured hair she was the daughter of an English army officer but became an Irish patriot who campaigned against the British Empire and advocated Home Rule for Ireland. As an aristocratic revolutionary she preached her message with great passion, and incited people to violence at a time, the 1890s, when most women were confined to the home. However, she was also one of the prime movers of the new amnesty movement and had a deep interest in spirituality.

Maud was involved in a thirteen-year long, illicit relationship with a married French politician, Lucien Millevoye, with whom she had an illegitimate child, Georges. Millevoye was, in Maud's eyes, her soulmate. At their first meeting, Maud was sure they had met before. They made a pact. He would help her free Ireland. She would help him win Alsace-Lorraine. Some commentators have felt that Maud, who in her autobiography relates that she had made a pact with the devil to give him her soul in return for freedom to control her own life, might also have included in that pact that he (the devil) would give her Lucien Millevoye. Certainly Maud had a feeling that her soul was lost and that much of the tragedy in her life was due to this pact – her father died ten days after the pact was made.

Maud and Lucien's child died young. Obsessed with keeping in contact with the spirit of her dead child, Maud went to a seance with Yeats. The seer, Moina Mathers, described a sad, dark-eyed lady in grey veils who was attached to Maud. Maud had frequently seen this 'grey lady' when she was a child. Yeats and Maud had performed a magical ritual a few days prior to the seance at which the grey lady appeared. She said she was Maud's *ka* from a former life. The *ka* is an aspect of the personality that survives death and can remain earthbound. It is a kind of 'etheric double' which holds the soul, or spiritual essence, in incarnation and also houses the personality. In Egyptian thought, it lived on independently in the astral world after the physical body died. The *ka* was the unsatisfied desires or unlived impulses that pulled the soul back into incarnation. But the *ka* could also continue its own afterlife when other parts of the soul had reincarnated.

Maud's *ka* told her story. Apparently she had been an Egyptian priestess who came under the influence of a priestly lover and gave false oracles for profit – strictly against the rules. As a consequence, the *ka* had remained 'a half-living shadow'. Yeats, in that life, had befriended the priestess and helped her to escape. Finally, she had died in the desert, but her *ka* remained split off from her soul. Now the priestess wanted to be reunited with Maud.

Moina Mathers felt the 'grey lady' was adversely influencing Maud, who had been almost verging on madness with her grief and blamed herself for being a 'bad mother' and neglecting her child, whom she had left in France – she had to keep the illegitimate birth secret. Maud herself said that when the grey lady had appeared at the end of her childhood bed, the apparition confessed to having killed a child and was full of remorse. Moina Mathers confirmed this in her own vision. Maud joined the Golden Dawn the next day so that she could learn to command and control such entities. It would perhaps have been more appropriate to do a soul retrieval and integrate this split-off, shadowy side back into Maud's own self or undertake a spirit releasement to free it, but this did not seem to have occurred to Maud or her magical advisers. As it was, the *ka* caused difficulties for Maud throughout her life.

Maud was determined to reincarnate her dead child's soul. The Golden Dawn were firm believers in reincarnation and had rituals for rebirth to 'call a soul forth'.[4] Maud eventually persuaded her unsuspecting lover, Millevoye, to visit the child's grave with her on All Hallow's Eve. This is the time when the veil between the worlds grows thin. Souls can cross. They made love in the memorial chapel vault and she became pregnant once again – and Maud no doubt, was convinced she was carrying the same soul. Her child was a girl. Some time afterwards, the relationship broke up. Eventually, Maud married someone else. When that marriage broke up, Yeats and Maud made their second mystical marriage.

Yeats remained her close friend throughout, although her marriage did release him into his own eventual marriage. But the two remained tied on the soul level. It was to Maud that Yeats wrote:

Others because you did not keep
The deep sworn vow have been friends of mine
The triangle plays out to the end.

Eternal triangles are often formed where someone meets up with two previous soulmates or members of the soul group, in one lifetime. Recognising that it is a soul link helps, but few people are this aware in the beginning. So often one person is happily married, and along comes soulmate number two. At other times, I have known people to leave their (often unsatisfactory) marriage for a soulmate, only to find another one comes along almost immediately. As someone said, "How can I possibly love two men with all my heart and soul at the same time? But I do!" In her case, the lesson was to let go of soulmate number one – who could not leave his wife and family – and drop all her illusions and dreams around him, and to go into a relationship with soulmate number two who was available. When she did this, she finally found the happiness that had been eluding her all her life.

[My love for you] has rescued me... from sterility, impotence, despair. It enables me in the daily stress of almost intolerable burdens and anxieties to see visions and dream dreams.

Herbert Henry Asquith to Venetia Stanley

---

4. Personal information from Christine Hartley in 1978.

11

Serial Soulmates

Sometimes we meet more than one soulmate. It all depends on what we have come to do.[1]

Early one summer, my phone rang. "Is that Miss Judy Hall?" drawled a Southern Belle. I could almost believe Scarlett O'Hara was on the other end of the phone, so I will call her Scarlett. It was Scarlett who said that she believed our soulmate is here to teach us the hardest lesson.

During that first call, Scarlett merely told me that she had met her soulmate, but he was dying. A previous soulmate of hers had already died. Could they come to see me urgently? Gradually over the years that I knew her, Scarlett revealed that this was in fact soulmate number three and that number two had also died. "I guess I'm stuck in a pattern", she said somewhat philosophically, "but it's a pattern I would like to change".

Scarlett's is a story of serial soulmates, and many other things besides. For the sake of clarity, I have tried to tell it not in the order in which it was revealed to me, but in the actual sequence of events in Scarlett's life. Many of the insights she had, however, were with the benefit of hindsight and, as we shall see, the tale meanders through several soul links as it winds its way to a conclusion. It is a complex and convoluted tale.

When Scarlett was eighteen she moved from a sleepy Southern town, where ladies still wore white gloves and napped in the afternoon on freshly laundered white sheets. Life in the big city was something of a surprise and working in a large insurance office a definite eye-opener. On day three, the door opened and there, in her words, was the hunk of all hunks. One look and she had all the classic symptoms: pounding heart, base chakra alight, wedding bells ringing. "Come and live with me", he

---

1. Judy Hall, *Hands Across Time*.

said. Being a properly brought up young lady, she waited a week before complying. She knew this was her soulmate, her one and only true love. But she was in for a rude awakening. Unbeknown to her, she carried the 'love hurts' scenario in the depth of her being.

Clark was a promiscuous drug addict who was not about to clean up his act on account of meeting his soulmate. Scarlett frequently came home from work to find the flat full of addicts or 'special friends' with whom he had been spending the afternoon in bed. Many times she left, and just as many times she returned. She could not get him out of her system. She "knew we were meant to be together", a view he continually reinforced by telling her how much he loved – and needed – her. She could see the potential he had and what he might be – "the pearl in his heart" – but she could also see the reality of his situation. Scarlett was not a weak and helpless woman for all her Southern ways. She was shooting up a somewhat ruthless career ladder and holding her own amongst much older and better qualified men. But, in the hands of Clark she was putty. Clark, however, was fast slipping down the spiral of addiction.

One day she finally left "for good". She had recognised that there was nothing she could do for her soulmate. For the sake of her own life, she had to get out. Two days later, Clark was dead from an accidental drugs overdose. Scarlett got on a plane to England – a pattern she was to repeat several times. She could not go to the funeral, she was terrified of death.

Five years later she met soulmate number two. He was Rhett Butler incarnate. Devastatingly handsome, debonair, just a touch dangerous: the ideal Gentleman to her Southern Belle. Their first date was a costume ball. Naturally they went as Rhett and Scarlett. A film producer was there. He was shooting a film set in the Old South. "Would they be extras? They so looked the part. She handled her dress as though she had been born to it". When I did a karmic reading for her, not yet knowing this, I told her she had had a life in the Confederate South. Her great love had been lost in the Civil War – his body was never found, and she mourned him for the rest of her life. She had vowed to wait for him "forever".

"Oh yes", she said matter of factly, "Here he is", and pulled out a photo taken at the costume ball. To clear the connection, I took Scarlett back to her previous life with Rhett and she amended that vow she had made. "Forever" became "for this life only". By making such adjustments back in time and healing the past, the present life can change and nothing need be carried forward into the next life. When, and if, they met again, they would be starting afresh, not bound by the past promise.

For the next five years Scarlett had handled that relationship a little differently to soulmate number one. Rhett lived at home with his wealthy parents and had no desire to move out. She enjoyed her bachelor apartment. But they saw each other most days and the families were very close – and have remained so. It was always assumed that one day they would marry. The only cloud on the horizon was that Rhett was always faintly unwell. Hypochondria, everyone thought, until one day his mother called to say he was in the hospital with terminal liver cancer and if Scarlett wanted to see him she should come quick. Scarlett hated hospitals. She went once but could not stand it and once again took off for England. When she came back, it was for the funeral.

Here we have to take a digression. Rhett was an adopted son. His parents had waited years for their own child, who was born when his mother was approaching forty. She had yearned for this child all that time, never wavered in her belief that he would come to her. A strict Baptist, she nevertheless "knew his soul". A pretty child, it soon became apparent that he was not strong. At five years old, he died of liver failure. Forty years later his mother told me that she still had not been able to grieve, she was so numb. Part of her shut down then and had not reopened. He was her most beloved child, and he was gone.

She could not conceive again and so they adopted a young child, Rhett. When she showed me the photos, it was uncanny. The two boys were so similar even she had difficulty telling them apart. They could have been identical twins. "I was sure my baby had come back to me", this deeply religious woman told me. So, the second loss was almost beyond bearing. It was something she is clearly carrying forward to another life, a soul drama that will draw them back together yet again.

In another twist in the tale, when I visited her all those years later I was given Rhett's room. A sanctuary to her dead son, it was filled with silver framed photos, all beautifully posed. "Oh yes", said Scarlett when I commented on them, "He was always having his picture taken, he seemed to be obsessed with it. He so wanted to be admired. He sent them off to magazines. He really wanted to be a star".

Later that night, unable to sleep, I was watching late night TV. Suddenly there on the screen was Rhett. I looked from the image on the screen to the photo on top of the TV set. There was no mistaking it. This was the same person. It was a 1930s' matinée idol. He died just as his career was taking off. Heavy drinking brought on liver disease. Such diseases can be carried over karmically into the next body, or bodies, that the soul inhabits. Here was a link with both the young child who died and the young man who followed. I shouted for Scarlett to come and see. She too agreed, here was another aspect of her soulmate.

To return to the main story, Scarlett decided to give soulmates a miss for awhile. She moved to England and married an old soul friend, "Definitely not a soulmate, but someone I knew I had had other lives with". She felt safe, "as though he had promised to look after me" – a promise verified in a later past-life regression and confirmed by her husband's own spontaneous past-life memories.

Meanwhile Scarlett's sister had had a child. "I took one look and knew it was Clark (soulmate number one) come back again", Scarlett said. Although living on the other side of the world, she became very close to the child. A major influence in his life, she was the one he turned to when in trouble, the one for whom he expressed his "very special love". In the family, it was accepted that these two had a bond that stretched over the miles. They were soul companions.

Some years passed. On the surface Scarlett and her husband were happy. But then Scarlett felt this nagging doubt. Something was missing. Were they simply living out his old promise to look after her? She felt that she had a purpose she was not fulfilling. Was she meant to be with a soulmate? She went to one of the 'Find Your Soulmate' workshops so popular in the States at the time. Five weeks later an old friend phoned, "A friend of mine is coming to England and I want you to meet him. I just know you two have been together before".

When she opened the door, Scarlett too knew they had been together. Here was soulmate number three. Ashley was in her words, "Gorgeous, a real hunk, just like Tom Selleck". There was just one problem. On their third meeting he told her he had only weeks to live, he too had cancer. Later, he told her he was gay and had Aids. This was clearly not to be a sexual union although there was considerable sexual attraction between them. She felt it must be for some other purpose. That was when she phoned me.

I knew very little about them then, which is the way I prefer to work. She had told me that he was her soulmate and had cancer. I also knew that she had had a previous soulmate who had died. That was all. She said of her meeting with Ashley:

> It was magic, just like the time I met my first soulmate, we felt instantly attracted and each felt we had known one another before. We spoke about reincarnation on our first meeting. On our third he told me he feels we have to teach each other some lessons and that we don't have much time. We feel so close to each other he has asked me to be with him when he dies. How can fate be so cruel?

When I compared their horoscopes, there were clear indications that this was a soulmate connection, although an extremely difficult one.

Essentially, they were going in opposite directions. Clearly this would not be a lifelong relationship for Scarlett but it was an important contact nonetheless. Obviously there were major karmic lessons to be learned and tasks to be undertaken. The previous contact between them had been symbiotic and manipulative with a powerful mothering energy making itself felt. There was a strong need to 'let go and let God' rather than trying to make things work out how she wanted them.

In her astrological chart, and therefore in herself, Scarlett had an 'emotional black hole' that did not believe there would ever be enough love and therefore manipulated and manoeuvred to get what it so desperately needed, which was why she settled for 'second best' with her husband. This hunger for love can never be satisfied by human love, it has to come from the divine part of ourselves. She had to learn to give love out, trusting that it would come back, but not controlling the process.

She also had a 'love hurts' indicator. It was a huge test of letting go, allowing to happen what would happen. This was combined in her chart with a challenge for unconditional love that usually manifests first as an idealised and idolised lover who is placed on a pedestal and expected to be superhuman. When the natural human frailties and fallibilities begin to show themselves, total disillusionment sets in. So often with this aspect, what is seen is the 'pearl at the heart of the person', what they may be rather than what they are now. An idealised picture is presented, illusions abound. In this relationship she was being offered the chance to love and accept someone exactly as they were, no illusion was possible. The planetary energies were saying that she had the opportunity to move out of a pattern of merging into an ideal relationship and go instead into a 'higher level' of relationship. This would help her to develop herself unselfishly and release her from old manipulative patterns. It would also allow her to support Ashley in whatever he needed to do.

A particular issue that surfaced for him was the need to teach people around him that death could be creative and was not The End – as his family had so long believed. By nature an exuberant, fiery Leo, he came over as a rather passive person, always holding back. He needed to find his own strength. There was a pattern of deferring to other people because of a need to be seen as nice, in other words he was a people pleaser. In regression he went back into a pattern of always allowing other people to dictate to him what he should believe in – especially his father with whom he had been in other lives. He needed to take back the control of his life.

When I read Scarlett and Ashley's past lives together, the strongest one seemed to be in the pioneering days when the wagon trains went out across America. I saw them as a mother and child, the father having died. He was a sickly child but his extremely strong-willed mother kept him alive – it seemed – by sheer willpower aided by some rather nasty tasting herbs. In the end, he was begging to be allowed to die. When Ashley went back to that life in regression he kept whimpering, "Please mama, let me go, let me go. I want to die". She, on the other hand, kept promising to always be there for him, to be strong for him – a promise Scarlett felt called upon to keep in the present life.

Born in this present life with the indicator of her karmic purpose in headstrong, pushy Aries, Scarlett commented that, when she had first heard of the cancer, she had been aware of wanting to force him to live. She had run round making appointments for him with everyone she could think of. One of the reasons she had phoned me was that my then partner was an holistic doctor who works with cancer patients and who uses Chinese herbs that can taste absolutely foul. Once she recognised the pattern, she could work on letting go and allowing Ashley to take responsibility for himself. She had to channel her positive Aries energy into strengthening herself so that she could offer him support rather than doing it for him.

Scarlett decided to leave her husband and follow her soulmate-orientated life plan. After all, she had made that promise to be with Ashley when he needed her and she felt she could learn a lot from their relationship however long it lasted. She also felt that she had, unknowingly, failed to keep her promise to Rhett and so in some sense this would be reparation for that too. She released her husband from the promise he had made to her, and the marriage was ended amicably as she was anxious that no karma attached to that relationship be carried forward.

Ashley and Scarlett went back to the States and Ashley underwent treatment that prolonged his life for three more years. Much of this treatment was experimental or unconventional. As he said, he had nothing to lose and maybe it would help someone else in the future. During this time he was in and out of hospital. Scarlett, who had had such a phobia about hospitals that she could not walk through the doors, stayed with him and nursed him. All those bodily functions that had so disgusted her in the past were dealt with quite naturally and lovingly. She learnt how to give him injections, how to change dressings and perform other intimate tasks. His doctors offered to give him drugs so that they could have sex together, but neither felt that this was the purpose of the relationship. She said, "We were as close as we possibly could be, we did not need sex".

As a Virgo, one of her purposes in being here was to give service and another was to explore 'dis-ease' in all its manifestations. She did all she could to support him in whatever choices he made about his life. They worked through a great deal between them. Everything was said that needed to be said. They went through all the emotions together. They shared every possible feeling. They both felt that all the karma was wiped clean.

Eventually, he became very weak, but he did not want to return to hospital, so Scarlett nursed him at home. One day, he caught hold of her hand saying, "I'm so tired. Can I go now?"

"You know I am the one person who can't answer that", she replied, "but I will be with you all the way whatever you decide". Later that day, after saying goodbye, he drifted into a coma. She held his hand as he slipped peacefully away. She said he looked radiant, so happy to be moving over to the other side. This time, she laid out the body as he had requested, and arranged that the funeral service be a celebration of his life rather than mourning the past. As she said, "It was the last service I could do for him and I did it willingly" – a long way indeed for someone to travel who could not bear death. The gifts she had received from the relationship were obvious, she'd developed the art of unconditional compassionate loving and faced her deepest fears around death.

The last I heard from Scarlett, soulmate number four had just arrived in her life. But, she was certain, that relationship would be different. This one would last. As Scarlett O'Hara would say:

Tomorrow is another day.

12

Cleaving to What is Akin

Those who are halves of a male whole pursue males. . . because
they always cleave to what is akin to themselves

Plato[1]

When speaking of soulmates or twinflames, the assumption is generally
made that this is a male-female phenomenon – that the original soul
was split between male and female. But this is not how Plato describes
it. As we have seen, he is insistent that, in the beginning, there were
beings that were wholly male and, therefore, when split became two
male halves. Similarly, the female soul became two female parts. It was
only the hermaphrodite soul that became one part male and one part
female. Plato is somewhat scathing about these latter souls:

> Those men who are halves of a being. . . hermaphrodite, are lovers of
> women and most adulterers come from this class, as also do women who
> are mad about men and sexually promiscuous.[2]

To Plato the ideal is the man who pursues his other, male, half. He says:

> Such [men] are the best of their generation, because they are the most
> manly. . . .It is not shamelessness which inspires their behaviour, but high
> spirit and manliness and virility, which lead them to welcome the society
> of their own kind. . . Whenever the lover of [men] – or any other person
> for that matter – has the good fortune to encounter his own actual other
> half, affection and kinship and love combine to inspire in him an emotion
> which is quite overwhelming, and such a pair practically refuse ever to
> be separated even for a moment. . . No one can suppose that it is mere
> physical enjoyment which causes the one to take such intense delight in
> the company of the other. It is clear that the soul of each has some other
> longing which it cannot express.[3]

---

1. Plato p.62.
2. ibid.
3. ibid.

Plato could perhaps be accused of bias towards the Greek ideal of his day, but nevertheless, he is making a valid point. There is no reason at all why soulmates, or twin souls, should actually be of a different gender. It is quite clear from regression work to other lives that we all take on not only various roles but also become male or female in gender as appropriate to those roles. So, if we insist on being with our soulmate throughout eternity, we may find that same-sex relationships occur from time to time, or on exploring the past, we may find that this has always been the chosen path of our soul. We may also find that, just as with heterosexual couples, we have chosen to incarnate with our soulmate or twinflame to support, or be supported by, someone we love at a deep soul level. On the other hand, it may simply not matter to us what sex our partner is. What may matter is that we learn to relate intimately.

I have undertaken a considerable amount of regression and astrological investigation for both gay and lesbian relationships. There is no one answer. Plato's theory may well be correct: that there were three 'sexes' and this has been continued on. It may be better to view sexuality as a continuum not an either/or choice. People tend towards the middle, heterosexual, or towards either end, but with the possibility for moving anywhere along the spectrum and exploring homo- or bi-sexuality.

What has emerged during regressions, and especially those relating to the planning stage in the between-life state, are various scenarios according to the lessons being worked on. For some, same-sex relationships have been a positive choice – and this often includes people who become HIV positive and go on to develop Aids. These can be some of the most caring soulmate or twinflame relationships experienced today. Souls choosing same-sex orientation want to experience, or to go on experiencing, relationships that are not the conventional male-female union and which bring out a different side of themselves. Sometimes they are choosing to develop their feminine or masculine side, so that they can integrate this into their whole being. At other times, they want to explore the aggressiveness of same sex male relationships and channel that energy in a new way, or find a new outlet for the nurturing side of female union. For others, where there is little planning, same-sex relationships may be a repeating pattern: there have been many cultures other than the Greek that saw homosexuality as ideal behaviour just as others viewed it as deviant and banned it.

In other cases, where someone has been, say, female for several lives, they may decide to experience life in a male body – quite often to break out of a soulmate deadlock they find themselves in. That choice may be forgotten when in incarnation and they find themselves pulled towards an old soulmate. The soulmate may retain the previous gender. On the other hand, they may find themselves unable to make the switch in internal gender. This happened to one client of mine. She saw herself as a young gay man. Her apparently conventional relationships with older men were actually based on her inward perception rather than her outward gender. In regression, she had been a gay man many times. So, despite the fact that the soulmate she was seeking would have an appropriate body to supposedly complement her own female body she knew that inwardly she would still be in the same kind of homosexual relationship as she had enjoyed before. She was not changing her way of relating despite having changed gender.

Souls may also choose a homosexual orientation in order to experience rejection, isolation and humiliation. In other words, being the alienated outsider who is cut off from soulmate union. Not necessarily as a masochistic action (although there have been cases where souls believed they needed punishing and this was the way it would be achieved), but as a way of empathising with others in the same situation or as a way of being thrown inwards to find self-worth and love for their own self. From the perspective of earth, it is impossible to judge why people choose such incarnations, but, when in the between-life state, the rationale always make sense and the life reflects the choice made.

Miracles do happen

> Whatever you choose to do, trust your passion, it will awaken
> your creativity, keep you in touch with your divine purpose
> and help you to feel alive.
>
> David Lawson[4]

In 1994 my then literary agent suggested we meet up with two more of her authors, Justin Carson and David Lawson. I have written elsewhere about their extraordinary relationship and how they met but wanted

---

4. Lawson, David, *The Eye of Horus – An Oracle of Ancient Egypt*, (London: Piatkus Books).

here to explore how Justin's transition to the next world can give us all hope. I also wanted to explore the idea of learning through and with each other, something David wrote about very eloquently. Some years before Justin's death, a psychic friend had suggested to David that they had been exceptionally clever in making a karmic choice to share their experience of Justin's illness. As David explained:

> In choosing to go through this process together, we were both undergoing the alchemical transformation of karma through 'dis-ease', and the spiritual evolution that can come with the role of carer. We were each simultaneously experiencing and learning from the two roles.

Through their powerful soulmate connection – which may well have been a twinflame union – and emotional empathy, they shared the impact of what each one individually experienced. So David, a sensitive Pisces, felt the subtle energetic impact of Justin's illness within his own body.

> Sometimes I could even feel the energy of his medication coursing through my veins.

After Justin's death, David realised the wisdom of their psychic friend's insight:

> Karmically, Justin and I were able to accomplish an enormous amount in a short space of time. I now wonder whether I will need to manifest a major illness in my body this lifetime. I feel like I have been through the process already and emerged with a new sense of wholeness, even in my loss. Almost by osmosis, the finest qualities of Justin have been absorbed into my psyche and have enhanced similar aspects of myself.

A typically Piscean way of David owning aspects of his own personality that had previously been embodied by Justin, thereby fulfilling the promise of the relationship. By his death, Justin gave an enormous gift not only to David but to everyone who knew him.

Living with Aids for seven years, Justin had 'walked his talk' and put their joint healing philosophy into action with great effect. But faced with a particularly unpleasant manifestation of the HIV virus, he chose not to have toxic treatment. He set off on his next 'awfully big adventure' as he called it when he phoned to tell me the news of his diagnosis and I feel exceptionally privileged to have shared a part of that adventure with him. As Justin said in a personal note in one of David's books:

Not everyone will get well again, but we can all learn to live with honour, dignity and courage whatever the future holds. While self-healing is primarily concerned with extending and celebrating life, for some, the process of dying can produce the greatest healing of all.

When Justin came home from the hospital to die, David was his primary carer with my assistance and it was a privilege to be part of this extraordinary man's passing.

Justin made a leisurely and peaceful decline into death: his loving, courteous and charming self to the last. Indeed, the atmosphere in his room became steadily more serene until, shortly after his death, it became quite extraordinary with a powerful perfume and a deep sense of stillness and peace. David and I had spent our days dealing with the practicalities of someone confined to bed by a final illness and working with healing techniques to assist his passing. Justin said goodbye to all his friends and family, telling each one exactly what they needed to hear and helping them come to terms with the idea of his leaving. With David, he planned the thanksgiving service for his life in great detail, he wanted it to be a celebration and as joyous as possible. His body slowed down, becoming virtually immobile. Only his eyes kept their sparkle and great joy at living. Justin savoured each moment – and the things that had given him pleasure in the past: his favourite ice cream, the finest single malt whiskey, a last cup of the best coffee we could brew. He was saying his goodbye to earthly life in the most positive way he knew.

The nights, however, were a time when Justin and I journeyed out of our bodies and began the great adventure. For him it was a time of freedom, the restrictions of his paralysed body dropped away. His sense of fun and his crackling aliveness were most apparent. One night I was surprised to find that we had risen up from the house and hitched a lift on a passing angel – and the angel was twelve miles high. It was quite an experience. Next morning talking to him about our trip I said that it had been a surprise because I wasn't into angels. "Well, they are in to you", he assured me with a grin. Justin was a true soul companion to me.

Before Justin died he had been working on a book: *Making Friends with God*. In it he said:

> Reincarnation is not about 'past lives', [it] is more a continuation of the essence rather than a continuation of a person's being.

This was something we had discussed at great length because I have seen time and time again the effects of such lives carried into the present and, therefore, I believe that the same essence is reborn time and time again, but with some adjustments, additions and subtractions according to what has gone before. Justin however, took a somewhat different view, typically looking more to the future than the past.

Justin's essence shines on as brightly as it did before he left the earth and his communications from the other side have been just as lively and humorous. Indeed, when David and I went to register his death we could both clearly see him skipping alongside us, giggling happily to himself. It was difficult to feel sad with such a strong presence. And it was even more difficult when we found out what he had been giggling about. He had said to both David and I individually that he would send us a signal that he was alright. The signal was to be '42' – the answer to life, the universe and everything from one of his favourite books *The Hitchhiker's Guide to the Galaxy*. When we entered the registrar's office we were both transfixed. On her computer screen was a large 42.

"What's that?" a stunned David managed to ask.

"The next number on the register", was the reply. So Justin was registered as death number 42. And so life goes on.

13

Pacts, Promises and Soul Contracts

Too long a sacrifice can make a stone of the heart.

W.B.Yeats

One of the most frequent causes of relationship difficulties is old vows and promises carried over from the past. Our soulmate may be here to help us break free of these vows and move on. The pacts and promises made to another in a previous life, or in the between-life state, can strongly affect the present. Not so long ago and in some cases today, in many marriages a couple stayed together because there was no option, but with the heart – in the words of Yeats – turned to stone, and love, if it had existed at all, metamorphosed into hatred or indifference. A couple were locked into a 'forever and ever, amen' scenario.

However, a pair of souls can become trapped by a vow that only one person makes, or even by the wishful thinking of one of the parties. You may find yourself part of a vow that says, "I'll make him, or her, know what it is to suffer", or "I could make him so happy if only..." You may also have demanded of someone else, "Be there for me". If so, you need to release them. You may also have made a soul contract in the between-life state that holds you fast but which is no longer possible or appropriate. People may also be held by old personal vows such as to celibacy or poverty, which can create difficulties in a present life relationship. Vows that were made to you may also be inappropriate and may need to be dissolved or renegotiated. But such vows work equally potently when they have been made earlier in the present life – you do not need to believe in reincarnation to be affected by earlier promises.

"I'll always love you", "always be there for you", "never let you go"; or to yourself, "I'll get even", "I'll never forget" or "I'll never let him/her go", are all equally debilitating. If a soul promised to always be there for someone or to 'always look after you', or never to leave, it can create relationship karma even though the previous life scenario was not as partners. But if the declaration was made that "you are the only one for me" this holds across lifetimes. The vow binds the two souls together beyond death.

A woman found her life partner at the age of thirty eight. She 'knew from the moment she saw him that they were meant to be together', although their path to a committed relationship was not easy. Before that commitment, she had always been held back from relationship by caring for her alcoholic sister and acting as support to her large family. Now, the woman wanted to have a child but worried about her sister as she 'wanted to be there for her'. In regression, she went back to promising her, sickly, sister that she would indeed always be there for her. She hadn't envisaged the promise lasting several lifetimes. She reframed her vow "for one life only" and asked that her sister be helped to make her own spiritual progress. Almost immediately, her sister went into treatment, which proved successful, and the woman found she was pregnant.

There are other kinds of vows, words such as, "One day he'll know how it feels", "I'll get my revenge on you", "I'll never forgive you" are powerful chains that draw souls back together. In these cases the marriage vow 'for better or worse' usually turns out to be the latter. The promises we make also draw us back, "I'll always look after you", "I'll love you forever", "whenever you need something, just call me" can hold us in thrall throughout lifetimes. We need to revise the past – to set ourselves, and the other person, free.

Forever and ever amen?

> It is so far from being natural for a man and woman to live in a state of marriage that we find all the motives which they have for remaining in that connection, and the restrains civilized society imposed to prevent separation, are hardly sufficient to keep them together.
>
> Samuel Johnson

The declarations made in marriage, especially as marriage is a sacred bonding in most religions, exert a powerful hold. 'Until death us do part' is one thing, but 'eternally' is quite another. Such a declaration binds both parties and may not be appropriate in a new incarnation – it may not even be appropriate for the whole of one incarnation. Couples do grow and change and may need to move on. If they do not, they become stultified. But a vow could still bring a couple back into incarnation again if it was not rescinded. If you have ever demanded that someone be there for you, you need to release them as that is sufficient to create an enmeshed or trapped scenario.

The power of these vows is extraordinarily strong – but they don't always work out quite as the soul thought they would. Nor are they necessarily negative, they may bring an unexpected creativity to the present life. Canadian author Jewelle St. James is convinced that she and John Lennon were soulmates in a past life but that he had died before they could marry. She wrote a book[1] about her experience. She says:

> My soul always knew that John Baron and John Lennon were the same soul, but the modern, doubting cynical kept me waiting for the ultimate sign to verify this. When I viewed my past and present lives as a script in one giant play, the whole pattern was obvious. I've realized that our relationships across the centuries are like those wooden Russian dolls; one fits neatly inside the other and so on and so on.[2]

She is certain that contact with John Lennon after his death propelled her into fulfilling her life purpose: to write a book about how past lives and patterns intertwine. In writing the story she picked up the promise that, as she saw it, had 'reunited' them:

> "Katherine", he said, reaching for her hand and smiling faintly, "I promise I'll always be with you. Always remember we are a part of each other... remember...'tis in the stars". Katherine sat for a very long time watching him sleep... When she awoke, she saw that she would never again see him smile, feel his touch, or gaze into those sky blue eyes. John [Baron] was gone.[3]

When Jewelle had written the book, she thought she was ready to move on:

> I was tired of living in another century. I wanted a life in the new century. I wanted to look forward, not backward.

---

1. St James, Jewelle, *All You Need is Love* (reissued 2008) [hereinafter Jewelle St James]
2. ibid p.221ff.
3. ibid p.85.

Such a release could only come if she had released John from that vow, however. When I emailed Jewelle to ask her about that she first of all replied that, in this life, John Baron had been guiding her towards completing her latest book on a Holocaust life, recollection of which had been accelerated when John communicated to Jewelle a poem about the Nazi death camps.[4] I quickly received another email in which she said she had never considered the angle of vows so she supposed had not released John. Recently she emailed again and said:

> About a year ago, I had decided to let John go. Shortly after, I received a message via a psychic friend in England. The strange thing is my friend didn't know I was letting him go – she was only relaying his message. I still have it tacked above my computer:
>
> "My Katherine, I'm taking you on a journey, please hold my hand, don't leave me yet, I have much to say. We have done well, have we not?" Months later I began the Holocaust book – and without his 'holding my hand' it wouldn't have been written.

As Jewelle said, she hadn't even realised that John Baron's last words to Katherine were a vow. But that vow has led to two remarkable books that show the workings of karma and past lives in great detail and it doesn't sound as though John, or Jewelle, are yet ready to sever the productive connection.

On New Year's Day 2008 she emailed me to say:

> It's now obvious to me that John and I are living out the life we should have had, way back when. Some may say I'm wasting this life, but my convictions lie very deep... without his spiritual guidance my quest would have stopped decades ago. This fact gives me the strength to endure, and often surprises me.

Spiritual divorce

> What God hath joined together no man ever shall put asunder.
> God will take care of that.
>
> George Bernard Shaw

---

4. Jewelle St James *Jude: My Reincarnation from Auschwitz* (Revelstoke, Canada, St James Publishing 2006).

Listening to people, I sometimes get the feeling that God was having a day off when a marriage was supposedly blessed by him. Shaw's ironic comment can be taken two ways, and all too often we do find that what seemed to be a marriage made in heaven was actually conceived in hell. The pregnancy just took a little time to come to fruition and deliver the demons.

So, what do you do when you find yourself in an impossible position? Well, there is something called the karma of grace that says when you have done all you can, you can leave without incurring more karma. Nor do you have to go on paying over and over again for a single mistake:

> It is by no means necessary to do penance for a lifetime on account of one karmic debt.
>
> Pauline Stone

Of course, you do have to be certain that you have done all you can and are not merely running away – and that your partner, or ex-soulmate, really is not prepared to work with you in this present lifetime and that you didn't make an indissoluble soul contract that has been forgotten. But if you have done all you can, it is possible to seek a spiritual divorce or to dissolve an inappropriate soul contract. It may also be that it was not your soul's intention to be with that person in this lifetime, in which case the divorce may well have to extend back into a past life. This technique is also useful where you feel, or know, you have made a mystic marriage in the past and no longer wish this to bind you. It is a good indication that a spiritual divorce may be called for if all is not going smoothly with your soulmate.

Exercise: The spiritual divorce
[Follow the relaxation instructions in the Introduction p.xii].

When you are in a relaxed state, picture yourself entering a temple or a church or other sacred place. (Allow the picture to come into your mind's eye rather than thinking about what it should be). If you are a woman notice how you are dressed, are you bride or widow? Either may be appropriate.

You are there to meet with your soulmate (or marriage partner). You have come before a priest (or priestess) to have the breaking of your union blessed. If you are wearing a ring or other symbol, take it off and return it to the priest.

Looking at your partner, rescind the vows that you have made. Take back all those promises. If necessary, let the tears flow as you do so. Where healing and forgiveness are required, let these pass between you saying that you forgive unconditionally and ask forgiveness for all that has occurred without apportioning blame.

Say quite clearly, "I divorce you, I set you free. I become whole again". The priest (or priestess) will then bless your dis-union, allowing the divine energies to flow over you both bringing more healing and forgiveness. Then say goodbye to your soulmate, or partner. Wish them well in their future. Accept their blessing and good wishes for your own. If appropriate, forgive yourself for any mistakes you may feel you have made.

Feel yourself wrapped in love.

Turn and walk out of the temple. Accept the congratulations of those who await you. Be joyous in your separation. This is the moment when you reclaim your soul.

When you are ready to close, surround yourself with a protective bubble of light. Feel yourself whole and healed within that space. Then slowly return your awareness to the room and open your eyes. Feel your feet on the floor and your connection to the earth with a grounding cord going deep into the earth holding you firmly in incarnation. Get up and do something practical or have a hot drink to ground you.

Note: If you are working with dissolving a soul contract, amend the exercise to picture the contract being torn up and you both being set free.

If you are non-visual: Take off your wedding ring and find an appropriate way of disposing of it. Using a wedding photograph or drawing of two people, cut the two figures apart, saying as you do so, "I divorce you, I set you free. I become whole again". Allow forgiveness to flow both ways so that you forgive and are forgiven. Feel yourself wrapped in love.

You could also take a crystal heart that symbolizes the union and split it into two halves or pulverize it with a hammer (wrap it before hitting it so that splinters do not injure you). Then throw the pieces into the nearest water saying as you do so, "I forgive you and ask forgiveness for myself. Go in peace".

Take a new heart and dedicate it to your own wholeness and healing.

The mystic marriage

> The joys of marriage are the heaven on earth
> Life's paradise, great princess, the soul's quiet
> Sinews of concord, earthly immortality
> Eternity of pleasures

John Ford

One of the strongest soul bonds of all was created in the ancient temples and in occult and esoteric orders. The mystic marriage was meant to last 'forever'. An Egyptian papyrus still exists with the steps for making the mystic marriage set out – unfortunately, or fortunately, depending on how you look at it, the last steps are missing. This was a carefully coordinated joining on the physical, emotional, mental and spiritual levels. The couple developed their psychic powers together; telepathy was a fact of mind, as were out-of-body experiences. It took years. Both parties had to be ready: one could not advance without the other. Once the souls were joined on all these levels, they were intended to stay together throughout eternity. They had spiritual work to do. Work that would not cease with death but would carry over into future lives.

Such contacts have a powerful hold and may lie at the base of many soulmate 'recognitions' and also twinflame reunions. The participants were taught telepathy and soul contact. So, at least one of the partners in a former mystic marriage will usually know exactly what the 'other half' is doing in present-day life even though they may be far apart. We can see the present-life effect of a mystic marriage by W.B. Yeats and Maud Gonne (see Chapter 10) – one which may have been a repeat of an earlier union. Some participants have not even met yet in their current life but still they share experiences. Comments vary from, "We met in our dreams long before we met physically" to "There hasn't been a moment since we met that I did not know exactly what he was thinking and feeling even when I was on the other side of the world", and "I hated the feeling that he knew every thought I had, and even that he could be controlling them to make me behave in a certain way".

Whilst it may be romantic and wonderful to 'feel as he is feeling, think as she is thinking', this can get in the way of individual development and feel exceedingly intrusive. After a time most people feel invaded by the other person and simply want to put up some boundaries – and, of course, the present life meeting may have exactly that purpose. If the partnership is too symbiotic, separation may be essential. As Plato pointed out, when two souls are totally entwined with each other, death is often the result.

What confuses the issue even further is that it is possible to have made more than one mystic marriage over several lifetimes. Even an arranged marriage in cultures that called for this can act as a mystic marriage in holding people together through the ceremonies performed at the time. A spiritual divorce may well be called for (see above). You may need to see yourself making that vow but with the proviso, "for this life only", or "for as long as appropriate".

A different, more positive and present-life growth-enhancing, kind of mystical marriage is the marriage of our own inner male and female. This can be seen as uniting the various parts of oneself that have been male and female in other lives, or uniting the anima and animus we have carried, or as bringing together the two halves that Plato says were split so long ago. It unites all our masculine and feminine qualities and brings us into inner wholeness. Making this mystical marriage can be a step in our spiritual evolution. It means we no longer have to look 'out there' for our perfect partner. We find, and integrate, all the qualities within our own self.

As a step along the way, we may meet a 'perfect' partner 'out there' – our soulmate or twin flame – who mirrors to us the unseen and unrecognised part of our soul, but, at some stage, we then need to move to seeing that part in our inner self. This is the moment when our soulmate must leave, or our twinflame stand aside long enough for the inner union to take place (although it is much more usual to meet a twinflame after the inner integration is complete). Then we can go into relationship not as a lopsided person looking for someone to make us whole – seeking our 'other half' – but as a whole person who has something to offer in relationship: the unique self of our true being. The integration of the inner mystic marriage can be encouraged by a simple visualisation.

Exercise: Making the inner marriage
When you are comfortably settled, close your eyes. Take ten slow, deep breaths. As you breathe out, let go of any tension you may be feeling. As you breathe in, draw in a sense of peace and relaxation. Consciously let go of your everyday worries and concerns and allow yourself to be at peace.

Now breathe gently, establishing an even rhythm. Allow your eyelids to grow heavy and lie softly. Then let waves of relaxation flow through your body with each breath. Draw your attention deep inside yourself allowing the outside world to simply slip away.

When you are ready, picture yourself standing in the entrance to a vast temple. Before you, you can see the huge walls with their high, ornate gates. These are the gates to the inner courtyard. Slowly these gates will open inwards. A temple guardian beckons you in.

The guardian will conduct you to a chamber in the inner courtyard. In this chamber a bath has been prepared. Servants will bathe, dry and perfume you and dress you in new robes to prepare you for your marriage.

When you are ready, the guardian will then take you to the offering chamber. Here you can make an offering to ensure a successful inner marriage. Whatever is most appropriate for you to offer up will be on the altar before you and you can dedicate it to whichever deity you wish, or to your own soul. Make the offering reverently and turn to leave.

Now the guardian takes you into the bridal chamber to await your partner in this inner marriage. Food is prepared, drink awaits you. Behind thin, gauzy curtains your marriage bed awaits. When the guardian withdraws, your partner will come to you. This will be a total merging, a marriage on all levels. Allow your inner partner to come into your heart, to merge with you. Spend as long as you wish with your inner partner.

It is now time to leave the bridal chamber. The temple guardian will come to conduct you and your inner partner back to the doors leading back into the outside world. Walk with the guardian across the courtyard.

As you step out of the gates, know that you are whole within yourself. You have integrated your masculine and feminine energies. No longer will you need to look outside yourself for the complementary energy, it is within yourself.

As you stand outside the temple, picture yourself surrounded and protected by a ball of white light. Then take time to slowly bring your attention back to your physical body.

Breathe a little more deeply, move your hands and feet.

Gradually bring your attention back into the room and get up slowly. Standing with your feet on the floor, picture a grounding cord going from your feet deep down into the earth to hold you in incarnation. Then move around to become fully alert and back in everyday reality.

If you are non-visual: create the scenes in your own home using candles, oils and props as appropriate. Walk in through your front door, go to your bathroom, bathe and change into a clean robe. Go into a room where you have already prepared an altar with an offering. Make the offering and then move into your bedroom. In your bedroom, hold out your arms so that your partner can walk into them. Go to bed and allow your imagination to take over.

Note: if you find that the inner partner who appears is someone known to you in your everyday life, check out most carefully whether this really is your true inner partner. Projection, wishful thinking or someone else's intense desire can affect who you see. Do not make the inner marriage unless you are absolutely sure. If you make the mystic marriage with someone who is in your life now, be sure to say, "For as long as is appropriate". It can be a powerful unifying force bringing the two of you together on all levels, and may be just what your relationship needs. Then again, it may not.

Religious vows

> Although distinct from physical celibacy... psychic celibacy is a more pervasive and imposing phenomenon. It consists in keeping women mentally and emotionally at arms' length. Women can be exalted as wife, virgin, mother or deprecated (and enjoyed) as temptress, playmate, whore.[5]

Religious vows are an obvious difficulty for many people who have had past or present-life experiences in a monastery or convent. They vowed poverty, chastity and obedience – forever. Then they wonder why they are always poor, have sexual difficulties, and are constantly waiting for someone to tell them what to do, or feel powerless, at the mercy of someone else's control. When a soulmate comes along, they willingly surrender their life and then find that the lesson is to take control for themselves.

We do not necessarily have to go into another life to see instances of this, but the present-life experience is usually an echo of a former life. I have seen several experiences where people have been drawn back into a convent or monastery in the present life, or lived as though they were in one.

---

5. Bianchi, Eugene 'Psychic celibacy and the quest for mutuality' in E. C. Bianchi and R. R. Ruether (ed) *From Machismo to Mutuality* (New York: Paulist Press: 1975).

In one case, a woman felt she simply had to be a nun. She went into the convent and took her vows. For her, Christ was her beloved soulmate. It took her twenty years to realise that she had made the wrong choice. As soon as she came out of the convent, she caught sight of the man who was to become her husband – her twinflame. It took several years before they married, despite the fact that she 'knew it had to be'. Even then, she came under considerable sexual confusion until she deliberately rescinded her vow of chastity. Up until then, she felt subtly 'wrong' and wanted to run back into the sanctity of her beloved convent. She knew she had taken a vow, but just imagine how much stronger is the effect of such a vow lived out for a whole lifetime, or even several lifetimes, and then forgotten at a conscious level. Deep down, the soul does not forget. The person holds back, cannot give of his or her self in a relationship because, at the innermost level, it feels 'wrong'. Where a soul partner or twinflame understands this and is patient, it may be possible to overcome that vow, but so often the experience hooks into the other partner's greatest fear – rejection, lack of love, betrayal, abandonment and so on – and an old pattern is reactivated. Unless the two people then consciously work at healing the past, even the closest of soulmate relationships finds itself in trouble.

In a similar story, a young monk came to see me. He had converted to Catholicism at the age of fourteen. He then went into the novitiate. One of his reasons for going into the monastery was to leave his sexuality behind – he was strongly pulled to homosexual relationships but felt them to be morally wrong. On his first night in the monastery, he was brutally raped by one of his fellow monks. To enter into full monkhood, he did not have to take a vow of celibacy, simply to make a profession of faith in order to be accepted. It was understood, however, that celibacy was part of his new way of life. Notwithstanding, the rape was the beginning of a seven-year sexual relationship, one full of abusive rage and domination. But, as he said, he had found his soulmate. He was torn between expressing his sexuality through this sadomasochistic contact and denying his soulmate.

Eventually, the monastic leaders took action. He was sent back out into the world 'to find himself'. However, when returned to the everyday world, he was totally lost. He felt like a part of himself had stayed at the monastery with his soulmate. He also found it impossible to enter into any new relationship, he was still bound by the ideal of celibacy that he had been unable to keep within the monastery. The result was a very lonely life indeed. He failed to find the gift of independent living, of setting himself free from the past and of embracing his sexuality no matter what form it took.

Renegotiating vows and soul contracts

It is possible to renegotiate vows whether given in the present life or a past. It is not always necessary to consciously know what the vow is, if appropriate your subconscious mind will let you know during the renegotiation – if you allow it to. It is perfectly possible to use the power of your intention to renegotiate or reframe any vow or promise. The process also works well for soul contracts. Soul contracts are agreements you made with another soul in another life or in the between life state. These contracts are not always beneficial in the present life, they may tie you to the past and can prevent you from being with someone with whom you have a more powerful soul connection and purpose which would be for your – and their – higher good. As we all have free will and as people and situations change once they are in incarnation and their personality and nurturing makes itself felt, it may well not be possible to fulfil a soul contract but it may still hold you back. Fortunately, it can be broken or adjusted.

Exercise: Renegotiating a vow or contract: the quick method

When you are relaxed and ready (see page xii), say firmly and clearly, out loud, "I hereby rescind all vows, promises, pacts, arrangements and soul contracts that I have made in this or any other life, or in the between-life state, that are no longer appropriate and no longer serve me. I forgive myself and set myself free. I also set free anyone from whom I have exhorted a vow, contract or promise anywhere in the past or who has willingly or unwillingly made such a vow and ask their forgiveness". Clap your hands together loudly to signify the end of those vows. Stamp your feet firmly on the ground, and walk forward freed from the past.

Renegotiating a vow: the more specific method

Follow step one above.

Now picture yourself back at a point in time when you made a vow, a promise or a soul contract (if you are unsure of when this was, or with whom, ask to be shown). Rerun the scene as it happened but do not become involved in it – see it as though on a screen. Observe but do not become part of it, do not take part. Notice who is present and what you are saying. If it is someone you do not recognise, ask who that person is in your present life.

Look carefully at that vow, promise or contract. Is it still appropriate? Is it something you want to continue? Does it need to be reworded, or rescinded? Is it something from a past life that has inadvertently been carried over into the present? Have you demanded a vow from someone else that is still holding them to you? If appropriate, ask for an advisor to come to discuss the matter with you. If it is a promise made to a soulmate or twinflame, have them be with you outside the scene to join in the discussion. Check whether it needs to continue. Check also whether you made a promise to, or a contract with, a soulmate or twinflame between lives. Then see yourself in that scene using new wording. Be firm and clear, "It is for this life only". If a soul contract cannot continue, set out why it is no longer appropriate. Or state clearly, "I cannot do that" if what you are being asked will fetter your soul unreasonably. If the promise has to carry over into the present life, or if it has been made for or in the present life, set out the conditions under which it can operate, or state firmly that it will be released. If the contract is to continue, make it clear that if your soulmate, or the other person, does not stick to the new terms of agreement, or if circumstances change, then the promise will no longer apply.

When you are sure that the scene has been reframed or the promise or contract renegotiated to your satisfaction, let it go. Bring your attention back to the present moment. Take a deep breath and be aware of your body once again. Picture yourself surrounded by a bubble of light to protect you – you can use this bubble during the visualisation if you feel the need for energy containment or extra strength during the reframing. Then, when you are ready, open your eyes and get up and move around.

If you are non-visual: State very clearly that you are now released from all former vows, promises and pacts that you have made in this or any other life and specify those of which you are aware. If you are aware of a specific vow that you wish to rescind, write it on a piece of paper, tear it up and burn it affirming that it is dissolving as it burns.

You can follow up this exercise by using positive affirmations. Tack up where you will see it frequently a note saying, "I am free from the vows and promises of the past" and repeat this regularly. If the promise was made to a soulmate or someone with whom you are in relationship, discussing it allows change, and may bring hidden issues to the surface for exploration. Adding forgiveness to the exercises and affirmations strengthens their effect. (See Chapter 15).

14

Soulmates – the Positive Experience

Will it alter my life altogether?
O tell me the truth about love.

W.H.Auden

At a reincarnation conference back in 1995, I happened to mention I was writing what I laughingly called 'the antidote to soulmates book'. An elderly man came up to me afterwards and asked anxiously, "Don't you believe in soulmates?"

"Well, yes", I said, "But I also believe they can be the exact opposite of what everyone thinks they are looking for". He told me that twelve years ago he had met his soulmate, now his wife. She had supported him through much depression and many troubles. "But", he said, "There isn't a day goes by when our love does not grow stronger". Pointing to his heart he said, "In here I know I have found my soulmate, and she makes my life worth living". He may well have been with his twinflame (see Chapter 17). Such stories do come my way from time to time – just often enough to remind me to adjust the jaundiced view that comes over me when I delve through my postbag.

When I was in the middle of writing *Hands Across Time*, and beginning to feel I needed some positive, life-affirming soulmate experiences to add to what I had already written, I happened to meet an old friend. She was looking radiant and said she had met a man:

Remember you told me it would take time and to wait for the right person because he was there and would come unexpectedly into my life? [She had consulted me some two years previously]. Well, I went out to see Mother Meera in Germany. Suddenly a man came up to me and said he would give me a lift back to the station in the next town. A friend had told him I was going to call a cab. We chatted like old friends as we drove to the town and, as I got out, we exchanged phone numbers. I casually said, "Give me a ring when you are in town and perhaps we can have a drink". As he was an American pilot, this was possible but not imminent. Two days later he rang me and said, "How about that drink?"

"Oh, does that mean you are in London", I asked.

"No", he said, "I'm coming over specially to take you out".

The relationship has progressed from there. He's been over to see me several times and I've been to see him in the States. I'm going over for Christmas. We both feel we have things to teach each other. Our beliefs go along the same pathway, and although we are both independent people with a life of our own, we fit together well. I have never felt so much for a man before, never been so loved by a man. I really do feel I have met my soulmate and it will be a positive experience.

This was an enormous turnaround in her life. Her marriage had ended a few years previously, very unhappily, after almost thirty years of devoted service to her husband and his career. At the end, she 'felt like a non-person'. She had picked up the pieces, trained for a new career and was beginning to carve out a place for herself where she could be of service to others and fulfil herself at the same time. She had met great personal tragedy since her marriage broke up. She had lost, in different ways, two soulmates. A beloved grandchild had died and her much loved son had had to be hospitalised with a psychiatric condition that seemed intractable.

She had had to deal with great guilt around this son, with whom she had a soul companion relationship of deep understanding. He had had a difficult relationship with his father, who took no further interest in him. To compensate, she gave him a great deal of her time and energy. She had badgered the doctors in an attempt to find the best treatment for him, and had so investigated the condition as to become something of an expert. Prior to meeting her American soulmate, she had done considerable work on letting her son go, so that he could be the person he needed to be. Indeed, she had gone to Mother Meera with the specific intention of leaving him in the hands of the Great Mother. This, she felt, had been beneficial to their relationship, they were 'not so symbiotic now'. It created space for another soulmate to enter her life, one with whom she could have a full relationship, one with whom she could move into the future with confidence.

As with so many of the case histories in *Hands Across Time*, however, this was not her one and only soulmate. Having healed her heart, she realised that there was still something missing in the relationship. It turned out to be a dress rehearsal for the real thing. Some months later she met 'a lovely man', one who was extremely supportive of her, her son and her spiritual work. They have been happily married for some years now.

Ultimate concerns

> Living life to the full comes when the ultimate concerns have been faced: death, freedom, isolation and meaninglessness.
>
> Irvin D. Yalom

So, if we change our attitude to love and loving, we can change what we attract in the way of a soulmate and may well be ready for a twinflame relationship, or for a practice run at the very least. Our soulmate relationships may still be difficult, but they will be different. It may well be that we now have something to offer our soulmate, a chance for them to grow too. One of my clients, who had worked hard on accepting herself and on changing her way of loving, felt that it was time to find a soulmate – which with the benefit of ten years' hindsight may have been more constructively phrased as 'twinflame' but neither of us were aware of this at that time. As she said, she had a good life, one that was rich and satisfying, but she felt she would like a partner. Thinking it over carefully, she advertised. Her advert was different. Instead of listing what she was looking for, she set out what she felt she had to offer. Her argument was that this would then attract someone who was looking for the qualities she had to give. Sure enough, she met a man with whom she had much in common. They got on extremely well.

There was only one problem. He had never had a long-term committed relationship. He always had several women on the go 'to be on the safe side'. Having the belief within himself that he was not lovable, he expected to be hurt in relationships. So, he would do all he could to push away his partners. He could then say, "See, I knew it". My client was wise to this game, she had played it for years. So, when he tried to push her away, she simply said, "I'll always be here. It doesn't matter what you do, I love you and I'll be here for you".

Gradually, he began to trust her. Finally, he asked her to go to Australia – his home – with him on a trial visit. He wanted to see how things would work out. She agreed to go for six months, not to see how things worked out with him, but to see if she could make a life for herself there which would enable her to be in relationship with him. She wrote to me from there:

> I'm in no hurry to try to formalise a lifestyle – will I ever be again, I wonder! I'm simply enjoying the journey very much: it is bringing me riches and pleasures I had only glimpsed before. All 1 can say is that it feels very right to be here with Peter and the future will take its own course as we develop it by living fully in the present.

When I contacted her in 1996 for permission to use her story she said:

> We are both very happy for you to do so. On this journey I'm learning a great deal about myself. Having opened my heart so fully, the vulnerable child seems often to be present. His vulnerable child is often evoked, as though in our openness to one another we inhabit some of our deepest hurts. The important thing is that we are both then able to understand what is happening, thus taking back the projections. It's bloody hard work at times but also very life-enhancing. It really feels like we've been drawn together for the lessons we each need to learn. The other women in his life have disappeared completely. Peter is very clear about his commitment and revels in his new status. He says now he feels fulfilled, like he's come home and he has absolutely no desire for anything or anyone else.
>
> Learning to live with someone again after years of fierce independence is interesting: a euphemism for rewarding, challenging, joyous, scary and hopeful! This is true for both of us as we learn to communicate and adjust, to be both interdependent and independent, to understand and be understood. Wish us well as we continue our separate and joint journeys.

So, it seems that the key to resolving the soulmate enigma is to move beyond our expectations and demands, to let go of our dreams, and simply to live each day as it comes. Accepting whatever a relationship offers in whatever way it presents itself whilst at the same time maintaining our own inner 'rightness'; what Jane whose story is told in Chapter 1 calls living in grace. This is the gift our soulmate offers. Whether we accept it or not is up to us.

But my client had more learning to come. Some years later she rang me, she was back in England, Peter was dead. She had nursed him, they had said everything that there was to be said, she had carried his coffin and had even taken his memorial service. Now she had returned to her homeland to begin again, 'wiser and more ready to go into relationship than ever'.

Acknowledging the gifts in what is

So many people have said to me, "what if you're in a relationship that is okay, nothing wrong with it, just not very exciting, it's lost its magic, or it seems to have lost its direction, what then?" – that I turned my attention to finding an answer. Does a relationship like that have to be quietly endured, or abandoned? Or is there another option? Working on a book that included material about the attractor factor, and having written another that included a blessings journal, made me consider this question again. If, having chosen self-love and self-acceptance and committed to choosing to feel good in our everyday life, we are able to have gratitude for what is, to find the blessings in our relationship, and to put our energy into the positive, then nothing stands in the way of raising that 'it's okay' relationship up to another level of intimacy. One much closer to what most people mean by a soulmate, and maybe even up to twinflame. If we accept ourselves as co-creators of our life, then we can create the relationship we long for within the one we have.

More easily said than done, you may be saying at this point. Well, yes, but isn't it worth giving it a try?

There are several parts to this creation. The first is forgiving and forgetting. How it has been doesn't have to be how it is. So, first thing, don't harp back to the past, let it go. Secondly, don't have expectations and you wont be disappointed – or have it constantly confirmed how bad things are. We get what we expect, so stop expecting the worst and start focusing on the best.

Bring an open heart to the relationship with no baggage attached; stop hoping and start accepting. Learn to listen to what is instead of thinking to yourself 'here we go again', getting all your defences up, and having your answer all ready before your partner has even finished the sentence. Don't think you know what is being said, or judge it, listen as though it's the first time you've heard it and respond accordingly. Non-judgemental listening from an open heart can work wonders. If what you hear means you have to forgive yourself for some flaws and foibles (who moi?), then recite the mantra 'I'm sorry, I love you, please forgive me' to yourself night and morning. You are not asking forgiveness of your partner at this stage – although you may come to do this. You are simply working on forgiving yourself.

Then have gratitude for what is good in the relationship, list all the things you have to be thankful for, all the blessings in your life. (You may like to do this in a special Blessings Journal).

And finally, list all the positive points you admire and appreciate in your partner, even the smallest things. Look for and list all the finest qualities and the smallest things. Don't include 'yes buts…' or 'if onlies' in this list. There is plenty of evidence that when we start thinking of someone positively, they respond. And even more evidence that people respond positively to praise and being thanked so share your thoughts with your partner. A little and often is the prescription and it can work miracles.

15

Healing the Wounds

To be wounded by your own understanding of love;
And to bleed willingly and joyfully,
To wake at dawn with a winged heart and give thanks for
another day of loving.

Kahil Gibran, *The Prophet*

Many people believe that in refusing to let go, they are proving their undying love. I knew a woman who had been married fifty-four years although she did not see her husband for the last thirty years of the marriage. It was a wartime marriage, supposedly the result of love at first sight – on her part at least. She certainly believed she had found her soulmate. She had made her vows for eternity. He had expected to die at any moment. He made his vows lightly, believing it would all be over soon. He found himself trapped. For the next fifty-four years (he died aged 88) he lived his life as though imminent death was the answer, the only thing that could relieve him of this terrible burden called love. For the first twenty of those years, whilst she may have believed herself happy, there was not a day went by when he did not want out. He had many other women. She threatened to commit suicide if he left. Eventually, he did leave her for another woman with whom he lived for thirty-four years but remained married to his wife. It was a classic eternal triangle.

For thirty-four years she sat at home and waited for him to return. She simply could not let go. It was as though she was in suspended animation. Her life was on hold. She saw herself as a helpless victim. He experienced her as an all-powerful, vampiric, controlling force that dominated his life even though he had not seen her all those years. She would not countenance divorce. Only death, she said, could dissolve their union. Only death, he believed, could release him – for a reason known only to himself he was not prepared to divorce her. The woman with whom he lived was waiting for the wife to die so that she could marry her soulmate.

This woman had been diagnosed with terminal cancer before they met almost forty years previously but she clung tenaciously to life to marry the man she loved. Eventually they all three of them died within six months of one another. However, death did not release them. I was consulted by the daughter (from the husband's marriage) after their deaths and she filled me in on what had occurred in the interim since I wrote *Hands Across Time*:

> My mother died in hospital, she took several days to die and I knew she was waiting for my father to arrive. She had said several times as she fought death, "I don't want that woman to have my house". This was the first time she had ever acknowledged that my father was with someone else. Any time I had tried to talk to her previously about it she had always insisted that he would be home soon.
>
> As she lay dying but resisting death to wait for him, I kept telling her that he wouldn't come and the best thing she could do was let go and wait for him on the other side. After she died, she seemed to be standing by the bed looking very lost so I said to her, "Go to the light and wait for him there". Reluctantly she eventually did so.
>
> I hadn't seen my father for many years and about three months later he phoned me to ask me 'if anything had happened'. I told him my mother had died if that was what he meant, and I also told him about her comment about not wanting the other woman to have her house. "That won't happen now" he said wearily and suggested we meet to discuss things.
>
> He told me that his soulmate had also died. When we looked at the dates, she had been taken, kicking and screaming and resisting to the very last moment, into hospital on the same day at exactly the time as my mother died. She had died at the moment my mother was being cremated, without realizing that she was finally free to marry my father. He, of course, would have had a death-bed marriage had they known. I was stunned by this coincidence of dates. I knew they had been held together in some weird triangle but this was too much. My father said he had a lot of unlived life to get on with but he died within a couple of months.
>
> I have heard from a psychic who lives next door to my sister-in-law that the three of them are 'locked in mortal combat'. They are making life very difficult for my sister-in-law, who is also psychic and very aware of them and their bickering.
>
> Please do something!

I talked to all three of them, but had to put them into a pentangle while I did so. Each of the women was adamant that he was 'hers'. Neither was prepared to let go. Nor did he help matters. All he wanted to do was escape from both of them. He was not prepared to discuss matters.

I called in guides, helpers and higher beings, everyone who could possibly assist them to resolve this ages old struggle. I told them all that they could not be released until it was resolved. Every day I inched the pentangle higher up the vibrational scale, hoping that one of them would finally receive some insight and let go. All I could do was leave it with those who were overseeing the process. To date, there has been no sign of progress and that was a few years ago. Both women are still clinging tenaciously to their man and the wounds remain unresolved.

So, where do they go from here? What does anyone in this position do? There are certain steps we can all take to heal our relationship wounds, to change the pattern so that it does not carry forward into the future, to rework it so that our relationships become positive, life-enhancing experiences. Whether or not we are already in a soulmate relationship, if we hope to be, or if we have left one behind, or if we wish to find a twinflame, we still need to work on our partnership issues. In its simplest form, it comes down to five things:

- ♥ acceptance
- ♥ forgiveness
- ♥ letting go
- ♥ moving on
- ♥ living – and loving – with grace

Believing in karma makes parting a little easier and also helps us to understand why we may be going through some of our less desirable experiences. It can also assist us in ensuring a happier future – after all, what we set in motion now determines the course of the rest of our life (and lives). As we have seen, understanding our soul's purpose in drawing us into the relationship in the first place also brings us healing insights, as does standing in the other person's shoes, seeing it from their point of view. So often, we have a preconception of what we expect from a soulmate: perfect love, shared expectations, certain standards of behaviour, total understanding, fidelity and so on. The list varies little from person to person. We seldom look at what we have to offer. Nor do we examine the baggage we bring with us to the relationship: our expectations around love, our ingrained responses, our past experience. Where the preconceptions and the baggage differ is where we find our pain. So often our response is to try to change the other person, when in reality we can only transform ourselves.

We need to start with our illusions. Is what we are seeking too perfect, too unattainable? Have we set impossible standards? Is what we are seeking really love or some clinging, parasitic symbiotic dependence that will suffocate both of us? Are we in love with the idea of being in love? Are we besotted, or in lust, rather than loving? All of these may need to be re-visioned. Are we seeing ourselves as perfect, not recognising our own all too human flaws and fallibilities? Or are we seeing only our – or our partner's – flaws and not recognizing our own perfection. Are we seeing our partner as a god (or goddess)? Do we need to look at their true nature? Do we need to be dis-illusioned – a painful process but a very necessary one if we are to see what really is. We may be putting onto our partner an heroic, idealised role that simply cannot be fulfilled. We project our aspirations for ourselves onto others; we invest in them what we are not ready to own in ourselves. We may need to take back this projection. To see ourselves, as well as them, as we really are. We may also need to accept that we can be in a good and fulfilling relationship that is not with a soulmate or twinflame without 'missing out'.

We may need to break an old pattern of dependence and passivity, to take back our power and individuality, to recognise that we do indeed make our own future. We may also need to see where we dominate and control, where we seek to have power over the other person, where we manipulate. If we only see one side, we can never heal. We have to offer loving acceptance to ourselves, as well as to our partner.

If we allow our partner simply to be who they are, to accept the worst, as well as recognising the best, then they have a space in which to flower. If we accept what is instead of wishing for more or better, then maybe we will find that we have all we need. If we constantly condemn, what hope is there? In the same way, we need to learn from mistakes instead of condemning them. This is how we evolve.

If we let go of karma, step off the eternal round, things change. If we refrain from retaliation, don't strike back, choose not to react but instead to forgive (without becoming a victim or martyr), we can transform the pattern. If we let go of our most powerful emotions – grief, anger, compulsion – we create a space for love.

In letting go of those we love most, we allow them to fly, to be, to grow. And we leave a space for them to come back. If we hold on tightly, we strangle and suffocate. If we let go, we are being truly loving.

If we have been hurt, if we grieve, if we are angry, our greatest tool is forgiveness. It sets both of us free. If we hold onto those feelings, no one benefits. They are death-dealing instead of life-enhancing. Forgiveness, especially self-forgiveness, on the other hand creates new possibilities. In that space, we may well find all we have sought. But if we do not, well then, we can be okay with that too. In a state of need, all we can do is attract neediness. In a state of incompletion, all we can find is an inexact fit. From a position of completeness, we can go into true relationship.

Did you give your heart away?

> What of soul was left, I wonder, when the kissing had to stop?
>
> Robert Browning

Giving away our heart is perhaps the commonest theme that arises in soulmate situations. Many people unthinking give away their heart – you have only to listen to pop songs to realise how common this is:

Right from the start, I gave you my heart. . .

I gave you my heart but you wanted my soul. . .

That kiss you stole held my heart and soul. . .

But few realise how devastating the effects of leaving their heart in someone else's keeping can be – or the dire effect of having it 'stolen' by a needy or manipulative person. Handing your heart over to another, having your heart shackled to a memory, suffering from a 'broken heart' or being 'hard hearted' is almost certainly linked to past and present heartache and will certainly create dysfunctional relationships if not healed.

We live in a culture that equates love with giving away our heart and our soul, handing over a part of ourselves into someone else's keeping. In adolescence, and later life too, we carelessly give away our heart and, when we part, we forget to take it back. It is not only the twentieth century that has seen things this way. Shakespeare speaks of 'her, where I my heart, safe-left, shall meet'. Ancient Egyptian papyruses speak of the 'Lord of my heart'. The heart has always been equated with love. How often when a lover leaves, or we leave, do we think to say, "Excuse me, but can I have my heart back before we part, and, oh, by the way, I release us both from all those declarations of eternal love that we made?"

If we extend this tendency to hand over our heart back into other lives, how many parts of ourselves have we left behind? And who now holds them? Exercises to recover our hearts often produce surprises. As we change roles, interact in different ways, these 'keepers of our heart' may become our friend, our enemy, our parent, our child even. No wonder the soulmate boundaries blur. To free ourselves to find true love again, we need to recover these fragments of our heart: to go back into the past and reclaim them.

Signals that the heart has been lost, stolen or broken

No passion to life	Defensive	Guilty	Naive
No fire and zest	Sacrificial	Scared	Cynical
Takes but does not give	Remote	Bitter	Fearful
Life has lost its colour	Burned-out	Alienated	Greedy
Defines oneself by roles	Dissociated	Separate	Judgmental
Unavailable for relationship	Selfish	Needy	Cold
Circulation problems	Uncommitted	Addictions	Fragmented
Promiscuous	Dead-eyed	Masochistic	Heartburn
Hollow-chested	Angina	Impotence	Hardened arteries
No-one home behind the eyes	Cruel	Commitment-phobic	Remote

(after Chuck Spezzano with additions by Judy Hall)

A broken heart may well lie behind a tendency to define oneself by the role of 'parent', 'wife', 'husband' 'carer' or 'loner'. The net result of a wounded heart is that life loses its zest and passion. A desperate soul whose heart is pained may well be both needy and greedy, but could become judgmental, bitter or cynical. There will certainly be a lack of love.

The heart in a box

Just how complex this handing over of the heart can be, how many layers can be involved, is shown by Anita's experience.

I had been working for sometime on freeing myself from the control of a very powerful man who ran the company for which I worked. I considered him as a friend, and originally had been very attracted to him. Indeed, for a couple of years I believed myself in love with him. I secretly harboured romantic visions of his becoming my lover or even my husband.

Through doing past-lifework, I soon learned that this attraction did not belong to this lifetime, but was a residue from a past life in which we had been lovers, after which he had rejected me. I had remained unmarried and had died in traumatic circumstances. In that life, he had no longer wanted me as a lover, but had become very jealous if ever I had associations with other men, and had beaten me in his jealous rage. In my present lifetime, from the time I met him, I had found it impossible to start a relationship. I would meet men I was attracted to, but nothing would ever get off the ground. I feel now that he had somehow in that other lifetime drawn a veil over my emotions so that I could not see anyone else and that this carried over into our present contact.

Eventually, I knew I had to pluck up the courage to tell him about the past life, to express the feelings I had for him then, and to clear it for myself. I was very scared but managed to tell him. After a week or so, the infatuation I felt for him began to fade, and I felt sure I was free of him and ready to find a partner.

However, I found that the situation was still blocked. I tried working with it in as many ways as I could think of but still couldn't resolve it. Then you suggested I should 'take back my heart'. A friend led me through the meditation. I saw the man, and could sense both aspects of him – past and present. He was carrying my heart in a box. I asked why he wanted to keep it and he said 'power'. I asked for higher help, and he eventually handed the heart over, and began to shrink and disappear. I then sent love to him, while keeping my heart. He said, "Be happy. Bless you".

Before coming out of the meditation, I asked if there was anything else I needed to do. I saw the man saying in mock irritation, "Clear off. You've finished!" I felt wonderfully free and clear of the situation.

Nevertheless, the relationship situation was still blocked for me. A few months later, I went into another regression to the previous lifetime. I found myself again talking to the man in question. The therapist said, "What has he got that's yours?" and told me to go through his pockets. When I did, I found a ring I took it back, and returned another one to him. Then I saw what had happened. We had exchanged rings to hold us together forever. I saw the scene the day it happened, back in the eighteenth century. I was very young, and we were in the garden together, very flirty, but with a sinister undertone. I said, "I give you my heart forever". He said, "Ah, but I want your soul!" To my horror, I saw myself saying to him, "I give you my soul" and we exchanged the rings. To me it was just playfulness and an expression of love, but to him it was deadly serious – he wanted total control of me. I had innocently allowed him to do this. So now I reframed the scene and saw myself saying to him, "I give you my heart for as long as it is appropriate". He asked, "Will you give me your soul?" I replied, "No! I will never give you my soul" and faced him with arms crossed. He nodded to me, acknowledging my power. It felt as if he had met his match.

I wanted to share this story as I was amazed at how many levels there can be to be released. If you think you've cleared something, but an area of your life still isn't working, then have another look. It was also interesting that this problem with relationships was not triggered until I met the man again in this lifetime. It was as though the veil came back and I could not see anyone else. However, once I let go of my view of him as a prospective lover, I was able to feel unconditional love for him. This was very different to how I felt when he still had the hold over me. Now I know I have reclaimed both my heart and soul.

Reclaiming the heart

You can do the following exercise with someone with whom you know you have had a close connection in your present life and feel you may have given away your heart (which can be very different to sharing your heart or opening to another person), or you can ask to be shown connections from other lives as well. It may not be necessary to know details of who they are, but you may need to listen to their story and renegotiate any old promises made.

Visualisation: reclaiming your heart

Allow yourself to relax and then focus your attention on your heart. Feel its beat, hear its sounds. As you listen to the rhythm of your heart and feel its pulsating energy, allow yourself relax a little deeper. Slowly, let your heart transport you into another time and space.

You find yourself standing in the temple of your inner heart. Its colour and dimensions are unique to you. Explore this temple; notice if it is broken anywhere. Notice if you meet anyone else (if so, remember to work with them in a moment). Recognise if there are heartstrings pulling you in a certain direction. If there are, use a pair of golden scissors to cut the connection and then heal and seal this place with golden light.

You may already have become aware of someone who holds your heart, if so picture that person standing before you. If you have not yet recognised who holds your heart, ask to be shown this right now. (If there is more than one person, work on one at a time).

You can see that this person holds a portion of your heart. It may appear symbolically. If so, look at its colour, shape and form. You may find that it is freely offered back to you, or you may find that the person wants to hold onto it. If they do so, ask their reason. They may well feel that they have to look after you, or you may have made them a promise, or you may have given your heart into their keeping. If necessary thank them, release them, release yourself, whatever is appropriate. State firmly that it is now time to reclaim your heart and that you forgive them and yourself.

Now take a deep breath and focus all your attention. Firmly and clearly, reach out and take this heart back. Say out loud: 'I take back all that is mine and I freely give you back all that is yours'. (You may need to purify your heart before taking it back if it holds the other person's energy. If so, see it coming back to you through a cloud of pink light). Welcome your heart back with love and place it once more within you. (You may like to place a piece of Rose Quartz or Rhodochrosite over your heart to symbolise this return).

[If you experience any problems, ask for a guide, a helper, your higher self or an angelic being to come to your aid].

Repeat this reclaiming until there is no one left who holds a part of your heart and your heart is whole once more. Check that you yourself do not inadvertently hold a piece of someone else's heart. If you do, then surrender it willingly and allow it to return where it belongs and ask for forgiveness for taking it. Then check the inner temple of your heart once again. You will probably find that it is looking much better. You may well find that the symbolic pieces of your heart decorate the walls. If it needs any further repair, use golden light or place a crystal over your heart.

Take a few moments to open your heart and offer forgiveness to the other person and, if appropriate, allow yourself to receive their forgiveness and place it in your heart. Open yourself to divine love and fill your heart from that source.

Now consciously step out of that inner temple, but know that it is within your own heart, which is now whole and healed. Become aware of your breathing once again, and the beat of your heart. Slowly bring your attention back into the room. Take your attention down to your feet and ground yourself firmly. Picture a bubble of light enclosing you, sealing your energies, so that you are safe and contained. When you are ready, open your eyes. After a few moments of reflection, get up and move around the room.

If you are non-visual: Put your fingers on the pulse points on your wrist. Feel the beat pulsing through your whole body and listen to your heart (if you put your fingers into your ears you will hear it clearly). Hold a Rose Quartz crystal heart in your left hand. Say out loud: 'I call back any pieces of my heart that I may have given or had stolen away, no matter how inadvertently or lovingly this may have occurred. I claim back my heart now'. Place the crystal over your heart and feel pink light and unconditional love suffusing your heart purifying the returning part and helping it to integrate. Keep the crystal in a safe place.

Forgiveness

> To forgive wrongs darker than death or night... is to be
> Good, great and joyous, beautiful and free.
>
> Shelley, *Queen Mab*

Guilt and resentment are deeply debilitating. Both occur frequently in 'soulmate' relationships. We tend to know when someone else is holding on to one of these emotions, but we may be less clear when we are ourselves. Having said somewhere in the past, "It's all my/your fault", or "I'll never forgive myself/you" are clear indications that you may still be holding on, even though you have forgotten, at a conscious level, what it was all about. Whether you were on the receiving end, or gave it out, it is very freeing to go back to these moments and consciously forgive and let go. If you do find something for which you would like to make reparation, it may be possible to apologise to the person in person, to drop them a line, send them some flowers, or perform a service for someone else which you dedicate to the object of your guilt.

All too often though, you have lost track of the person – or you might not want to approach them. If this is the case, it can nevertheless be freeing to write an apology or a letter of forgiveness, using a photograph of the person or a 'mind picture' to link up. Once you have expressed your feelings, you can either tear up the letter or burn it and let the cosmos take it where it needs to go. You can release guilt by lighting a candle and, as it burns away, seeing all your guilt dissolve in the flame. You can follow this up with flower essences, which are excellent tools for emotional healing.

A simple visualisation will also help you to give and receive forgiveness. If you are giving forgiveness, write a letter setting out your love and forgiveness for the other person, although you could also speak from your heart.

Exercise: Giving and receiving forgiveness

Write a letter setting out all the reasons you are seeking forgiveness – either for yourself or the other person – and apologising where appropriate.

Settle yourself in a comfortable, relaxed posture. Close your eyes and breathe gently, concentrating your mind on the area immediately above and between the eyebrows.

When you are ready, picture in your mind the person from whom you wish to receive forgiveness or the person to whom you are giving forgiveness (if this is difficult, use a photograph).

When you have a strong image of this person, either picture yourself reading out your letter and the other person receiving it in a loving, kindly way. Or, picture the other person reading their letter to you and open yourself to them in loving forgiveness.

When the letter reading is finished, ask them to forgive you and allow yourself to feel that forgiveness flowing towards you and into your heart. At the same time, let your forgiveness flow towards them. Allow the forgiveness to spread through your body in a warm glow until it settles in your heart.

When the forgiveness is complete, thank the person, wish them well and make any gesture you feel is appropriate, such as hugging or holding hands.

Then allow them to fade from your mind, sending them on their way with love. Notice how much lighter you feel now that you have let go and received and given forgiveness.

When you are ready, breathe a little more deeply and become aware of your surroundings once more. Then open your eyes slowly and stamp your foot to bring you firmly back into the here and now.

If you are non-visual: write your letter as above and read it out. Holding a Rose Quartz crystal in one hand and a photograph of the person you wish to forgive or receive forgiveness from in the other (or write the name on a piece of paper) say out loud, "I give and receive forgiveness". Place the crystal on the photograph. Hold a strong intention in your mind that the forgiveness is taking place. Then place the crystal over your heart and absorb its loving pink vibration.

Non-specific forgiveness

When you are in a relaxed and receptive state, picture in front of you radiant white light which grows until it completely envelopes you. This light is all-loving and all-forgiving. Feel it spreading through your body in a warm glow, filling your heart with unconditional, loving energy. Rest in its peace until you feel you have been totally forgiven. Notice how much lighter you feel now that you have received forgiveness.

When you are ready, breathe a little more deeply and become aware of your surroundings once more. Once your attention is back in the room, open your eyes. [Holding a piece of Rose Quartz on your heart as you do this exercise can greatly strengthen its effect.]

If you are non-visual: use the light of a candle to assist you.

Cutting the ties

> Sacred bonds may be dissolved when the meet and cheerful conversation
> for which they were entered into falls into a melancholy and intractable
> silence.
>
> John Milton

As we have seen, our difficulties from the past are often, seemingly, inextricably linked to people with whom we have become enmeshed and with who we have created bonds that are not always good for us particularly at subtle, unperceived levels. This is especially true in soulmate or love relationships but can apply to any interaction. For over thirty-five years I have used a method of cutting the ties that involves letting go of all the oughts, shoulds and if-only's which make our contact with other people conditional and which hold us, and them, back from developing as people in our own right. This tie-cutting has always had positive, beneficial results.

Cutting can be carried out with anyone regardless of whether or not they are still alive, which makes it perfect for releasing people from other lives, as well as present life, parents, ex-husbands or lovers. It is useful to do this exercise with a partner from time to time, even if you are in a happy relationship as it keeps it clear and working well. The Australian Bush Essences *Stuart Desert Pea* and *Sunshine Wattle* assist in letting go the past, and the Bach Flower Essences *Walnut* and *Honeysuckle* are helpful in cutting the ties and can be taken prior to the cutting and for several days following. The Australian essence *Boab* is indispensable for breaking family patterns.

The work involves cutting the emotional ties that have built up and sets both parties free to be themselves and to take their own place in life. It does not cut off the love, but it does remove all the expectations, buts, oughts and shoulds, karma and so on that can attach themselves to what masquerades as 'love'. For rather too many people 'loving' their children or partner involves a subtle radiation of acceptance or non-acceptance based on whether the other person is conforming to what is required or is considered to be good. Love, unfortunately, is all too often a method of control.

Paradoxically, in letting go, the bond of love often becomes stronger and the relationship improves as the other person is perceived as a person in their own right. The imaging is also useful for working with people, such as parents or grandparents, whom you have loved very much but who have now passed on, as they can still be having a deep influence in your life and you may still be living out their hopes for you.

As the visualisation frees you from the past, and particularly from people that have been holding you back without your realising it, it can be helpful to do a 'blank' cutting, creating the circle and then asking that whoever you most need to cut away from will appear in the circle.

This work is powerful and should only be undertaken if you really feel it is right. It has been suggested that it may interfere with another person's autonomy and rights. However, the meadow, in the visualisation, represents your own inner space. In doing this exercise, you are inviting another person to manifest in that inner space. They are there by your invitation, not by right – although they may well already occupy part of that space without your invitation, which interferes with your own autonomy. By using the circles you delineate the space which each of you can occupy while doing the work. You should not let the circles overlap, or allow the other person to move into your circle. When the work is complete, you set them free and send them back to their own place. In other words, they move out of your inner space and into their own. Thus, you are each set free to inhabit your own space.

Thanks to a recent experience of an old client of mine, I have now become even more aware of just how subtle and long lasting some of these ties can be, and the different levels at which they can operate. The levels are vibrational – and extremely subtle. Working together on earth healing, for example, as my client did with a spurious soul companion, tied them together at a vibrationally high level, and the work was on-going so disconnection was problematic – although eventually she realised that even the idea of on-going work was in itself an illusion. Although I had done several of my usual tie-cuttings with my client, they had not fully worked. Neither I nor she had not recognised how high up the vibrational scale, and higher chakras, they had become connected. She felt that they had met to do that work, but the purpose had become subverted by his trying to make money by publishing a book of hers the contents of which he, privately, ridiculed. There was, therefore, a huge dilemma. Did she allow the, as she felt much needed, earth healing work to continue which meant her energies would continue to interact with his, or should she cut off completely? Her initial solution was to take back the publishing rights and hand the earth healing work over to their higher selves (the part that is not fully in incarnation) and ask that the 'me-down-here', which was still trying to deal with the repercussions of what had quickly become an extremely abusive and vampiric relationship, would be freed.

However, a year later she had to do a full-blown higher chakra and higher selves tie-cutting because it became apparent that this man was still vampirising her energy through the, alleged, earth healing. It was an enormous learning curve. We discovered that, merely thinking about him and his demands for compensation, she opened up an energetic channel between them. In addition to the high level tie-cutting she also found she needed to do a forgiveness exercise in which she not only gave forgiveness but asked it too for any actual or perceived wrongs she had done him. This is, in slightly different forms relevant to many people, and I have confirmed with her that the channel has remained closed, an excellent test that the tie-cutting worked and emphasising the value of forgiveness in this process.

The meditation for tie-cutting is set in a meadow, but some people find it easier to picture the sea-shore, the side of a lake, or some other peaceful place. It is important to use your own images, rather than ones I suggest to you, so adapt the wording if necessary. During the imaging work, the ties can manifest in many ways, as nets, hooks, umbilical cords and so on – and in many places. It is quite common to find a sexual tie linking you to a father or brother or your mother no matter what gender you are. These images are the subconscious mind's way of symbolically representing an emotional and psychic truth and should be accepted as such. Part of the work involves removing the ties, the place where they have been on each person being healed and sealed with light, and the other part involves destroying these ties. I find the most useful way of doing this is to have a large fire, as the symbolism is important. As the fire burns, it transmutes the tie into energy which you can use to re-energise yourself. It is also possible to use water to dissolve or wash away the ties. The one method I do not usually recommend is to bury them, as symbolically this does not free you from them, and they may well sprout and grow again. Having said that, I have learned from years of experience that it is impossible to be dogmatic as, just occasionally, a tie may be transformed through death and rebirth, of which the ritual of burying can be a part.

Exercise: Tie-cutting visualisation

Take time to relax and settle, breathing gently. Slowly raise and lower your eyelids ten times and then leave them closed. Without opening your eyes, raise them to the point between and slightly above your eyebrows as this helps images to form. Then picture yourself walking in a meadow on a nice, warm, sunny day. Really let yourself feel the grass beneath your feet, the cool earth below. There is a gentle breeze playing around your face, keeping you cool and comfortable.

Spend a little time exploring your meadow and then choose the spot where you want to do this work.

Draw a circle around yourself as you stand in the meadow. The circle should be at arms length and go right around you. You can use paint, chalk, light or whatever comes to mind. This circle delineates your space. (If you use a hoop of light, it can be pulled up around you if needed).

In front of you, close to but not touching your circle, draw another circle the same size. Picture the person with whom you wish to cut the ties in the circle. (If you have difficulty in seeing the person clearly, you can picture a photograph being placed in the circle). Do not let the circles overlap, peg them down if necessary.

Explain to the person why you are doing this exercise. Tell them that you are not cutting off any unconditional love there may be, but that you wish to be free from the old emotional conditioning and bonds that built up in the past, and any expectations in the present.

Look to see how the ties symbolically manifest themselves. Then spend time removing them, first from yourself, healing and sealing the places where they were with light, then removing them from the other person. Make sure you get all the ties, especially the ones around the back that you may overlook and those that are far out in your subtle etheric bodies. Pile the ties up outside the circle. If you have problems with ties at high vibrational levels, ask your higher self to deal with these on your behalf. Hand it over and allow the process to complete.

When you are sure you have cleared all the ties, and sealed all the places where they have been, let unconditional love, forgiveness and acceptance (where possible) flow between you and the other person. Then let that other person go back to where they belong.

Gather up all the ties and find an appropriate way of destroying them. You may wish to have a large bonfire onto which you throw them, or a swiftly flowing river into which you cast them. Make sure you have destroyed all the ties.

If you are using a fire, move nearer to the flames and feel the transmuted energy warming, purifying, healing and energising you, filling all the empty spaces left by removing the ties. This is your own creative life force coming back to you in its released and purified form. Absorb as much of this energy as you need. If you feel able to, move into the fire and become like the phoenix, reborn from the flames.

If you are using water, you might like to enter the water, or to use the heat of the sun to purify heal and energise yourself. Then wrap a bubble of light around you to protect yourself.

Repeat the cutting with another person if you wish. When you have completed all the cutting you wish to do, bring your attention back into the room and allow yourself plenty of time to readjust, breathing more deeply and bringing yourself into full awareness with feet firmly on the ground. Have a hot drink to bring you fully back into your body and the present moment.

If you are non-visual: place two photographs (or write the name of the person with whom you wish to cut the ties) within two circles that do not touch – you can use a large dinner plate for this. Place coloured thread or a net (the kind that fruit is wrapped in is ideal) or whatever your imagination tells you would be appropriate to link them. Carefully remove the threads from your picture and then from the other person. Burn them. Place a piece of Rose Quartz on each photograph and allow its healing energy to seal the places where the ties were. Then move the circles wide apart, certainly into another room and preferably out of your space entirely. If you were using a piece of paper with a name written on it, this can be burnt.

16

Why Some People May Never Find Their True Mate

Truth waits for eyes unclouded by longing.

The Mirror Cards[1]

To make life bearable, to avoid loneliness, to fill a huge hole, to enable them to feel complete, to give them children, are all reasons given by my clients who ask how they can find their soulmate. Such reasons are inherently selfish, they seek to make the small-self happy, rather than the other person or the eternal Self and that is not a good basis for relationship. Rarer, but more positive, are the people who ask how they can find someone with whom to grow and evolve. Occasionally, someone will say, "I feel I have much to offer a partner". The one thing all these people have in common is that they are searching for someone with whom to spend their life and become whole. And yet, I have as many if not more letters from people who are married and trying to find a way out as it has not lived up to their expectations. In her book on the work of the American seer Edgar Cayce, Gina Cerminera comments:

> The French have a brilliant epigram on the subject of the married and the non-marital state: 'Marriage is like a beseiged fortress: those who are outside want to get in; those who are inside want to get out'. . . Marriage has brought so much psychological misery to so many people that it seems almost surprising that other people should still consider the married state a desirable one, that they should still be able to disregard its many threats to peace of mind and see only its promises of felicity. And yet ... the unmarried generally have a sense of having been cheated of something precious – a sense of frustration and failure.[2]

---

1. Charley, Geoff *The Mirror Cards* Edison Sadd Editions.
2. Cerminara, Gina *Many Mansions* [hereinafter Gina Cerminara] p.131.

That sense of frustration and failure is extremely real, judging from the mail I receive. Whilst the single state may well be a positive choice, with the soul learning lessons of self-sufficiency, self-worth and other such qualities, it is rarely seen as that. From over thirty-five years of looking at this issue, it appears that some people are simply not destined for marriage. They may well have made that choice at a soul level but are having difficulty adjusting to it here in the physical world. Comparatively few people are happy with their single state – and those who are rarely need to consult a karmic astrologer to find out why. Most souls for whom the single state is an issue either do not find a partner or, having found a partner, the marriage is not destined to last. I regularly get letters from both men and women whose partners have died shortly after marriage, or who move out of the relationship swiftly, leaving them alone again.

In the past, such people often dedicated themselves to the church, or to family obligations. Men could go off to war or some solitary pursuit, but women were limited in their alternative outlets. Nowadays, of course, sex is more widely available; women as well as men devote themselves to their career, and women can conceive children without having a partner just as men can adopt. Nevertheless, I am regularly consulted by women, and men, who feel that, whilst perfectly happy with their lives, they nevertheless suspect that they may be missing out on something – and equally by people who are in a perfectly good marriage with a non-soulmate who wonder if there could be something more.

In some charts there may be astrological indications of a 'blockage' – such as an old vow or ingrained belief or an unresolved issue around sexuality and gender or intimacy. But there are times when there is nothing obvious in the astrology. In such cases, it can be helpful to go back to pre-birth to look at their life-plan for the current incarnation or to examine the karmic reasons for not attracting a mate – something which requires a skilled guide or expert in far memory.[3]

Edgar Cayce did many readings on this kind of question. He told one frustrated spinster, for example, that several lifetimes back she had been married with two children. Her husband 'fell into disgrace in his community' and she committed suicide in a fit of post natal depression. According to Cayce, her failure to find a partner now was because she

---

3. For details of my karmic readings please see www.judyhall.co.uk.

deprived her husband and children of the love they needed then. As she had not honoured her responsibility to her family, nor appreciated family bonds, in her present life she was to go without these things because through their lack she would appreciate their worth.

In my experience, such an extreme measure would only occur after several lives as karma is not a punishment but rather a balancing out. It is usually undertaken with the cooperation of the soul after careful planning in the between-life state but can occasionally be a wake-up call that is imposed on a soul who is deeply entrenched in a negative pattern.

In another reading Cayce told a woman who had had a love affair which was purely physical with great psychological incompatibility, since when she had been alone, that she too had committed suicide and abandoned a child, and so was deprived of one in her present life. In that other life she had been proud, haughty, self-willed and arrogant and died rather than suffer humiliation. In her present life, she exhibited exactly those same qualities again, together with an independence and brusqueness of manner that put prospective partners off. She was prone to fits of black depression, during which she contemplated suicide. After the reading, she never again wished to commit suicide [suicide is not necessarily a negative karmic choice although Cayce usually seemed to feel it was]. Cayce also told her that she could expect to marry much later in life after she had made herself as helpful as possible to all with whom she came in contact. In that way she would make herself 'worthy of marriage' (Cayce's words), which was the karmic purpose of her present incarnation. For her, it was not the suicide which led to her single state, but rather the carry-over of the traits that had caused the suicide in the first place.

What many people are looking for in a partner is someone to make them feel complete, to fill in the gaps as it were. The doctrine of karma, however, says that they should seek to develop the missing qualities within their own self. So, if they are looking for love, they should practice love at every opportunity – which does not mean becoming promiscuous but rather showing unconditional, compassionate love and an open heart whenever and wherever possible, even in the smallest of ways.

Lack of a partner is so often regarded as being a negative condition when it can be a positive one. Being single may have been part of the soul plan for the present incarnation. You may be learning the difference between being alone and being lonely. Being lonely often brings dependence and barriers. It shuts off from spiritual comfort or insight and is constantly looking 'out there' for answers. Being alone can, however, bring strength and independence, an ability to be happy in your own company and to practise self-love and self-cherishing. It can offer the opportunity for spiritual insights gained through meditation, and the possibility of knowing your inner self more intimately. People usually encounter what they expect. If at a deep level you feel unlovable, unworthy, inadequate or inferior, for whatever reason, this is what will be attracted. So, one of the most powerful ways to find a true mate can be to learn to love yourself – not in a selfish, self-centred way but in a way that validates and appreciates who and what you are in the fullness of your whole being – and change your expectations into something positive and life-affirming (see Chapter 17).

Setting too high standards can be one of the pitfalls in finding a mate. If a previous experience was of perfection, then anything else tends to disappoint. If it wasn't perfect back then, at death or in the between life state the soul might have decided it has to be now. Many people go into relationship expecting – or demanding – that everything should be instantly right. If it were there would perhaps be no way to evolve or grow together and you would stultify unless you were in a twinflame relationship. On the other hand, if you have always settled for something less, and therefore been disappointed in love, then, once again, that expectation will probably manifest once more unless you reprogram it.

If a soul has taken a vow of celibacy in another life, unless this was rescinded, there will remain a certain 'untouchable air' about that person. They may make subtle movements of distaste and rejection that are perceived subliminally by a potential partner, who backs off. Disappointment or hurt in love, the decision that, 'I'll never risk that again', can have much the same effect. It is as though the aura freezes as well as the emotions – and prospective partners intuitively read the signals the aura gives out and so stay well away. There will be a deep conflict, consciously the person wants to receive love, subconsciously a little voice inside is warning, "Remember that decision you made, well it was good sense, you'll only get hurt again". Once you recognise that voice and, where possible, find out where it is coming from and shut it down or reframe it, then a new attitude is possible.

Why it may be inappropriate to marry

> Times are changed with him who marries; there are no more by-path meadows, where you may innocently linger, but the road lies long and straight and dusty to the grave.
>
> Robert Louis Stevenson

Edgar Cayce did a great many relationship readings – some of which specifically referred to the karma embedded in a prospective relationship. In response to a question as to whether marriage would be best for a couple's mutual development, he replied that it might be so, but that there were other potential partners with whom their growth would be better served, especially as they had some karma which would be particularly hard to deal with as husband and wife.

In that case Cayce clearly felt that the couple should not marry although he didn't say so outright. When asked a similar question by another couple, however, he stated starkly, "No" but gave no reason. In other readings he left the couple to make up their own mind – which is what an astrologer or other counsellor, no matter how intuitive and spiritually aware is well advised to do. You can set out the factors as you read them and then leave your client to make the decision. Anything else is risking karmic enmeshment with your client. In response to one couple's enquiry as to whether they should marry or was there someone else with whom they could each be happier, Cayce retorted that he could name twenty-five or thirty – going on to say that marriage was what you made it. But he followed this up by saying that the couple did have an issue that would have to be worked on together sooner or later, and so the choice was up to them.

In commenting on this and the inadvisability of marriage in certain cases, Gina Cerminara points out that the souls, despite having mutual karma, may well have other lessons to learn which are more important than the one they would learn together. In my work, I have certainly found this to be the case. The couple may also have lessons that they could learn better apart than together – although sometimes a couple are 'rehearsing' for a later relationship where they will face the deeper issues with the person with whom they arose in another life. It may be that one soul actually needs an experience of being alone, for instance. Gina Cerminara goes on to say that some couples should not marry because one of the souls may be 'spiritually insolvent'. In other words, he or she has not yet developed the inner strength needed to face and work through the karmic difficulty. There are also cases, she feels, where the marriage would be 'too extreme a penalty for the delinquency, or the punishment does not fit the crime'.[4] That is to say, whilst there may be some karma between a couple who are attracted to each other, it would not be sufficient reason for them to become embroiled in what would, or could possibly, develop into a difficult passage due to other considerations. Karma is, of course, an on-going process and what is set in motion now will have to be met in the future.

Some people are still dealing with the consequences of unwise choices in previous lives, setting themselves the task of learning discrimination in relationships. If this is so, it would be wise to postpone marriage until the issues have been unpicked as it were, as otherwise the couple may find themselves tied together for a repeat lifetime in which they go round and round over the same old ground.

Sexuality and gender may be hidden agendas behind failure to find a marriage or life partner, or in a marriage breaking down. There are souls that are suffering from a resistance to a gender change that has taken place. Extremely masculine women, for example, or effeminate men may be resisting moving into a new experience and, therefore, do not find a suitable partner because they are unconsciously looking in the wrong direction – something which can affect all and anyone at one time or another not just those who have changed gender. As we have seen, the incarnating soul may have intended to have a same-sex relationship in order to develop certain qualities only available through that interaction, but society's mores may have pushed them into a more conventional marriage. As many men, and women, with same-sex leanings have found to their cost, marriage to the opposite sex does not provide a cure. If anything, it exacerbates the yearning. Until such time as the soul adapts to the new gender in whatever way is appropriate, it might be more constructive to be alone.

Still other people remain working on the continuity principle or karmic treadmill. Many people believe they will recognise their perfect partner instantly, and dismiss anyone that does not match up to this

---

4. Gina Cerminara p.128.

idealised picture – usually without even recognising the selection process has taken place or that they are looking for a partner from the past rather than for the present life. If such a person does find a match, they will marry for that reason – deluding themselves that everything will be perfect but it seldom is. In other continuity cases, old messages around love could still be operating and affecting the possibility of attracting a partner. Until such messages have been changed, it may be better not to enter a relationship. On the other hand, a soul in a previous life may have made a decision, or taken a particular stance, and it carries over from life to life as attitudinal karma. So, for example, a woman may have decided in another life to resist love, or maybe to keep herself pure for Jesus. Or a man may have formulated a heartfelt desire to remain single and unattached. Such decisions carry forward and may need reframing but it might be better for the soul to live out the consequences of that earlier decision until it has been fully experienced and the soul is ready to move on.

Notwithstanding, there are people for whom an informed decision to remain single will be a positive act. I knew a man who had become a monk in his present life, at a young age, despite his determination not to. He thought he had no vocation, and yet found an aptitude for the work. Having been a teacher, he moved into counselling. In his forties, he fell in love. Totally, head over heels, blissfully. But he decided not to marry. Having carefully considered the matter, he felt that he could help far more people through his spiritual and counselling work than he could gain personal satisfaction from marriage. He lived within a small community of brothers who shared a spiritual life that sustained him. When he looked at his past lives, he had already experienced relationships and children. He then had an interim life where, although married, he felt a powerful pull to solitude and spiritual work. Something which was only resolved at the very end of that life after the death of his wife. By the time his present incarnation came along, his soul felt ready to move onto a different way of giving and sharing of himself. For him, his single state was a positive affirmation of who he was.

Once people view their single state as complete in itself rather than as a lack they can be much more positive about their relationship to the wider whole. This gives them an opportunity to find strengths and develop qualities within themselves that could not have been accessed had they married.

17

Twinflames

One does not earn the love of another person. One has the love of another person because one is, and thereupon it follows naturally.[1]

So, if you need your soul scoured of its karmic encrustations, ingrained attitudes and ancient debts, or if you want deep soul learning and accelerated emotional evolution, a soulmate can be the answer. But, you might well be asking by now, is there an alternative to a soulmate? What if you feel ready to step off the treadmill of relationships and find a new way of loving? To seek someone who has all the positive qualities of that so-yearned-for soul partner but none of the drawbacks? A true soul-mate, what I now call a twinflame: a companion of the heart. A twinflame is epitomised in this email I received from a friend who has been married for over twenty years when I asked her what she thought made her relationship so different – they zing out as a couple who are happy together without being cloying in their togetherness:

> We are very different and also very much alike. Odd thing to say, but true in our case. I think that's why it works, we don't interfere in each others life, but also have great understanding for each other. We can be in a crowded room, at other ends, one look across and we know what the other feels. We give support without props.

It wasn't odd to me and I loved her description of 'support without props'. A perfect summation of the twinflame state.

Companions of the heart

> What unfolded over the following months was an unforgettable, fairy-tale romance, long-distance, crowded with synchronicities and incidences of telepathy... it was clear that this was a re-connection of twinflames, so

---

1. Viederman p.1.

deeply and powerfully connected in love that we wished for nothing more than to walk together through the rest of this – and any other – life.[2]

A twinflame is a mutually supportive, interdependent, unconditionally loving and accepting relationship between two souls with a deep connection but no karma to work on, no unfinished business to complete, and no hidden agendas. They are two individuals who come together to make a third entity: a relationship. They do not complete each other, they complement each other. They do not demand, they willingly share. They mutually respect and honour each other in their wholeness and uniqueness and they do not try to change each other although they may facilitate each other's growth. The relationship works, it does not have to be worked at. Although having said that, it does not mean that it is perfection personified, the participants are, of course, still human with all the foibles and fallibilities that includes, but obstacles are flowed around and encompassed rather than causing discord. The two people grow alongside each other, willingly and lovingly adapting and adjusting to circumstances and personality quirks without feeling put upon. They have mutual respect for each other. And the relationship may be a far from conventional one; twinflames are not necessarily destined to live together, certainly not for all time, and sometimes one partner is in incarnation and one not.

The concept of twinflames is summed up in a Buddhist analogy used by Justin Carson to illustrate reincarnation in *Hands Across Time*:

> If you light a candle, and from that candle light another candle, and from that one light another, and so on for a hundred candles, is it the same flame, or is it different? Its essence and nature appear to be the same, but the flames, especially when side by side, are quite distinct from each other.

Twinflames are like two of those candle flames side-by-side. Sharing the essence but nonetheless distinct, they may well have been together for many lifetimes, and almost inevitably go way back into time – if there really is such a thing as time, in my experience that is a very fluid concept indeed. They may well have had karmic lessons to work on

---

2. Gunn, Celia. M, *A Twist in Coyote's Tale* (Chichester: Archive Publishing: 2006), p.360.

in the past, but they are beyond that stage now and into what Chuck Spezzano calls the vision stage (see Chapter 4). They come together out of pure love and for no other reason. They give each other space, and support. They allow each other to be who they are, and to become more of that person. Nothing is held back. There is total honesty, intimacy and trust between them and they evolve at their own pace as Celia and Anthony's story shows.

Celia: In finding and being with each other, Anthony and I feel we have come 'home'. In joining ourselves together, we feel liberated, having uncovered the deep wellspring of what can best be called unconditional love that springs within us all, given the opportunity. We both feel that we have found 'The One'.

We meet many soul-mates in our lifetime – I believe it is an earlier, other than this life agreement. We each have something to give the other, and then – usually – we move on. This special connection is one that our society for the most part does not recognise at all, so that the profound connectedness felt by the soulmates, which is often first experienced at the level of the sacral chakra, is expressed sexually instead of being raised to the spiritual level of the brow chakra. And then we wonder why the relationship eventually blows apart. . .

The twinflame is another – I feel higher but this is not about better or worse – level of connection; often telepathic in nature. Before Anthony and I actually got together, we had, during our months of correspondence and phone-calls between here and Canada, a number of extraordinary experiences of telepathic contact – as for instance the example I give in A *Twist in Coyote's Tale*, when we were both asking at about the same time how we would be together, and the cloud showed me the map of the UK.

For the first few months we were together in the UK, I often experienced the most extraordinary sensation of 'melting' into Anthony, even when we were just sitting together, chatting. I've never felt anything like it before. It was like joining with the rest of myself that I never knew had been missing, or that I would lose myself in him, and it was a sooo delicious feeling. . . Perhaps an energy connection shared and experienced by two energetically-compatible souls?

It is a joyful and joyous connection that is affording me a greater consciousness of my Higher Self. I feel that together, we are acting as a channel (not that I care for what we understand as 'channelling') or conduit, or accessing something of the greater Creative Intelligence. Not to have children together, that is behind us, but in manifestation according to our divine purpose, or what we came to Earth for in our case, the sacredness of Mother Earth.

In another incident (there were so many!) sometime in early 1994, after we'd been together a few months, we were walking over the downs behind the cottage we were renting in Upper Woodford, near Salisbury, and watching the starlings doing their amazing dusk flocking; you know, where they gather in a mass and swoop and soar in silent oneness. As we watched, hearing only the whirr of their wings, they drew together in a cloud then right in front of us formed themselves into the most elegant and accurate heart-shape, which hung there for several seconds before they moved on and began to drop away into their roosts. We were speechless.

Although I happily feel totally bound up with and to Anthony, I am more than ever aware of my individuality. There is absolutely no conflict between our Oneness and our individual consciousness. I believe this is because we strengthen and empower the ego in each other in our Oneness, and the higher (spirit) and lower (ego) self are united and maintained in balance.

But first of all, before we ever got together, both of us consciously worked to become one with ourself. We both did a lot of inner work to strengthen and balance our male and female within, to create a sort of foundation to be able to release the Oneness, I believe.

I also understand that the twinflame relationship need not necessarily be sexual: I know of a brother and sister who have attained this level of connectedness.

It's ultimately about being a channel for the Greater Intelligence. Spirit, which knows no gender; the masculine and feminine principles are complementary. I believe that in Anthony and me, these energies unite to create One Energy: a Divine Marriage.

I also believe that more people are beginning to understand the flow of these energies. And I pray and wish and hope they do, for there is to me no better way of Being.

Anthony and Celia first met on the pilgrimage in 1990, six months before his first wife left him but at the time there was no feeling of being twinflames, although they 'recognised each other'. As Celia's extraordinary book relates, they finally got together in 1993, having corresponded for some time because Celia was living on the far side of Canada. At the time, Anthony had asked me to do a reading on their charts, I remember telling him that this would be the most amazing relationship of all time – or the biggest illusion, but it was impossible to tell. That can be one of the indicators of twinflame relationships, it is beyond the conventional astrological indicators of soulmates although it can incorporate certain components, and time is the test.

> **Celia**: Throughout that initial correspondence, and in the years since, we have had what we both consider to be a quite awesome deepening and widening continuity of the initial experience of oneness/synchronicity/telepathy. One example that has come back to me as I write was in 2004, when I was taken with my sister by my mother on a two-week cruise in the Caribbean. First of all, I found (as did he) that being away from him like that (it was the first time in 11 years) made me almost physically sick – I missed him so deeply (but not pathologically), it was like there was a hole in my side, or part of me was simply missing. I was also concerned about his state of health at the time and how he was still uncomfortably working in the medical-legal field in order to maintain our mortgage etc., and after a couple of days of deep, private contemplation, decided that we should sell our house. I had just firmly come to this decision and that I would tell him this when I got back, when a voice said in my head, quite clearly, 'Don't make a decision like that; you don't know the whole story'. It was quite a shock, because I was quite happy with my decision and it almost felt like there was someone else sitting in my head, something to which I'm not particularly used or prone.
>
> When I got back and told him about this whole incident, he told me how he had had a mental crisis re the medical-legal work and how much he couldn't bear to go on doing it (I believe he actually phoned you up at one point and talked about the astrology?); and had sat down with the I Ching, and after appropriate preparation asked of the oracle whether we should sell the house. He was given an unequivocal 'No'.
>
> When we sat down and worked out the timing of our two incidences, it was synchronous.

Anthony had indeed phoned me. We were born a couple of months apart and, having been friends for many years, have found that our lives tend to go in parallel. When he phoned me about the crisis with the medical work and his health, my relationship was ending and our mutual astrology indicated that there were great changes to be made. We were looking at nodal returns, one cycle for me, two for Anthony, which culminated in a solar eclipse. Ancient astrologers would have seen this as highly symbolic and 'fated'. For me it was my relationship that had to go, for him the ending of a career that had been extremely successful but which had never really allowed him to be fully who he was. Each of us went through a powerful rebirth in the following months. But to return to Celia's story:

> **Celia**: As for the eight weeks I was just away in Canada/US promoting my book, well, even though it was an amazing time, I'll never again go away without Anthony – almost painfully, again I felt like I was half a person.
>
> Even when we lie in bed at night, reading: he'll be reading some weighty academic tome such as Plato, and often as not I'll be reading fantasy; and I'll make some comment about some pithy truth I have come across and he'll laugh and show me what he was just reading, which was saying the same thing, or dealing with the same matter. That happens so often, but we still find it amazing.
>
> And perhaps one of the most vital things to say is that I still find Anthony to be a daily wonder to me: never a day goes by that I'm not in awe or wonder of who he is, that we are together and that we have such a deep and ever-deepening connection. The love I have/hold/feel for him is likewise a daily wonder to me; it's like I can feel that deep wellspring in me that is always bubbling up, whenever my mind goes there. We express this to each other every day.
>
> We have never had an argument. I know this doesn't sound healthy according to present-day relationship gurus, but we don't; perhaps because of the fact that we are in constant communication about all and everything, so nothing can ever escalate; or because each of us is fully prepared to hear and cares about the other's point of view.
>
> I guess the bottom line is that each of us is primarily concerned with the other's happiness and fulfilment; and perhaps this is one of the prime indicators of the twinflame connection.

Celia and Anthony are a couple who give me hope for better relationship in the future, for myself and for others. I have observed their relationship from their first meeting and it has been a joy to see it grow and develop – and to read Celia's inspiring book. Parts of their story, however, sound remarkably similar to soulmate stories in this book that ultimately ended badly. So how can you tell the difference you may well be asking? The answer seems to be that you can't, at the beginning. It has to stand the test of time. But there are pointers to watch out for and it can be commonly defined by including the following negative indications:

Non-twinflame relationship indications

- ♥ One partner is reluctant to fully commit to the relationship in whatever form it is to take.
- ♥ There are uncomfortable or disharmonious 'edges' in the energy between you.
- ♥ One person tries to force change, bullies the other or attempts to retain control or hold power over the other.
- ♥ One partner has to suppress large parts of their own self to fit into what is expected.
- ♥ There are conditions to be fulfilled to maintain the relationship.
- ♥ The relationship starts on a high but inexorably deteriorates or needs constant working on.
- ♥ There is a sense of duty, debt or being owed something, needing retribution or reparation, or 'having to do'.
- ♥ One person feels vastly superior or inferior to the other.
- ♥ One or both people are so absorbed in the relationship that they cannot function in the world.
- ♥ Physical intimacy is forced upon or demanded by one of the partners.
- ♥ One person is subsumed by the other, is dependent on the other, and the relationship is parasitically and vampirically symbiotic (that is, one person feeds off the other to their detriment and could not exist alone).
- ♥ There is a sense of unfinished business, karma or a hidden agenda.
- ♥ There is competition between the couple, or resentment of the other person's successes.

- One partner feels jealous, insecure or abandoned when the other is perusing his or her own interests.
- 'Ephemeral and irrational passion'.[3]
- No reality, only the fantasy of what might be.
- Constant illnesses or physical, emotional and mental dis-ease.

The key may be that if you have to carve off great portions of your soul in order to fit in to a relationship, if you suppress who you are or make compromises and adjustments that force you, consciously or unconsciously, to lose sight of who you are, then you are with a soulmate no matter how much you may yearn for a twinflame relationship and labour under the delusion that you are experiencing one. A twinflame relationship allows, and maybe even impels – but never compels – you to be all that you are and can be – at your own pace and in your own time.

Twinflame indications

- Unconditional love.
- Mutual respect and recognition.
- A feeling of being met halfway.
- Mutually supportive.
- Interdependent and independent.
- Accepting.
- Deep soul and heart connection.
- Complementary and non-competitive.
- Allow each other to be who they are, and to become more of that person.
- Total honesty, intimacy and trust.
- Reciprocal feelings and behaviours.
- Each takes responsibility for his or her own thoughts, feelings, actions and happiness.

---

3. This particular point has been taken from *Passionate Attachments*, p.17. Milton Viederman was not speaking of non-twinflame relationships but I see it as relevant.

- Different needs and outcomes are encouraged.

- The reality of the other is recognised and accepted.

- Exalted and energized by the sense of loving and being loved.

- Each evolve at their own pace.

- Positive symbiosis – the association functions to the mutual benefit and advantage of both equally (but one partner can survive without the other).

- The magic and wonder never fades, it is renewed each moment.

- An embodied recognition of each other that is beyond the merely sexual.

- Adjustments are made willingly (such as living arrangements, changing countries, or adapting to living with someone else in your space), and intimacy and trust are there from the beginning, which enables the adjustments to be made together, each lovingly supporting the other through the process.

Celia added to the above that there is a sense of liberation that results from extraordinary closeness, complete trust in each other, and the delight when the other follows their dream and finds their bliss. She also suggested that there is a gentle, unforced, daily physical interaction that is not necessarily sexual but which encompasses touching and hugging – part of what I would call a fully embodied relationship. Another of my clients who has had such a relationship says that she felt it in her sacrum (the 'sacred bone') rather than the sacral chakra, "it was as though the relationship formed an integral support at the core of my being, it was earthy and earthed as well as profoundly spiritual".

The sense of a twinflame moves fluidly through time. One of my clients described having reached the end of a difficult relationship, cutting the ties and turning round and finding someone who had been there all along but suddenly the relationship was different. She said:

He is my twin in every respect – date, time and rising sign. Our happiness goes from strength to strength, hourly, daily… But I must tell you something very strange, I knew him a long time ago, thousands of years ago. I did a painting years ago, long before I met him again in this life, and one of the characters in the painting had a particular attachment for me. To cut a long story short, I had painted my twinflame as he had been in a time I had once known him.

Since that time she has found other similarities, they have the same markings on their bodies, scars, moles and dimples. They had similar upbringings but at opposite ends of the earth. She has uncovered more details of the life in ancient Egypt that she painted, and a life as half brother and sister. But it remains to be seen if they are true twinflames.

The downside to the twinflame?

I know not if I know what true love is,
But if I know, then, if I love not him,
I know there is none other I can love.

Alfred, Lord Tennyson

Twinflame relationships are clearly rare, and yet they are possible. But are they too idealistic and perfect, you may well be asking? There is another side of the twinflame union that I had not considered until I began to write this section, one that Celia hints at in her pain at being parted from Anthony even temporarily. While speaking to author Moyra Caldecott, who had introduced me to the concept of twinflames, she mentioned the daily grief she had endured since the death of her twinflame husband. On the same day, Sue Minns had emailed me to say that she was, "not even sure I understand why a soul might have an earthly union of that nature, unless it was to deal with the searing grief when one of them died?" However, when I mentioned this on a workshop, one of the participants told me that she had recognised her twinflame when they met again after thirty years having known each other in childhood. She said that they spent two years "adjusting", sorting out the karmic patterns and then two blissful years as twin flames before he died. She said yes there was grief, but it was not searing. There was enormous joy in remembering their time together and, in any case, he was around her all the time, encouraging and supporting her. Their beyond-death connection gave her the courage to go forward in her life knowing that they would be reunited.

A story I included in *Hands Across Time* shows that these meetings with someone from another time can be galvanising and life enhancing.

The almost middle-aged poet Elizabeth Barrett, a reclusive opium addict who had been slowly dying from a chest complaint for twenty-five years, found new life when courted by the younger Robert Browning. I am now wondering whether these two were also twinflames. After Elizabeth's death, Robert, who never remarried, wrote in her bible these lines from Dante's *La Vita Nuova*:

> Certain am I – from this life I shall pass into a better, there where that lady lives of whom enamoured was my soul.

Years after Elizabeth's death, Browning told a woman who pursued him, "My heart lies buried in Florence" – Elizabeth's last resting place.

Elizabeth's tyrannical father had not allowed any of his children to marry and would not allow 'courting' under his roof. Any love affairs his adult children conceived had to be kept strictly under wraps. The Barrett-Browning courtship was, initially, conducted by letter. Elizabeth at that time was a well-known and much respected poet, Robert an up and coming one. She mentioned Browning in one of her poems. His picture hung on the wall by her bed, so we can surmise an attraction to him was already at work. Indeed, one of her friends was later to insist that Elizabeth was in love with him long before they met.

Certainly when Robert wrote to her, ostensibly about her poem, he declared his love for her. This was not love at first sight, it was love before meeting. In that first letter he says, "I do love these verses with all my heart and I love you too". Even making allowances for the flowery Victorian style of prose, it is a pretty direct statement. Elizabeth replied the next day, "I thank you, dear Mr Browning, from the bottom of my heart". They clearly had a powerful connection. Over the next twenty months they wrote each other 574 letters.

When they finally met, five months after their correspondence began, Elizabeth found her 'ideal man fleshed out'. The visit unsettled her. She could not sleep, despite her opium. She could not get him out of her mind – alien feelings, for a woman who had led such an emotionally sheltered life, although she was no stranger to emotional trauma, her beloved brother's drowning had led to her prolonged illness. Robert, on the other hand, was much more straightforward. He was in love and declared so again in the letter he wrote immediately after that first visit. In a later letter he was to say, "My heart will remember". Hearts played a great part in their relationship. The poetic lines that had put them in touch in the first place have an allusion to the heart:

> Or from Browning some 'Pomegranate' which, cut deep down
> the middle, shows a heart within blood-tinctured of a veined humanity.
>
> *Lady Geraldine's Courtship*

Within months of their meeting, Elizabeth had moved from being virtually bedridden to someone who could go out and about, marry secretly, travel with her new husband to Italy, where they would spend the next seventeen years, and even give birth to a son. It was the first love relationship either had had. Robert never remarried after her death. He remained a widower for twenty-eight years. As Elizabeth said, "If God choose, I shall but love thee better after death".

A collection of poems *Sonnets from the Portuguese* came out of this union. These contain what is perhaps Elizabeth's best known line: 'How do I love thee, let me count the ways'. But they also included a poem that, in its first draft, was entitled 'Death or Love'. This was the choice Elizabeth had had to make – to continue under her tyrannical father's rule and inevitably wither and die, or to take up her unlived life, marry her soulmate – or twinflame? – and experience love. She chose 'Not Death, but Love'.

What they both found was a mature love that expected and demanded nothing from the other and which may have had a twinflame basis. As she said, "If thou must love me, let it be for naught except for love's sake only". Like so many soulmates and twinflames before and since, they knew each other intimately from the start. From the letters it is clear they shared thoughts and feelings without words, although words did, of course, instigate their love. But it was what lay behind the thoughts that mattered most to them. They shared 'intuitions of the heart'. There were no barriers between them. As Elizabeth put it, "I am inside of him and hear him breathe". Robert said, "[we] know each other for time and, I trust, for eternity". And yet, at the same time they remained individuals and of independent thought. They did not lose themselves in each other totally, but they accepted each other absolutely. An old friend told them, "If two persons were to be chosen from the ends of the earth for perfect union and fitness, there could not be a greater congruity than between you two".

However, even in this most blissful of marriages, dark clouds blew. There were disagreements, most noticeably over Elizabeth's espousal of Spiritualism, of which Robert disapproved. Elizabeth was prone to deep dark depressions, as well as her physical illness, and these, although much lessened after her marriage, continued to plague her. She was deeply affected by the loss of key figures in her family and sought solace in contact with them.

This brought another woman into the picture – not for Robert but for Elizabeth. She came under the spell of Sophie Eckley, her 'sister in the spiritual world', a soul sister who idealised and idolised her. The two shared a mutual interest – the spirit world – but the friendship went far beyond this. Their letters declare their love – a love which, on Sophie's side, was obsessive and, as it turned out, deceptive. Her false soulmate finally revealed, Elizabeth had to break free. She wrote to Sophie breaking off the contact. Her marriage was renewed. But is it perhaps an echo of Sophie we hear in Browning's lines:

> If two lives join, there is oft a scar.
> They are one and one, with a shadowy third,
> One near one is too far.

So, were they twinflames or soulmates? It really is impossible to tell but on balance this does feel like a relationship in which, because of the holding on of the heart and the eternal triangle, two soulmates may well have to return to earth and continue their unfinished business and then develop into twinflames. The same conundrum applies to the following story. In 1995 I couldn't decide whether this was a soulmate experience, now knowing that many twinflames do not actually incarnate together, I am wondering if it is actually a twinflame or soul companion saga.

More than just an illusion?

> Pause after pause that high old story drew
> our eyes together while we blushed and paled,
> but it was one soft passage overthrew
> our caution and our hearts. For when we read
> how her fond smile was kissed by such a lover,
> her who is one with me alive and dead
> breathed on my lips the tremor of his kiss.
>
> Dante

One of the most extraordinary love stories I have heard came from someone who had fought in the Vietnam War. He maintained that the drugs he took then, many of them unknowingly, had literally blown his mind and that he now inhabited a different level of consciousness. As I discovered later, he had been diagnosed schizophrenic and hospitalised for some time. Everyone he had consulted so far had said he was suffering from delusions, that his experience was unreal, a psychotic fantasy.

When I met him, he was in England trying to make sense of his experience. His story had an internal structure and consistency that made sense to me, no matter how others viewed it. It incorporated aspects that I had heard from many people, and some I had experienced myself. Was it all an illusion, were we all mad, or was he tuning into a universal experience? Did he indeed have access to another level of consciousness and to glimpses of the future? Certainly much of the seemingly more weird and way out beliefs he had have since come into mainstream thought, but as these are not a part of his soulmate experience we will not be looking at them here.

He came to see me for several sessions, during which his story gradually unfolded. One of his first questions to me was whether I believed that we had a soulmate, and if so, could someone have a soulmate who was not in a physical body. I told him I did indeed believe in soulmates, but not necessarily in the conventional fashion. And that, yes, I did believe we could have a soul companion who was not incarnated but who remained very close to us. At the time I had not encountered the concept of twinflames so did not mention this.

He recounted to me that he had met his soulmate briefly and then she died. As this part was too confused and painful for him to relate coherently and he became agitated whilst talking about it, it was something I went back to much later. He wanted to do a regression to find out more about their previous contact – of which he had had several glimpses.

I asked him to tell me more of his story first. Partly I felt I needed to check out his mental state before we looked at the possibility of regression as it is not something I would undertake with anyone in a psychotic state, but I also felt that he needed simply to be heard at that stage. Listening to someone's story in an accepting way can help to clarify exactly what is going on for them. I did not make a judgement as to how true it was or how much of a delusion he was under, if any. Clearly this was his reality and if I could enter into it with him, then maybe we could both understand.

Eventually it emerged that after his 'soulmate' died, she began to appear to him. At first in dreams, and then more and more often he would 'see' her around him. Then, he found himself out of his physical body and able to be with her. They inhabited a world that was, superficially, solid and real but in which they could move around at will and in which thoughts and feelings were totally visible. To me it sounded exactly like the less physical realm to which we pass after death and into which we can venture from time to time when we leave our physical body behind. I had had enough experiences of this place myself, having accompanied many people there, and read sufficient accounts, both ancient and modern, to accept this as a valid experience.

He said that, right from the start, they had sexual experiences together which were like nothing in the physical world. It was a total merging, a joining at the soul level. Again, this is supported by many accounts of such experiences. Eventually a soul marriage was performed. They took vows of eternal fidelity. He considered himself married. The only difference to ordinary, everyday marriage was that he had to leave his body to join his wife. His wife had then communicated to him that they had a mission. They were to help those on earth understand about these other levels of being. To accept that death was not the end of existence. Soon, many people would find themselves in similar soul marriages. It was when he began to talk of this to his family and friends – and of the other somewhat more bizarre communications he was receiving – that he was hospitalised.

Now he wanted to know more. He, like so many so-called 'schizophrenics', was convinced of the validity of his experience. Although the content of much of what he told me was 'bizarre' and some could be described as paranoid, it was nothing I had not heard before from other, supposedly sane people. I suggested to him that he should write it all down in the form of a novel as the world might not be ready yet to read it as fact. He began this task, but was insistent that some of the answers at least would be found in the past.

I took him into regression to check out his previous connections with his 'wife'. In every one, he seemed to have met her and then one or other of them died before the relationship could develop. Eventually he vowed, "Next time we will have a relationship no matter what".

I asked him to go right back to the beginning of their association. What he came up with was like something out of Plato and other, much earlier esoteric writings. A being, non-physical, and totally one was drifting blissfully through the cosmos. It was struck in half and the two pieces went hurtling off to opposite ends of the universe. Across aeons of time they searched for each other. When they met again, it was at a time of great cataclysm. Scarcely had they met when they were parted again. This was the beginning of the cycle of meeting and parting, joining and losing, which seemed to spread over a great time span. It really did feel as though these were two parts of one soul weaving and entwining only to part again. He was quite convinced that she was literally his other half. Eventually, when they had done the work they had to do, he would leave earth and they would merge and become one again.

Clearly there are psychological and psychotherapeutic explanations that could be given here. We could look on his lost love as representing his own inner feminine energies, the anima, from which he felt cut off, particularly by the dehumanising experiences he underwent in Vietnam. We could also see it as an externalisation of the enormous shock his psyche underwent in that trauma – the killing of all that was female: kindness, compassion, receptivity, sensitivity, caring, love. All qualities he had received from his soulmate in that brief contact before she was so brutally taken from him. We could see their marriage as his way of reintegrating this lost part of himself. If looked at from the shamanic perspective, he might have become possessed by this woman, as the kind of trauma he had gone through would have created a gap or vacuum in his energy field into which another spirit could slip. This could have been his way of integrating that spirit into himself. It could also, once I had heard the whole story, been his way of expurgating intense guilt.

When we were finally able to talk about where he first met his love in his present life, he told me she had died in Vietnam. They had met and spent a little time together in the town near his base. Later, his platoon had been attacking a village, they opened fire and suddenly there she was. He had reached out to her as she reached out to him, but his buddy, convinced she was Vietcong and was trying to kill him, had shot her. She was ripped virtually in two by the bullets. He then had a complete breakdown, but in the madness that was Vietnam, no one seemed to notice. Taking refuge more and more in drugs, he eventually returned home to the States, a bombed-out wreck. But, at the same time, he was experiencing a rich life on another plane. He certainly felt his soul marriage was both valid and fulfilling. Who am I to say what was fantasy and what was reality? With another twelve years of soulmate experiences behind me, and having investigated twinflames more deeply, I'm even more with Shakespeare's Hamlet on this one than I was in 1995:

> There are more things in heaven and earth, Horatio, than are dreamt of in (y)our philosophy.

Twinflames: some thoughts

Perhaps we can return to the Anthony and Celia story for more enlightenment as to exactly what a twinflame relationship is all about.

> **Anthony**: I've read all the bits that Celia has sent you and agree with all she has said, but I would like to add a few thoughts as it's such a fascinating subject. Celia and I are six years apart in age and we grew up in Northumberland thirty miles apart but never met in childhood; nor as far as we know did our paths ever cryptically cross, as some lovers later find out. Like 'Oh yes! I was at that concert as well! Fancy you being there. Our paths must be destined!' We never had anything like that – as far as we are aware.
>
> We have often thought about what would have happened if we had met earlier in life. Would the chemistry have worked then? Would the Twinflames have ignited? We think an earlier meeting probably would not have worked.
>
> By the time we met in 1990, we were already going through huge life changes, Celia was nearly 40 and just entering her long dark tunnel with a big Pluto transit, and I was at 46 just moving out of my 3-year Pluto transit, and all the rest of the mid-life astro-bumpy stuff. The two people who got together in 1993 had both moved on a lot. But still in 1990 we both acknowledged a sense of easy friendship, but it was not at all a sexual or lustful attraction; as you know there was no affair or infidelity. So earlier in our lives I doubt we had enough in common to make it likely that we would have had a successful and lasting relationship. We were very different people leading very different lives. Landscape and mysticism drew us together, but we both had to get to that point

through a lot of hard work, analysis, astrology, workshops, and painful and difficult relationship work.

After I knew my relationship with the only girlfriend I had had since my marriage broke up was definitely over I was feeling intrigued (almost academically) as to when I would next say to a woman, "I love you". I knew I would never say such a thing unless I really meant it, as I have no history of flirtations and casual relationships (no regrets in my case!). So I asked the I Ching in very early 1993 (in a rare consultation) for the date when I would say these words again. The date given was July 15th and the year surprisingly was 1993! I could think of no one I would say such a thing to at that time and was inclined to dismiss the I Ching answer as so much nonsense. But then I only used the I Ching very sparingly (half a dozen times in ten years and only over very important advice). I also did the 1993 consultation very seriously with meditation, preparation, facing north etc. So I thought, well, I will ask the Tarot the same question, and found a Tarot technique for fixing times and dates from one of Jane Lyle's books. I carefully and seriously asked the question a fortnight later of the Tarot. The answer came back quite plainly: July 15th 1993. I was staggered that the answer was the same date, but then as the weeks went by I forgot about it.

Celia and I began writing to each other during March 1993. By June the phone calls/letters were practically daily, and by early July I felt I wanted to say to her 'I love you'. I had of course forgotten the readings and on July 12th phoned Celia to share my feelings and tell her that I loved her. But she wasn't at home and I had no idea where she was. I phoned again over the next two days but there was still no answer.

Then a letter arrived to say that she and a friend had suddenly decided to go on a visit to some native medicine people up country for a few days. I phoned again on 14th but still no Celia at home. No mobiles in those days! So finally I phoned on July 15th and she was back at home, and I said (in the course of a long conversation), "I love you". She said, "I love you", and you know the rest.

But the I Ching/Tarot accuracy staggered me as I suddenly remembered my readings, and this was one of those synchronicities which I now associate with our being Twinflames. I had had nothing like this kind of intensity of synchronous connectedness in any previous relationship.

Celia: Now that this bit has come out, I thought to give you my side of this intriguing 'destiny' story.

In that fateful month of July 1993, I had written to Anthony to say that I would be away for three or four days, getting back home on the 11th or 12th July. However, the pipe-carrier that Nadine was taking me to meet and share a pipe with was not at home and we had to wait a day for her to get back; afterwards, we stayed another night and then as we had taken separate cars and a route that brought us close to the Okanagan Indian Reserve, I decided that while I was in the area (this was a round-trip of some three hundred miles) I would visit with some folk I knew there, which kept me away for another couple of days, so I only got home late afternoon on the 15th. Because by then we were speaking almost every day, I was feeling a little concerned that he might be worried; it was almost as if I could feel his spirit questing.

When I got in, there were two letters and a little parcel from Anthony waiting for me. Thrilled, I sat down to open them up and found I was shaking/trembling uncontrollably, something which hadn't happened to me before when reading his letters. I had a definite sense of something about to happen, not ominous but mighty, nevertheless, which I couldn't understand. I could barely read any words, I was so shaky, and put down the letter unread just as the phone rang, and it was he. We chatted briefly, as I told him where I had been (I'm sure my voice was shaky), and then he said, "Celia, I love you".

It felt like one of those moments that stretches into eternity, as a voice said in my head, "You can't say those words to this man, Celia, unless you mean it now and forever". (I don't know if you know that, notoriously, Taureans find it quite easy to say, 'I love you').

So I said, "I love you Anthony", knowing that I did mean it, now and forever, and feeling like I had just jumped off the trapeze swing and there was no safety-net!

Later, when Anthony eventually told me about his side of this story, I found it fascinating that it was Native spirit that had kept me away until the I Ching/Tarot could be proven accurate.

Anthony: Another interesting synchronicity: when Celia and I wrote to each other, we each had a private symbolic logo on the top of our letters. Celia's was a circle with a long, equal-armed cross through it and mine was a round circle with a candle flame coming out of the top. When we finally met in Canada on August 28th 1993 at Castlegar Airport in British Columbia, and made physical contact for the first time (what a risk you say – but we were both deeply confident that it would be right, and so it turned out), Celia immediately bundled me off to a sacred cave above a beautiful river just twenty minutes from the airport. Above the cave, on a rock known as the Wolf's Rock, were painted ancient red ochre Native American petroglyphs: the figures of a man and woman standing holding hands, their head blazing beams of light like a halo or crown chakra explosion. Standing close by them was a child or a being of their union or creation. But we were both staggered to find, when we got the photos developed, that above them and part of the whole symbolic piece were two symbols: one a circle with a long, equal-armed cross, the other a circle with a flame above it. Our chosen logos, completely accurately represented! Celia was using her logo before she first visited the cave and had never noticed that part of the petroglyph before our visit. We still have photographs of the petroglyphs and I checked them again before typing this piece. This was another Twinflame experience. There were lots of incidental synchronicities during and connected to the many phone-calls and they continue to the present.

I was going to write down the starlings in the sky story but I see that Celia has already done so. What was staggering for me about that experience was the way the moving cloud of starlings seemed to freeze in the heart shape for a few seconds to emphasise the reality of the symbol for us both, as we watched in awe. Then the cloud resumed their fluid dance in the air changing shape continuously. They didn't stop to freeze any further shape, so only the heart showed up.

These kinds of experiences strengthen the knowledge that Celia and I have a profound connection and make 'distancing' a difficult experience to imagine or indeed have. So the connectedness is a continuous strengthening of our bond together. There is a strong sense of timelessness and eternity about our feelings for each other – which has never faded.

Another feature I would want to emphasise is that both of us want to care for and support each other as a basic way of being together. My greatest joy is to be giving Celia her greatest joy and it is the giving which is the basis of my reward and pleasure. Fortunately I also receive Celia's great love and concern for me at the same time, so I am nurtured as I nurture. But I am not out to get what I can out of the relationship or selfishly 'take only', whether that is in intimate lovemaking or being in the kitchen together, but only wanting to provide ultimate pleasure and emotional support for her. This attitude of 'pleasuring the other' has given both of us an enduring depth of experience in both our intimate lovemaking and our total life together, and somehow staleness or boredom has never had a look in. We are also both very creative and startle each other continuously by the novelty that we can produce for each other.

I think our mutual creativity is a turn-on for both of us but it applies much more widely than simply in the bedroom! It is more than just mutual creativity. It is also about being freed or liberated by the other. So many relationships are about combat and issues of dominance, often very subtle, but nonetheless a battle – indeed, the battle of the sexes. In our twinflame relationship we have both commented to each other many times how the love and acceptance of the other has liberated each of us to follow our own individual path of experience or creativity or interest. There is no sense of envy or jealous ownership from Celia to me and vice versa, perhaps because of some partial but satisfactory sense of wholeness or completeness (no one is entirely or ever completely whole or 'complete'!) which may be a feature of all the personal work we did on ourselves in the years before we eventually met. Being so completely freed and liberated in what is a very close and powerful relationship may seem to others like an impossible paradox, but for me it is probably the most significant and telling thing about my whole life with Celia.

Thus I have found it most exciting that Celia is the first strong relationship I have been in where my partner has not been envious of my creativity and has locked themselves into a power struggle, ultimately an important component of the demise of my past relationships. Celia has never been phased by my creativity or ideas and ambitions but has supported me enthusiastically and wholeheartedly. She of course is secure in her own creativity and I love to support her and see her thrive creatively. Hence her writing etc. is very exciting for me, and I know my ideas, writing etc. are very exciting for her. There is no competition, only complementarity and support.

In 2005 when we concurrently polished up the novels each of us had written, then edited and advised each other through that process, we achieved a creative and inspirational high for a two-month period which permeated into every aspect of our personal and social lives in a way we have never experienced before. It was quite a shock to experience such a new level of intensity after being together 13 years. And it hangs around!

But then it is the continuous 'shock of the new' which has delightfully supported and sustained us through the whole experience of being together. Although we have different writing interests and approaches we were able to combine (most effectively and harmoniously) this last autumn a joint commission (60,000 words and an eighty-page gazetteer) for a report on the protection of sacred sites worldwide for the Gaia Foundation. A very exciting experience of 'one-ness'.

We are very content to just be together in a continuous and fascinating co-creative conversation, which can be about some very profound things. Some of this conversation then becomes part of our creative work that day. As Celia says in her Plato story, we are often bouncing off the same kind of ideas or insights from very different sources. We are both very taken up with natural synchronicities (flights of birds, animal appearances, nature in general, chance meetings, car numbers, etc.) and see these as significant on a daily basis for enriching and informing the web of consciousness through which we ultimately walk our walk together. We often talk about the reality of the deep connectedness in time and space that our lives together and with others (including animals and plants) are ultimately about. Such contemplation is not crazy or anxiety-making but incredibly profound and calming, a kind of sacred and spiritual flow.

When we go out to the cinema or to a restaurant together, we both feel a strange novelty, as if we are only on our third or fourth date. The outing carries a quality of newness, of excitement and intrigue. We never quite know what might happen next. We delight in each other's company, laugh at each other, look into each other's eyes or turn and kiss in the street like only new lovers are supposed to. Each outing has a quality for us of 'like being like new lovers'. We have often remarked and marvelled at this but it is still there after all our years together. These for me are some of the qualities of the Twinflame experience.

After all my pain working through my divorce, I read a huge amount about manifesting across the whole spectrum of life including relationships. I used a book to fashion a manifestation list for my ideal partner and then carried out ritual and affirmations to energise the manifestation, being careful that I had no specific person in mind.

Every feature that I listed for my ideal partner (excepting one very minor one!) came up in the person of Celia. Among many of the things I asked for was that the sense of being in love and the sexual experience with this person should not fade but always stay fresh and novel, and so it has been and is. Celia, of course unknown to me, made out a very similar list in Canada, and manifested me. Both of us had that marvellous conviction that 'somewhere in the world someone who is totally right for me is walking, right now, towards me', until we met in that consciousness and knew who that person was.

I think everyone should be encouraged to have this 'walking towards' experience as a creative visualisation. Celia has just told me this evening (shock of the new again in action!) that after writing out her list on a piece of paper, she took the paper and burned it ritually, offering it up to the creator spirit on the hillside above the same cave where together we were to find our petroglyph logos some months later. Thought precedes form.

Whilst Celia was in Canada recently being a grandmother and promoting her book in the seven weeks before Christmas we were apart for the longest period since we got together. I missed Celia greatly but not in the same painful way as in her Caribbean cruise story. Through the internet and phone calls we were in regular contact and I often seemed to sense what she was going through. I felt curiously alongside her in Canada and as if she was alongside me here at home, all at the same time. I think I had psyched myself up for the long apartness and was also determined not to dwell on her absence, but in the last week before she returned it became very painful and I was counting the hours in the last two days. Neither of us wants to be so long apart ever again.

Clearly I could go on but won't!

There are a number of books that I think cast important insights on the kind of experiences Celia and I have had and have together, so that we do not come across as freaky or unique. The best of these is *Dreams of Love and Fateful Encounters: the Power of Romantic Passion* by Ethel Spector Person. I remember reading before I did my manifestation list, the section in this book (she is a psychoanalyst and the book is academic, popular and full of literary examples) on enduring passion, finding that it was possible to have such an experience and deciding that that is what I wanted! I also got a lot from *Intimacy and Solitude: balancing closeness and independence* by Stephanie Dowrick. Especially the theme in this book of living in solitude but not loneliness, and learning to live and like yourself before you could let someone like you into your life so that the relationship would work.

We both believe that many (if not all) people can find a Twinflame kind of relationship. Soulmates: as you have always said, you meet and learn much from. You may stay with them for a short time or a long time but they may move on. Twinflames are more profound and more enduring, as Celia says, not necessarily sexual and about partnership, but most likely to be. I think there are enough books and dvds about manifesting such a partnership today, but it does involve (I think) a lot of hard life-work and preparation, and is probably more likely to occur in the second part of life than before 40 – but that is a personal opinion. We have helped at least four female friends through the manifestation list to find a better man for themselves in the last few years.

Some years ago I tried to summarise in a kind of pseudo-Confucian adage what it was all about for me. This is what I came up with and have passed on many times since:

'Life only begins to change for the better when you like yourself enough to let someone like yourself like you'.

I think perhaps this could be extended to say when you love yourself enough to let someone like yourself love you although I agree that liking is very important.

Anthony: I think the problem for most people is the first part: 'liking yourself enough'. Very deep down many people are really stuck in fundamentally not liking themselves and wanting to stay that way because the alternative, although apparently desirable and logical, is actually absolutely terrifying. You go on repeating the tape-loop of bad previous relationships again and again until you change your own tape… Enough of this wild waffle!

Twinflames?

Just when it began to look like Celia and Anthony's story would be the only twinflame saga included in this book, Sue and Simon Lilly sent me an account of their meeting and subsequent life together. Sue and Simon are a couple I have known for many years and have watched them expand and grow in their work and in living together. It had always struck me how much in harmony and how confident they were to be complementary and yet their own unique selves in both in their professional presentations and in their everyday life – one facet constantly spilling over into the other, as can be seen in Sue's account:

Sue: Back in 1987 I was going through a very rough patch in my personal life and was pouring effort into my spiritual development. Whilst trying to improve my clairvoyant skills I asked for some indication or sign connected with my future that would give me hope. The result was 'seeing' a pair of eyes – that's all, no words, just the eyes.

I parked the memory, like you do, deep in the back of my mind under the 'that didn't work very well, but who knows?' category.

A couple of years passed and after my marriage collapsed I went to work for a well-known colour therapy company as a girl-Friday. Having been through a divorce I had no intentions of getting involved with anyone for some time. However, six months after starting work there Simon arrived to help them out. In every way Simon was different from people I had been attracted to in the past. He was not taller than me, he did daily spiritual practice and actually seemed to find my interest in things like astrology, fascinating. Very slowly a relationship developed. After several weeks I happened to catch him cleaning his glasses. He looked up, minus his specs, as to my shock/horror, the eyes I saw two years previously, were looking back at me.

A few weeks later we represented the colour therapy company at a Healing Arts show in London. Whilst we were setting the stand up a friend of mine who was doing readings at the show arrived to have a hug and a chat. As she approached us she burst out laughing. When the giggles subsided she admitted to me that at many of the shows she had done in the Midlands Simon had come for readings, so she had known both of us independently for over four years and was surprised/not surprised to see us together.

We had a spontaneous simultaneous past life far-memory of being together, having two daughters and keeping swans. We both worked with plants and I have the painful memory of Simon being killed but being determined to carry on our work.

I recall explaining to someone what it was like when I first met Simon, I replied it was like finding a old favourite jumper in the back of the wardrobe and realising how comforting and snug it was and how much you missed it! When we first met Judy, we both 'knew' her. She picked up another link between us, this time as Simon being an older sage and me being a younger tearaway on horseback.

Our time with the colour therapy company began to draw to a close when others realised we had become a couple. Two people are harder to coerce than people on their own, let alone when they communicate with each other and become strong. Astrologically we are fairly opposite – me with four planets in Libra, Simon with four in Aries (signs that lie opposite each other on the zodiac wheel). Both of us have Earth-sign Jupiter and Water-sign Ascendants with all but each Jupiter below the horizon. So both are essentially introvert, apart from the Jupiters

– which says it all given how our work has progressed with the books and travelling. The Jupiters also define how we write and folks looking through our books can see the joint influence. Simon tends to be long-winded and very precise in his use of words. My written words are fewer, precise but tend to be easier for most people to understand. Hence my written work is worked through by Simon to broaden out ideas and his work gets chopped into shorter sentences by me.

We came to the West Country to live in 1991. Starting with nothing and from nothing apart from our knowledge and skill we have slowly built up the work we now do. In the beginning I used to clear tables at a local café and do astrology readings. Simon created his trademark prints and started making tree essences. Pulling on work I had done in 1984 and joint work in 1990 we began writing what was to become our first book *Crystal Doorways*.

We have learned a lot from each other, as could be hoped from having planets in opposite signs. Accepting each other for what and who they are is of course, the primary issue. I have learned to be more Arian, looking after my own interests in a way that a classical Libran never would. I have come to appreciate the 'finer' issues of male-female communication and behaviour, tinged by Simon's Scorpio Ascendant, which has ensured that the learning is thorough! I have also accepted that the way that I express my creativity is not the way Simon does through his artistic skills (Simon has an MA in Fine Art), but is nevertheless to be valued. When I asked Simon if he could verbalise what he had learned from me his Scorpio Ascendant engaged and nothing was forthcoming!!

Time twins

Astrologically speaking, if you are born on the same day and year as someone else you have a natural empathy with them because you share the same drives within you although you may not express them the same way, and significant events may well happen to both 'twins' at the same time. Being a time twin by no means indicates that you must be twinflames. Soulmates maybe but twinflames, no. Nevertheless, there can be exceptions as David and Adrienne's story shows. They came up to me after a 'soulmate or twinflame?' talk I gave and asked if I'd like to have their story. Naturally I said yes please.

Adrienne: I was born in Lancashire and moved to Nottingham in 1971, and at about the same time, David who was born in Wales and had been living in Birmingham, got a job in Nottingham at a town about a mile away from our house.

We met at a Yoga day where David was also manning a Biorhythm stand in the lunch break. He runs a small business selling Biorhythm charts. That day I went in to buy one from him and that is how we discovered that we have the same date of birth. He asked if we could keep in touch to check out the Biorhythm theory (that we would experience the same in all respects physically, emotionally and intellectually). From then on he rang me at random intervals, weeks and sometimes months apart, and we would always be experiencing the same things at the time. This means we have the same amount of energy available for projects, we like doing the same things, both feel tired together (recognise that more tolerance needed there) and so on.

This progressed to meeting infrequently for a chat and a cuppa and we discovered that we both felt very easy in one another's company and began to feel that we had known one another for a long time. Over the next few years we discovered we had both had bad falls at 4 years of age, and again in our teens, both failed GCE exams and had to re-sit them the following year, both been on holiday to the same place in Scotland the same year.

We had both married similar people although one was a Taurean the other a Piscean, so we had steady marriages with lovely people, however we had this inner feeling of something missing in the relationships.

By comparison, David and I seemed to have an unusual ability to effortlessly flow towards a goal. In 1987 we both had a strong feeling that there was something we needed to do that would only happen if we were together, so with a great deal of trepidation and trusting that this feeling was right, we left our marriages and set up home together, along with my 13 year old daughter and my dog.

In his previous marriage David had been a strongly controlling figure (he later realised) and I had allowed myself to be dominated in mine by a man who was afraid of his temper (Grand Cross with Pluto, Uranus, Moon and Mars), who subconsciously kept me well under his thumb but in a very caring way.

For David and I, strong Pluto [control, power and domination] in our charts was obviously a big issue in the early days, however, eventually we found ways of dealing with life from our joint strengths instead of a battle! Recognising that the issues were there, and leaving the room and processing them instead of projecting them onto the other one was our salvation. My daughter was angry and upset about the break-up of my first marriage and went wild, turning into a badly behaved teenager who hated David. What a great test for a relationship.

Once we stabilized, we then ran a cancer care group, used our home for talks, workshops, meditation evenings, meetings and all things spiritual and interesting. This confirmed our original sense that we were meant to be together in order to work in the Light. My daughter Emma and David became good friends over time, another plus after all that had gone before.

We have been together now for twenty years and still delight in one another's company. Every aspect of our relationship works well, we rarely fall out, but when we do it is soon resolved by looking at the problem, discussing it and solving it, again trying at all times to take responsibility for our part in the problem. We are used to our joint transits so try to use the energy positively. We make a great team and work really well together in whatever we do. We have similar interests, especially music, so we do a lot of things together, but are perfectly happy to follow separate pursuits as well.

We have other small similarities too which amuse us –

As this house has limited wardrobe space, my clothes are in an upstairs bedroom and David's are down. More often than not we get dressed separately and only when we meet in the hall discover we are wearing clothes with similar colours. My maiden name was Voce, four letters just like David's last name – Rudd. Our full names both contain a longer name beginning with A (Adrienne and Anthony).

When David was working full time in Bristol, he had a computer at his desk, and we were able to mail one another randomly during the day. Many times our e-mails crossed as we chose precisely the same time to send a mail to one another.

We feel we have a really special relationship – many friends have said they would like a relationship like ours. We feel that it is because of our joint birthday and feel very blessed to have been brought together.

Twinflames across the years

Victor and Diana are another couple whose relationship seems to me, as an outside observer, to have elements of twinflameship and a reincarnation aspect to it. Their story is told by Diana:

I was born in North London, locally to Victor, and since we met I have felt that I chose this rebirth to catch up with him. This would explain why when my parents moved to Kent (I was aged 8) I hated it and was unhappy deep down until I left school at 16 and joined Lloyds Bank in London.

Born before the war, Victor survived the Blitz. He joined the Air Training Corps to prepare himself for wartime service and was flying by the age of 15. He marched on the Victory Parade, then went back to college and finally into the army to do his national service, which led to his joining the Special Forces. Then accountancy filled the years until he too joined Lloyds Bank.

Sailing was a passion with Victor and he bought a yacht, which he intended to sail to Spain upon retirement. However, one day in 1984 he stood in the cockpit and looking skywards asked "How much longer must I be alone?" In a 'dream' that night he was rushing down through the ether to reach me but I was laid on a bier, dead. He had arrived too late.

Victor himself told me of the anguish he felt when he had that dream and thought that his twinflame, whom he had been expecting to meet all his life, could be dead, although he believed that it was a previous life experience rather than a current. Shortly after that 'dream', the two met at Lloyds Bank and he instantly knew he had found her. According to him, someone introduced them saying, "Here's someone who'll sail in your yacht". His thought was "no, this is the person I'll spend the rest of my life with".

Within two months we had rearranged our lives to be together. Our ages were 29 and 55.

We have been together for 25 years. We love and look after each other. Any problems usually come from outside, although we disagree on one issue [which she is hopeful will be resolved].

I met them on a crystal workshop in which Victor, when asked to introduce himself and why he had come, simply said, "I'm here to support Diana". However, we soon found he had much to offer and he came to the whole series but his initial response was typical of the loving, supportive energy of the twinflame relationship. Diana was interested in the subject and, therefore, so was he.

And finally....

Publication of this book was delayed from our intended launch because it didn't quite feel the right time and also because I particularly wanted to include a story that I had had the pleasure of watching unfold from its beginning and which seemed, in many ways, to sum up what I was trying to say and to offer hope to everyone – and to show the value of right timing.

Ironically, the story came into being partly because of the launch of another book of mine, serendipitously entitled *Good Vibrations*. But, as you will see, that launch was being used by the universe to bring together two very special people who have been intimately connected by books over a number of years but who had never met. The interview with these two was one of the most joyous I've ever conducted and I began by asking Stephen what stage he was at just before he finally met Margaret in person:

> **Stephen**: I was using a simplified version of astrology which suggested that my perfect partner would be a Capricorn 'Monkey' (in Chinese astrology) and, having never met one until that point, I met two in the space of six months. Neither relationship was right, and I remember being at a total loss – I really had no idea where to go from there.

I asked Margaret to describe how things had been for her because I knew quite a lot about her story and that she had put a great deal of time and energy into making a relationship work before she met Stephen:

> **Margaret**: I was in a 14 year marriage that ended with a huge amount of pain and trauma, then after a period of being alone I started a relationship with someone who turned out to be really emotionally abusive. I wasn't used to being shouted and screamed and sworn at, and I was really confused – I didn't know who I was. People like that really start to make you doubt yourself. You lose your self-esteem, your confidence, and you are walking on egg shells the whole time. My friends were really concerned about me, telling me I should get out of the relationship. I had this sense that – astrologically – it had to run its course, as we'd split up once and had got back together and I knew this time it had to be final, and that the end would come in May 2008. In the meantime, I'd started working through a book called *Creating Money* by Sanaya Roman and Duane Packer which is about creating abundance in your life and

one of the things they get you to focus on is what you actually want and talking as though you have it. I was doing a lot of running at the time and so I used to do these affirmations as I was running along. I'd often be almost crying because I was so upset and so angry. I'd be saying, "I have a fabulous boyfriend and a gorgeous home, and I've got lovely children and I'm wealthy and have everything I could possibly want" and yet I was so miserable it was really horrible. The good thing about affirmations and that book in particular is that the words get into your head and you do it automatically so you don't have to necessarily believe it. That's one of the things the authors really emphasise: you don't have to believe. You can be in the most horrible situation but once you open yourself up to that energy you are allowing it to come into your life. If you focus on what you haven't got and how miserable you are, that is exactly what you attract. So Barnaby, a work colleague, and I were working through the *Creating Money* book and we used to play this game because he wasn't in a relationship and I was having these massive lows in mine. I remember one day we were larking around and you remember that game "I went on a picnic and I took…" We started saying, "When I meet my next partner they will be really kind, fun to be with…" so we worked on the list and periodically we'd do it again and embellish it. It was just for a laugh and an extension of the *Creating Money* exercise. So I had this programme running in my head that I would really be with somebody who fulfilled everything on this amazing list.

So how did it all start? Margaret and Stephen had known each other for over a decade because Margaret publishes books, and Stephen produces the *Watkins Review*, in which he promotes new titles to the customers of the famous Watkins bookshop in London. They spoke regularly in this context, but the way they were edged together without either of them doing anything is fascinating. I was in Margaret's office doing some editing one day (unusual in itself) when Stephen phoned to discuss me writing an author article for the *Review*. I prompted her to ask for his birth data and we watched as the chart came up on screen, and it was obvious how incredibly compatible their charts were – Stephen picked up on this excitement and joked, "Maybe we should get together!" Once Margaret had put the phone down, the room positively fizzed as we saw more and more in the charts. From that moment on, I was absolutely convinced that they were meant to be together, even though they hadn't actually met.

Margaret: This was the last thing I needed. Judy's mantra became, "You two so need to get together" and I was getting really cross, saying, "It's so not going to happen is it? He lives in Southend, works in London, and I live in Bournemouth. And I've got one massive problem I'm still trying to get rid of". So it shows you really can't control your life.

The initial conversation where we had looked at the charts together had subtly changed the relationship between Stephen and Margaret, which had always been strictly work-related. They had a conversation a while later:

Stephen: I remember speaking to Margaret just after the second Capricorn Monkey relationship had finished and she asked me how I was. I'd got to the point of stopping being polite because I felt so miserable and I just said, "I'm not feeling so good", and we must have been on the phone for an hour and a half. It turned out that Margaret's partner was also a Capricorn and she was in the process of finishing the relationship, so we formed the Capricorn Recovery Club. It was quite amazing. And that was it really.

What was ironic was that this was June 2008 and I remember being in the bookshop the previous year on a grey rainy day and an elderly woman was there looking at the astrology books. I helped her with a couple of books, then as I went back to the office she said, "What you need is a Cancerian woman" without any prompting, and because it was such a strange thing to say it stuck with me. When Margaret and I got together I remembered it as one of the anomalies and strange things that led us together.

Margaret: You didn't even know I was Cancerian initially. And what is really interesting about that conversation when I asked Stephen how he was, is that we'd never done any personal stuff before despite talking to each other on the phone for twelve years. We'd had really good talks about loads of different things and were really good phone friends but never mentioned anything personal.

Stephen: That was the time when I really wondered, "where do I go from here?" That conversation was the catalyst for being able to open up and allow the space for the right thing to come in because I'd finally given up on what I thought I should be pursuing. It was almost like life said okay, let him go on banging his head against the wall, one day he's going to realise it doesn't work like that, and the moment I got fed up with banging my head against the wall, it happened.

I was having a book launch in July, at *Earthworks* book distributors in Poole, for the latest of my books published by Margaret and we'd invited all their customers and a load of our friends and other authors as a networking exercise. I'd asked Stephen because I felt he should be there – after all he'd be selling my book and featuring it in the *Watkins Review*, but it was more than that – I really wanted to see him and Margaret together. Margaret was convinced he wouldn't come as it was so far out of London. So when he said at first he couldn't come, I just kept saying to Margaret, "He'll be there" and of course he was. How did that happen?

> **Stephen**: I originally was not going to come down for the book launch as it was a long way to go and I didn't have a lot of money, but all the obstacles dissolved because the universe had decided this was going to happen. A friend, author Ian Lawton, who was also living in Southend, split up with his girlfriend and had moved into a flat which his landlady decided she wanted back, so overnight he upped and moved out, to of all places, Bournemouth! He could have gone anywhere, but now I had somewhere to stay if I wanted to go down to Bournemouth. But I still had the issue that my son and my nephew, who were staying with my ex-wife in North London, needed me to take them back to my sister's in Leeds. I suggested that Ian should go to the book launch to meet people in the same business. But suddenly the last obstacle was taken away when my son rang and said, "We're going up on the coach so you don't have to take us". So I could email Margaret and say "Right I'm coming to the launch!"

The universe had obviously decided to push things along somewhat faster:

> **Margaret**: I was still trying to get my previous partner out of my flat at that time, although I'd told him it was over some two months earlier. My fiftieth birthday was approaching – ironically the weekend before the book launch – and my friends were insisting I celebrate it in style with a party, but I didn't want to as my ex was being so horrible about it, and he was still in my flat. All this was in my head when I phoned Watkins for an order – something I do regularly. I was excited that Stephen was coming to the launch but was also somewhat shy. I felt fifteen all over again as I called, hoping he wouldn't pick up the phone.

Stephen: It was another of those strange coincidences where Margaret, because of the tension that was building up, was reticent about phoning up, so she thought it was safe by phoning at lunchtime and speaking to one of the others to give her the order, but it so happened that she phoned when I was out on the shop floor covering for one of them so I answered the phone –

Margaret: I couldn't believe that…

Stephen: – and she was talking in another voice and pretending not to be her. I said, "Isn't that you, Margaret?" and she owned up. We chatted for a bit and got over that hurdle and Hugh overhead me talking to her and came past with a sign saying "Happy Birthday Margaret". So I asked "Is it your birthday?" and there was a squeaky "yes". So I asked her which date and she said the 19th and I said, "But that's when I'm coming down", and there was yet another squeaky "yes". At that point I didn't know Margaret was going to be fifty although I did know she was born the year of the dog, so I thought she's either going to be 38 or 50 and I secretly wished that she was 50; having gone out with several other women in their late thirties, I'd rather she was nearer my own age so we'd have more in common.

Margaret: He asked if I was having a party, and I gave another squeaky "yes". I felt just like a fifteen year old, it was awful. . . Stephen asked if he could come, so I managed to calm down and explain the dilemma with my ex. He didn't want to put me under any pressure and just said to let him know when I had decided what to do.

This was the impetus Margaret needed – her ex vacated the flat – alas only for the night – and the party went ahead. As usually happens at parties, Margaret and Stephen didn't get a lot of time together.

Margaret: Stephen and Ian were the last to arrive so I was really nervous by then. When Stephen walked in I just remember his huge smile and gorgeous eyes. The few moments we did get to talk together it felt as though we had created our own special bubble – he was exactly on my wavelength, which probably isn't a surprise looking at our phone history!

Stephen: I think sometimes it's just about learning to get out of your own way. We get such fixed ideas about what we want or should have that we get in our own way and it's about allowing those things to fall to the wayside to let the universe bring you what you're meant to have. Quite often what you think you deserve and want and expect isn't what the universe has in store for you and it's about being open and trusting that the universe knows what to bring and what's right. It's difficult to do that in a society where we're used to thinking we control every aspect of our lives.

Margaret: The timing of the whole thing was so weird because I had known that John and I were going to finally finish when my Saturn transit ended in May. It had been a horrible time, just waiting, after months and months of knowing (on my part) that we had to finish; it was hanging by a thread waiting for that final thing. It was so frustrating but in terms of the astrology, you look at the cycles and you learn not to rush things and I think that helps. If I'd thrown him out the year before, then I wouldn't have been in the right position to have had that 'Capricorn Recovery Club' talk with Stephen.

The day of the book launch dawned. The connection between Margaret and Stephen was obvious from the moment they met. Even though I was busy talking to people, it was impossible to miss the frisson in the air, or the way they gravitated together as though pulled by magnets and they stayed there.

Margaret: The book launch for *Good Vibrations* was a completely magical day, we have decided that that's where our relationship started because we were both so aware.

Stephen: Ian and I arrived in an open-topped sports car and it was a lovely, lovely day. We were talking to the people from *Earthworks* and we'd been there about half an hour before I bumped into Margaret. We didn't get much time to talk during the launch, but towards the end we sat together and went through the crystals Margaret had been accumulating with a view to finally getting her ex out of her flat – and I remember feeling very strongly that we were a kind of unit within the larger unit of the book launch and I don't think we moved for quite a while. It was a real sense and feeling of togetherness which was quite unique.

Margaret: I felt totally and completely natural, as if I could have just snuggled under his arm or kissed his cheek – I actually had to stop myself, wondering, "what's going on here?" But I felt completely together with Stephen, and I'd never felt that in any relationship before.

One of the things that we've noticed is that wherever we are we seem to create this little bubble that's our world and it's almost like people notice it when we're walking along. When we were out shopping the other day, I kept noticing that people were looking at us. We've felt that total completeness right from the beginning and we definitely feel that this is like a reward for all the other stuff we've been through in other lifetimes. It feels like coming back together again after a long, long time of having to go off and do other things. We've been together so many times before.

Stephen: It was so relaxed, so normal, so natural. Our relationship progressed rapidly after the launch by text and phone – and I came down to Bournemouth in August 2008 for our first proper weekend together. And the rest, as they say, is history, or her story, or our story...

Margaret: The most ironic thing about all this is that I haven't been for a run for quite a while and last week I went out for the first time and the programme started in my head, I didn't even have to think about it. I was running along chanting "I have a fabulous boyfriend, I have a gorgeous life" ... then I realised I HAVE, I'VE ACTUALLY GOT IT!! And it was the most amazing feeling, because for so long I'd been affirming something I didn't have and no matter how miserable I might have been when I did it, it was working away, creating that space.

Stephen and I show that you can work as hard as you can to block things off that are coming – I was convinced we wouldn't get together because of the geography and everything else – and yet you don't have a part in it. If you focus on what you want, you attract it, without a shadow of a doubt, even if you don't recognise its approach in your life.

Stephen: I think if it's right or meant to be, all the obstacles are removed. I was living on the Essex coast and commuting into London every day, and Margaret was down in Bournemouth. I couldn't see any way it would happen. But at the same point, I have to be honest, I didn't see it as a problem because I had a gut feeling that everything would work out okay. I didn't know how but I just had that feeling. And every obstacle, and there were a lot at that time, was removed. I suddenly managed to rent out my flat after years of not selling it, and I was able to have a temporary stay with a friend in London before moving down to Bournemouth myself.

Margaret: Everything between us is absolutely in line, in tune, unforced. We've been together a while now, and before Stephen moved down here we only saw each other every other weekend; that can lead to quite intense times. When you're together, you're really, really together and I can honestly say that in all that time there hasn't been even one second of a sense of any irritation, unhappiness, nothing; and I've never experienced anything like it.

Stephen: We've never had a cross word or an argument or anything like that.

Margaret: It's not because we're trying, we've been together long enough and been close enough now that something would have come out, but there just isn't. It's like this is the good karma, we're here now because this is where we belong. We haven't got stuff to work on with each other. Whether you're in a difficult relationship, or not in a relationship at all, you can get a real complex about yourself: I'm too this, or I'm too that, and you build up a picture of yourself that can be very damaging.

Stephen: It undermines all your confidence. I can remember in one of my major relationships in the past I was accused of being clingy and needy. I was quite shocked because I didn't see myself that way. Different people bring out different aspects of you and I think for me the key thing is that how the other person makes you feel is a good sign of whether the relationship is working. For instance, I never felt confident or secure in any of my previous relationships. I never felt content or happy because there was always something not right. And this is the first time I've been in a relationship that actually makes me feel good about myself. I feel how I want to feel and I think you realise that even though you thought you were in love in other relationships, ultimately they weren't right – not because you didn't love enough or that the other person was wrong or you were wrong, but just because it wasn't right with that person. I think it is important to recognise that it is how the two of you work together – and the chemistry is either there or it isn't. No amount of trying can force something to be right that isn't there.

Margaret: We've both tried so hard in other relationships and it's like you're banging your head against a brick wall. We used to joke, semi-seriously, that instead of encouraging people to go to counselling to try and make it work, we should say, "Just accept that it isn't working, move on". I think so much damage is done when you're trying really hard to be everything your partner says they want, but you're turning into someone you're not really, deep down, and they're still not satisfied. We've both had that and I think I am now anti-counselling, which is ironic because I'm a trained counsellor myself. I think as Stephen says, sometimes it's just not right, it's not going to be right and you make yourself miserable by plodding on – that's not a relationship. Which might be a bit fierce but I'd never have dreamed I could be this happy and so complete and it's multi-layered. It comes from many, many lifetimes of us getting to know each other.

I'd also like to say this to all the people who are asking, "Is this the right one?". If you have to ask the question then the answer is no – because it is such a deep feeling that you don't even think about asking the question, you just know, "I've come home".

Attracting your twinflame[4]

Calling your twinflame into your life is essentially more satisfying and supportive of your spiritual evolution than seeking a soulmate. For this ritual you will need a twinflame crystal, which consists of two long, preferably equal, crystals side by side. The crystals may merge along their length, or spring from the same base – crystals that have the same base seem to ground the relationship more firmly in the physical level of being whereas two that are joined along their length but have no mutual base tend to attract a more mentally compatible kind of twinflame relationship. You will also need four Rose Quartz candleholders and tea-lights. If possible, carry out the ritual in the relationship corner of your house or bedroom – the furthest right corner from the door. Setting a time within which the ritual will work keeps it focused in the now rather than eternally in future possibility.

Before beginning the ritual, write down all the qualities you seek in a twinflame: phrase it positively, avoid negative statements. When you are sure you have all the positive qualities, write them onto a piece of gold or pink card under the heading 'My twinflame'.

The ritual

Choosing a time when you will be undisturbed, carefully prepare a place for your ritual. Cleanse the space and the crystals thoroughly including the

---

4. Taken from Hall, Judy *Good Vibrations: psychic protection, energy enhancement and space clearing* (Flying Horse Publications, 2008).

candleholders (you can use incense or a candle flame or a purpose made space-clearing spray), bathe and put on clean clothes. Place a clean cloth on a table and lay out the four Rose Quartz candleholders with tea lights lit within them.

Hold your crystal and programme it with the intent that it will attract your twinflame into your life. Read the twinflame qualities out loud from the gold card. Place the card underneath the crystal in the centre of the candles. Then place your hand over your heart and invite your twinflame into your heart. Welcome the energy of your twinflame as it moves towards you. Ask that your twinflame will manifest within the month. Then blow out the candles sending your unconditional love to your twinflame as you do so. Leave the crystal in place.

Visualisation: walking towards your twinflame

I am indebted to Anthony for the inspiration for this visualisation which also draws your twinflame towards you.

Settle down where you will not be disturbed. Close your eyes, relax and in your mind's eye take yourself to a favourite place in nature. Make sure that it is somewhere with a long view – a path or river down which your twinflame can travel. Spend a few moments enjoying the sights and sounds of this lovely place. Then let your eyes move to the path. In the far distance, at the furthest end of the path, you will see a tiny dot. A feeling of anticipation and excitement seizes you, this is your twin-flame approaching. Slowly, oh so slowly, the dot approaches, getting bigger and bigger. The wait is tantalising, your heart opens and you feel you can almost reach out to touch the figure.

At first, the dot may be indistinct and may not approach closely but in time the figure will come near to you. As it does so, the excitement mounts, you begin to feel an electricity in the air, a magnetic pull between your hearts and souls. So much so that you will be drawn down the path towards your twinflame. In time, you will see his or her outline clearly and then be clasped in his or her arms (try not to put a face to your twinflame at this stage). When this happens, ask that your twinflame will manifest physically in the world so that the two of you can be together.

If you are non-visual: find an appropriate place with a very long vista that you can walk down and allow yourself to believe that your twinflame is walking towards you. Feel the excitement that engenders within you, the bubble of joy that fills your heart. Hold out your arms and enfold the loving presence of your twinflame.

Anthony and Celia have reminded me to state how important it is not to put a face to the twinflame too early in this visualisation. If there is a face and especially if it is someone you already know, do assess most carefully whether this is wishful thinking, a hidden agenda, someone else intervening in your process, or whether it is a true seeing. It is far better to keep the face shadowy and be pleasantly surprised when your twinflame arrives physically in your life.

Anthony suggested that this should be timed to the cycles of the moon – something that is traditionally done with occult rituals, as the waxing moon 'charges up' the energy. Start at the beginning of a waxing moon – that is, new moon when the moon gets brighter and more visible each day. Practice it each day for a fortnight. Then, at full moon, stop for two weeks until the next new moon. Celia says that it took nine moon cycles for her twinflame to manifest – but it was worth waiting for! You can also remind yourself at idle moments during the day, or just before going to sleep, that you are walking towards your twinflame and that he or she is walking towards you. He or she is approaching through the mist, which gets thinner as time goes by so that the silhouette becomes more and more visible. This preparation time is very important, during it do all that you can to work on yourself to prepare for this new energy entering in your life. Be mindful of anything that emerges as an impediment or inner sabotaging voice – the quickest way I have found to work on these is the Emotional Freedom Technique which taps out these old programmes and brings in a new way of thinking and feeling. And, as this postscript from Celia shows, don't be in so much of a hurry that you inadvertently misidentify your twinflame:

> **Celia**: I believe that the preparatory work is a necessary part of the process of finding one's twin flame, although it's important to be mindful of how human weakness can interfere with it. While still living in Canada, I learned how to pendulum, and thought that once and for all I would try and find out if I should just give up on this idea of finding The One.
>
> After suitable preparation, but with some lingering reservation about my ability to use a pendulum in this way, with all my heart I asked of the wooden bobbin on a length of silk thread: 'Will I ever find the One, whom I will love and happily spend the whole of the rest of my life with?'
>
> 'Yes,' emerged from the gently-circling, clockwise response.
>
> Pleasantly surprised, I thought to ask: 'Do I already know him?'

To my amazement, another 'Yes'.

'Will this happen within the next six months?' I tried next. I had not prepared these questions; they were coming off the top of my head.

Slowly, the bobbin began a counter-clockwise rotation: 'No'.

'Within the next year?'

'Yes'.

I was thrilled, although part of me remained sceptical. But the one negative response seemed to lend an air of authenticity to the whole experience. I filed it away in the back of my mind.

A couple of months later, an old friend with whom I had a lot in common resurfaced in my life. In the intervening year or so, his long-term relationship had come to an end. Something 'clicked' between us and I remembered the pendulum-wisdom and thought to myself that it (I, that is) had probably just got the time-scale wrong. I embarked on a relationship with him.

WRONG! We were soul-mates; that much soon came clear, but within six months we had split up.

Some two months later, I received a letter with a UK stamp. It was from Anthony, the first of what was soon to become a torrent, reciprocated. It was about ten months from the time I had asked my searing question of the pendulum.

As I said in the Introduction, I'd like to be able to report that I've met my twinflame, that the rituals and visualisations worked for me, but not yet. I'm giving myself more love, cherishing myself, forgiving the past, and trying to radiate more positive loving vibes out to the world. Given my astrological chart, a twinflame relationship seems to be a distinct possibility – the last part of my chart to live out – and my intention is to manifest that potential as and when the timing is right. So, be patient, your twinflame will come to you if that is on your soul-plan for this current incarnation. Although, of course, you may prefer the challenging, soul-scouring, lesson-learning, karma-shattering world of the soulmate. Or neither. Whatever you chose, remember:

You cannot make someone fall in love with you, but you can work on loving yourself and radiating love and positive energy so that people are naturally more attracted towards you.[5]

---

5. Allen, Sue, *Spirit Release* O Books, Winchester, 2007, p.53.

Other Books by The Wessex Astrologer

www.wessexastrologer.com

CPSIA information can be obtained
at www.ICGtesting.com
Printed in the USA
BVHW040020160419
545609BV00003B/11/P